Fundamentals of
Internet of Things

Fundamentals of Internet of Things

Sudhir Kumar

CRC Press
Taylor & Francis Group
Boca Raton London New York

CRC Press is an imprint of the
Taylor & Francis Group, an **informa** business

A CHAPMAN & HALL BOOK

First edition published [2022]
by CRC Press
6000 Broken Sound Parkway NW, Suite 300, Boca Raton, FL 33487-2742

and by CRC Press
2 Park Square, Milton Park, Abingdon, Oxon, OX14 4RN

© 2022 selection and editorial matter, Sudhir Kumar; individual chapters, the contributors

CRC Press is an imprint of Taylor & Francis Group, LLC

Library of Congress Cataloging-in-Publication Data

Names: Kumar, Sudhir (Electrical Engineering), author.
Title: Fundamentals of internet of things / Sudhir Kumar.
Description: First edition. | Boca Raton : C&H/CRC Press, [2022] | Includes
bibliographical references and index. | Summary: "The main emphasis of
this book is on the building fundamentals of IoT networks by leveraging
the important and relevant concepts from Signal Processing,
Communications, Networks and Machine learning. The book focuses on IoT
protocols, energy harvesting, control optimization, clustering, data
fusion, data analytics, localization, fog computing, privacy and
security including Elliptic curve cryptography and Blockchain
technology. This book is primarily aimed at advanced undergraduates,
graduates and industry professionals. The book will also be useful or
researchers"-- Provided by publisher.
Identifiers: LCCN 2021032153 (print) | LCCN 2021032154 (ebook) | ISBN
9781032126449 (hbk) | ISBN 9781032126500 (pbk) | ISBN 9781003225584 (ebk)
Subjects: LCSH: Internet of things.
Classification: LCC TK7895.E43 K66 2022 (print) | LCC TK7895.E43 (ebook)
| DDC 004.67/8--dc23
LC record available at https://lccn.loc.gov/2021032153
LC ebook record available at https://lccn.loc.gov/2021032154

ISBN: 978-1-032-12644-9 (hbk)
ISBN: 978-1-032-12650-0 (pbk)
ISBN: 978-1-003-22558-4 (ebk)

DOI: 10.1201/9781003225584

*To my family
and almighty god wholeheartedly.*

Contents

Preface   xiii

Author   xv

Abbreviations   xvii

Symbol Description   xxvii

1 Things and Internet   1
   1.1   Introduction   1
   1.2   Things   2
         1.2.1   Temperature Sensor   2
         1.2.2   Pressure Sensor   3
         1.2.3   Proximity Sensor   3
         1.2.4   Air Quality (Gas) Sensor   4
         1.2.5   Humidity Sensor (or Hygrometer)   4
         1.2.6   Level Sensor   4
         1.2.7   Flow Sensor   4
         1.2.8   Accelerometer   5
         1.2.9   Imaging sensor   5
         1.2.10 Characteristics of Sensors   5
         1.2.11 Actuators   6
   1.3   Internet   7
         1.3.1   OSI Model   7
         1.3.2   OSI Model versus TCP/IP Model   12
         1.3.3   Devices at Different Layers   13
         1.3.4   Circuit and Packet Switching   14
         1.3.5   Some Protocols of TCP/IP Model   14
         1.3.6   IPv4 Addresses   15
         1.3.7   IPv6 Addresses   18
         1.3.8   Routing at Network Layer   19
         1.3.9   Distance Vector Routing   20
         1.3.10 Link State Routing   20
         1.3.11 Shortest Path Routing—Dijkstra Algorithm   22
         1.3.12 Interior Gateway Routing Protocol   23
         1.3.13 Exterior Gateway Routing Protocol   26

       1.3.14 Performance Metrics 27
  1.4 Summary 30
  1.5 Exercises 30

2 Standards and Protocols   33
  2.1 Introduction 33
  2.2 IEEE 802.11 Protocol 33
       2.2.1 Features 34
       2.2.2 Modulation Schemes 35
       2.2.3 Supporting a Large Number of Devices 40
       2.2.4 Throughput without Error 42
       2.2.5 Throughput with Packet Error Rate (PER) 44
       2.2.6 Path Loss Models for IEEE 802.11ah 45
  2.3 IEEE 802.15.4 Protocol 45
       2.3.1 Pseudo-Noise Sequence Generator 46
       2.3.2 Modulation Scheme 48
       2.3.3 Topology 51
       2.3.4 Time-Slotted Channel Hopping 52
       2.3.5 Blocking Techniques 54
  2.4 LoRaWAN Protocol 55
       2.4.1 Architecture 56
       2.4.2 Device Class 57
       2.4.3 Radio Propagation 58
       2.4.4 Link Budget 59
       2.4.5 Rate Definitions 59
       2.4.6 Time of Air 61
       2.4.7 Modulation 63
       2.4.8 Adaptive Data Rate 65
       2.4.9 Pure ALOHA—Access Protocol 65
       2.4.10 Slotted ALOHA protocol 68
       2.4.11 Duty Cycle, Dwell and Hop Time, and Robustness . . 69
  2.5 6LowPAN Protocol 70
       2.5.1 6LowPAN Stack 70
       2.5.2 6LowPAN Encapsulation Header 71
       2.5.3 Routing Protocol 74
  2.6 Application Protocols 77
       2.6.1 Request-Response model 77
       2.6.2 Publish Subscribe model 77
       2.6.3 Constrained Application Protocol 78
       2.6.4 Message Queue Telemetry Transport 82
       2.6.5 Extensible Messaging and Presence Protocol 83
  2.7 Summary 83
  2.8 Exercises 84

3 Clustering and Data Fusion   **87**

  3.1   Introduction   87

  3.2   Clustering Technique   87

      3.2.1   Algorithm for Clustering   88

      3.2.2   Example of Clustering   88

      3.2.3   Remarks on Clustering without Initialization   89

      3.2.4   Algorithm for Initialization   90

      3.2.5   Example of Initialization   90

      3.2.6   Remarks on Clustering with Initialization   91

  3.3   Energy Efficient Clustering   93

      3.3.1   Radio Energy Dissipation Model   93

      3.3.2   Radio Model for Receiver   94

      3.3.3   Optimal Number of Clusters   94

      3.3.4   Example of Optimal Number of Clusters   98

      3.3.5   Example for Verification of K_{opt}   98

      3.3.6   Remarks on Energy Efficient Clustering   98

  3.4   Sensor Data Fusion   98

      3.4.1   Motivation and Pointers for Data Fusion   99

      3.4.2   Fusion Architecture   99

      3.4.3   Bayesian Data Fusion   99

      3.4.4   Fusion of Data from Two Sensors   102

      3.4.5   Fusion of Data from Three Sensors   103

  3.5   Dempster-Shafer Theory for Data Fusion   104

      3.5.1   Sensor Data Fusion of Two Sensors   104

      3.5.2   Example of DS Theory   105

      3.5.3   Fusing Multiple Sensors   106

      3.5.4   Support   107

      3.5.5   Plausibility   108

  3.6   Decision Fusion   110

      3.6.1   Binary Signal Detection   110

      3.6.2   Probabilities of Detection and False-Alarm   111

      3.6.3   Centralized Detection Scheme   112

      3.6.4   Distributed Detection Scheme   114

  3.7   Summary   117

  3.8   Exercises   118

4 Smart Device Localization   **121**

  4.1   Introduction   121

  4.2   Taxonomy of Localization Algorithms   122

  4.3   Distance-based Localization Methods   123

      4.3.1   Multilateration Based Localization   124

      4.3.2   Time-of-Arrival Based Localization   125

      4.3.3   Time-Difference-of-Arrival Based Localization   126

      4.3.4   Angle-of-Arrival Based Localization   127

      4.3.5   Received Signal Strength Based Localization   128

		4.3.6	Multidimensional Scaling (MDS) Based Localization .	129
	4.4		Distance-free Localization Methods	131
		4.4.1	Centroid-based Localization	132
		4.4.2	Distance Vector Hop Based Localization	133
		4.4.3	Closest Point Based Localization	133
		4.4.4	Approximate Point in Triangle Test (APIT)	134
		4.4.5	Assumption Based Coordinates (ABC) Localization .	135
	4.5		Performance Metrics	137
		4.5.1	Average Localization Error	137
		4.5.2	Cramer-Rao Lower Bound	137
		4.5.3	Box and Whisker Plot	138
		4.5.4	Cumulative Distribution Function	139
	4.6		Summary	141
	4.7		Exercises	141
5	**Energy Harvesting and Control Optimization**			**143**
	5.1		Introduction	143
	5.2		Energy Harvesting	143
		5.2.1	Time-Switching Based Relay Protocol	144
		5.2.2	Power-Splitting Based Relaying Protocol	147
	5.3		Model Predictive Control	149
		5.3.1	Notations and State Space Model	149
		5.3.2	Solution of State Space Model	150
		5.3.3	Continuous to Discrete State Space Model	151
		5.3.4	Discrete Time MPC	152
		5.3.5	Solution to Constrained MPC	154
		5.3.6	Example of Unconstrained MPC	155
		5.3.7	Constrained Rate of Change of Control Input	156
		5.3.8	Constrained Control Input	157
		5.3.9	Constrained on Output of Plant	157
		5.3.10	Remarks on MPC	160
		5.3.11	Optimization in MPC Using quadprog	160
	5.4		Summary	162
	5.5		Exercises	162
6	**Things Data Analytics**			**165**
	6.1		Introduction	165
	6.2		Understanding the Buzz Words	165
	6.3		Supervised Learning	167
		6.3.1	k-Nearest Neighbor	168
		6.3.2	Naive Bayes Classification	169
		6.3.3	Linear Regression	170
		6.3.4	Logistic Regression	171
	6.4		Unsupervised Learning	173
		6.4.1	Principal Component Analysis	174

6.5   Bias and Variance Tradeoff 176
6.6   Artificial Neural Networks 178
      6.6.1   Perceptron Model 178
      6.6.2   Activation Function 179
      6.6.3   Loss Functions 181
      6.6.4   Back-propagation and Its Example 182
      6.6.5   Optimization in Back Propagation 184
6.7   Evaluation Method 187
      6.7.1   Cross-validation Method 187
      6.7.2   Performance Metrics 187
6.8   Summary 189
6.9   Exercises 189

7   Fog Computing   191
7.1   Introduction 191
      7.1.1   Motivation for Fog Computing 192
      7.1.2   Cloud Computing versus Fog Computing 192
7.2   Technologies for Fog Computing 192
      7.2.1   Virtualization Technology 192
      7.2.2   Terminologies in Computing 194
7.3   Mobility in Fog Framework 195
      7.3.1   Ethernet Virtual Private Network 195
      7.3.2   Default IP Gateway 197
      7.3.3   Locator/Identifier Separation Protocol 198
7.4   Fog Orchestration 199
7.5   Localization in Fog Computing Framework 199
      7.5.1   Fingerprinting Based Localization 200
      7.5.2   Getting Device Information 200
      7.5.3   Computing Cost Function 201
      7.5.4   Example of Offloading 201
7.6   Task Offloading 203
      7.6.1   Offloading Task 1 to Fog Nodes 203
      7.6.2   Offloading Task 2 to Fog Nodes 205
7.7   Summary 205
7.8   Exercises 205

8   Privacy and Security of Things Data   207
8.1   Introduction 207
8.2   Data Privacy 207
      8.2.1   Privacy Using k-anonymity 208
      8.2.2   Privacy Using l-diversity 209
8.3   Elliptic Curve Cryptography 210
      8.3.1   ECC over Real Numbers 211
      8.3.2   Dot Operations over Real Numbers 212
      8.3.3   Operations over Finite Field 213

	8.3.4	Trapdoor Function	214
	8.3.5	Beauty of ECC	215
	8.3.6	Key Generation and Exchange	216
	8.3.7	Encryption and Decryption	216
8.4		Blockchain	220
	8.4.1	Bitcoin	221
	8.4.2	Hash	221
	8.4.3	Blockchain and Its Versions	222
	8.4.4	Miner	223
	8.4.5	Tamper-Proof Blockchain	224
	8.4.6	Role of Digital Signature in Blockchain	224
	8.4.7	Transaction in Blockchain	225
	8.4.8	Distributed Ledger	225
	8.4.9	Byzantine Generals Problem	226
	8.4.10	Transaction Pool and Candidate Block	227
	8.4.11	Fork	228
	8.4.12	Bitcoin versus Ethereum	228
	8.4.13	Some Remarks on Blockchain Technology	229
	8.4.14	Applications of Blockchain	229
	8.4.15	Disadvantages of Blockchain	230
8.5		Summary	230
8.6		Exercises	231

9 Applications of IoT   **233**

9.1		Introduction	233
9.2		Smart Healthcare	233
	9.2.1	Human Activity Recognition Using Wearable Sensors	233
	9.2.2	Human Activity Recognition Using Channel State Information	235
	9.2.3	Human Health Monitoring	236
9.3		Smart City	237
	9.3.1	Smart Parking	237
	9.3.2	Smart Farming	238
	9.3.3	Smart Air Pollution Monitoring System	239
9.4		Summary	240
9.5		Exercises	240

Bibliography   **243**

Index   **255**

Preface

I am delighted to write the preface of this book. First, I am grateful to Prof. Rajesh M. Hegde (IIT Kanpur) who had directed me to work on Localization in Wireless Sensor Networks (WSN) during my Ph.D. study. Next, I would like to thank my colleague Dr. Sanjoy K. Parida who had given me an opportunity to deliver a few lectures on "Component and Applications of IoT" in Study Webs of Active-Learning for Young Aspiring Minds (SWAYAM)—Massive Open Online Courses (MOOCs) initiated by Government of India. I would especially like to thank Prof. Pushpak Bhattacharyya (IIT Bombay) and my colleagues of IIT Patna for their encouragement. I would like to acknowledge Ankur, Pritam, Mohit, Yasin, and Vivek, the members of my Sensor Networks Research Lab for their help in drawing/typing in few portions. The positive comments of reviewers helped me in developing better coherency and adhesiveness in the book by adding some sections/chapters and reorganizing a few chapters. The book is written by surveying references of the bibliography.

As we know, the Internet of Things (IoT) network has revolutionized the world and has innumerable real-time applications on automation. A few examples include remote order of tea/coffee of your choice from a vending machine, remote monitoring of elderly people, smart home, smart transportation, industrial automation, and driver-less car amongst others. The most of existing books are theoretical without many mathematical descriptions and examples. This may not create interest among readers. In contrast, the important benefits of the books are as follows: first, the mathematical descriptions of most of the topics in addition to relevant theory and insights. Second, illustration of the topics with numerical examples wherever possible. Several examples are worked out with pen and paper for building confidence on the topics among readers instead of programming on a computer. Needless to mention programming tools can be used for a large example or dataset. This helps readers in the visualization of the theory and testing of the understanding. Third, getting a complete package of cutting-edge topics of IoT networks that are missing in the existing books.

The main emphasis of this textbook is on building fundamentals of IoT networks by leveraging the important and relevant concepts from Signal Processing, Communications, Networks, and Machine learning. The book covers two fundamental components of IoT networks, namely, Internet and Things. In particular, the book is divided into nine chapters: Thing and Internet in Chapter 1, IoT protocols in Chapter 2, Clustering and Data Fusion in Chapter

3, Smart Device Localization in Chapter 4, Energy Harvesting and Control Optimization in Chapter 5, Things Data Analytics in Chapter 6, Fog Computing in Chapter 7, Privacy and Security of Things Data in Chapter 8, and Applications of IoT in Chapter 9.

In a 4-stage IoT architecture, there are things layer, network layer, middleware services, and application layer. The things layer deals with the collection of sensor data from an event. An actuator takes mechanical actions based on the decision made. We deal with the gateways and IoT devices in order to form a larger network at the network layer. Those devices communicate and notify among themselves using IoT communication protocols. In the middleware services, the sensor data is analyzed further using things data analytics. In order to make data meaningful, we often need the tag location and timestamp with the data. The Global Positioning System (GPS) is usually used for the localization of the smart device. However, the GPS fails in indoor or underground scenarios because of unavailability of the direct satellite signals. Also, the energy consumption of GPS is high. Therefore, we leverage localization techniques for estimating the location of the smart device.

Further, the resource-constrained devices of IoT networks cannot do heavy computations. We generally wish to do the computation near to the source of data to avoid delay or latency. We use a fog computing paradigm for facilitating distributed storage and computing capabilities. Additionally, energy harvesting techniques are utilized to harvest energy from external ambient sources such as mechanical energy, wind energy, water current, or electromagnetic waves. Importantly, privacy and security of the things data in an IoT network are achieved using data anonymization, elliptic curve cryptography, and blockchain technology. Finally, two use cases for smart healthcare and smart city are presented to grasp the understanding of theory. In particular, human activity recognition, human health monitoring, smart parking, smart farming, and smart air pollution monitoring applications in an IoT environment are discussed.

Sudhir Kumar.

Author

 Sudhir Kumar is currently an Assistant Professor with the Electrical Engineering (EE) department, Indian Institute of Technology Patna, Patna, India since May 2017. He received his B.Tech. degree in Electronics and Communication Engineering (ECE) from West Bengal University of Technology, Kolkata, India, in 2010 and a Ph.D. degree from the Electrical Engineering Department, Indian Institute of Technology Kanpur, India, in 2015. He has worked as an Erasmus Mundus Fellow with the Department of Computer Science, the University of Oxford, U.K from October 2014 to July 2015 and a Scientist with TCS Research, Kolkata, India from February 2016 to July 2016. Subsequently, he joined as an Assistant Professor at Visvesvaraya National Institute of Technology (VNIT), Nagpur, India from July 2016 to May 2017.

He published more than 50 research articles in prestigious journals, conference proceedings and book chapters. He has also edited a book titled "Innovations in Cyber Physical Systems", filed two patents, and undertaken four sponsored projects. His broad research interests include Wireless Sensor Networks, Internet of Things (IoT), Molecular Communications, 6G Wireless Communications Systems, Signal Processing, Machine Learning, and Deep Learning.

Dr. Kumar is a recipient of several awards and fellowships, such as the Best Teacher Award in UG Teaching from the EE Department; the best poster paper award at COMSNETS 2021; the CSIR, and SERB International Travel Grants; the National Award from L&T-ISTE for having guided the Best M.Tech. Thesis (Second Prize); the SERB Indo-U.S. Postdoctoral Fellowship, the India-EU Namaste Fellowship; the TCS Research Scholarship; the MHRD Scholarship; the IEEE ICC Student Travel Grant Award; and the COMSNETS Travel Grant. He has guided several B.Tech. and M.Tech. projects which won national awards. He is a member of ACM, a senior member of IEEE, and a life member of ISTE.

Abbreviations

ASN Absolute Slot Number

ACC Accelerometer

AP Access Point

ACK Acknowledgment

ADR Adaptive Data Rate

ARP Address Resolution Protocol

AIC Akaike Information Criterion

A All

AC Alternating Current

AoA Angle-of-Arrival

APIT Approximate Point in Triangle Test

AI Artificial Intelligence

AID Association Identifier

ABC Assumption Based Coordinates

AS Autonomous System

ASN Autonomous System Number

BO Backoff

BW Bandwidth

BIC Bayesian Information Criterion

B Beacon

BPSK Binary Phase Shift Keying

BTC Bitcoin

BGP Border Gateway Protocol

BIA Burnt-In Address

CSMA Carrier Sense Multiple Access

CSMA/CA Carrier Sense Multiple Access-Collision Avoidance

CPU Central Processing Unit

CO Channel Offset

CSI Channel State Information

CCD Charge Coupled Device

CSS Chirp Spreading Spectrum

CIDR Classless Interdomain Routing

CC Cloud Computing

CH Cluster Head

CR Code Rate

CMOS Complementary Metal Oxide Semiconductor

CON Confirmable Message

COAP COnstrained Application Protocol

CW Contention Window

CID Context Identifier Extension

C Continuous

CRLB Cramer-Rao Lower Bound

CDF Cumulative Distribution Function

CE Customer Edge

CRC Cyclic Redundancy Check

DAO-ACK DAO Acknowledgment

DIFS Data Inter Frame Spacing

DE Data Rate Optimization

DTLS Datagram Transport Layer Security

DL Deep-learning

DS Dempster-Shafer

DA Destination Address

DAM Destination Address Mode

DIPA Destination IP Address

DODAG Destination Oriented Directed Acylic Graph

DIC Deviance Information Criterion

DC Direct Current

DSSS Direct Sequence Spread Spectrum

DAG Directed Acylic Graph

DOA Direction of Arrival

DV-HOP Distance Vector Hop

DAO DODAG Advertisement Object

DIO DODAG Information Object

DIS DODAG Information Solicitation

DNS Domain Name System

ETR Egress Tunnel Routers

ECG Electrocardiogram

EDA Electrodermal Activity

EEG Electroencephalography

EMG Electromyography

ECC Elliptic Curve Cryptography

EID Endpoint Identifiers

EH Energy Harvesting

EVPN Ethernet Virtual Private Network

XOR Exclusive OR

XML Extensible Markup Language

XMPP Extensible Messaging and Presence Protocol

ERP Exterior Routing Protocol

FN False Negative

FP False Positive

FTP File Transfer Protocol

FIM Fisher information matrix

FR Flow rate

FC Fog Computing

FSR Force

FCS Frame Check Sequence

FC Frame Control

FHSS Frequency Hopping Spread Spectrum

FFD Full Function Device

GFSK Gaussian Frequency Shift Keying

GPS Global Positioning System

HC Header Compression

HT High Throughput

HAR Human Activity Recognition

HTTP HyperText Transfer Protocol

IH Implicit Header

IPHC ImProved Header Compression

IID Independent and Identically Distributed

ISM Industrial, Scientific, and Medical

IE Information Element

IR Infrared

ITR Ingress Tunnel Routers

IRP Interior Routing Protocol

ISO International Organization for Standardization

IANA Internet Assigned Number Authority

ICMP Internet Control Message Protocol

IETF Internet Engineering Task Force

IGMP Internet Group Message Protocol

IoT Internet of Things

IP Internetnetworking Protocol

ILT Inverse Laplace Transform

IPv4 IP version 4

IPv6 IP version 6

6LowPAN IPv6 over Low-Power Wireless Personal Area Networks

KKT Karush-Kuhn-Tucker

KYC Know Your Customer

LBG Linde, Buzo and Gray

LOS Line Of Sight

LSRP Link-State Routing Protocol

LAN Local Area Network

LISP Locator/Identifier Separation Protocol

LoRa Long Range Protocol

LoRaWAN Long Range Wide Area Networks

LPF Low Pass Filter

LEACH Low-energy adaptive clustering hierarchy

ML Machine Learning

MAP Maximum a Posteriori Estimate

MLE Maximum Likelihood Estimate

MAE Mean Absolute Error

MSE Mean Squared Error

MAC Media Access Control

MQTT Message Queue Telemetry Transport

MPC Model Predictive Control

MCS Modulation and Coding Scheme

MDS MultiDimensional Scaling

MIMO Multiple Input Multiple Output

NIC Network Interface Card

NH Next Header

NLOS Non-Line Of Sight

NON Non-Confirmable Message

NAC Number of Available Channels

OQPSK Offset Quadrature Phase Shift Keying

OSPF Open Shortest Path First

OSI Open System Interconnection

OS Operating System

OUI Organization Unique Identifier

OFDM Orthogonal Frequency Division Multiplexing

PER Packet Error Rate

PL Packet Length

PM Particulate Matter

PL Path Loss

PSK Phase Shift Keying

PSDU PHY service data unit

PHY Physical layer

Pl Plausibility

PS Power Saving

PSD Power Spectral Density

PSR Power Splitting based Relaying

PCA Principal Component Analysis

PDF Probability Density Function

PE Provider Edge

PN Pseudo-Noise

PAM Pulse Amplitude Modulation

QAM Quadrature Amplitude Modulation

QASK Quadrature Amplitude Shift Keying

QPSK Quadrature Phase Shift Keying

QoS Quality of Service

RF Radio Frequency

RFID Radio Frequency Identification

RAM Random Access Memory

RSS Received Signal Strength

RSSI Received Signal Strength Indicator

ReLu Rectified Linear

RFD Reduced Function Device

RDP Remote Desktop Protocol

RFC Request for Comments

RTD Resistance Temperature Detector

RESP Respiration

RAW Restricted Access Window

RARP Reverse Address Resolution Protocol

RIP Routing Information Protocol

RLOC Routing Locator

RPL Routing Protocol of Low Power and Lossy Networks

SHA Secure Hashing Algorithm

SSH Secure Socket Shell

SIFS Short Inter-Frame Space

SIG Signal

SINR Signal-to-Interference-plus-Noise Ratio

SNR Signal-to-Noise Ratio

SMTP Simple Mail Transfer Protocol

SNMP Simple Network Management Protocol

SVD Singular Value Decomposition

SA Source Address

SAM Source Address Mode

SIPA Source IP Address

SF Spreading Factor

SFD Start of Frame Delimiter

STA Station

SGD Stochastic Gradient Descent

TEMP Temperature

ToA Time of Air

TDOA Time-Difference-of-Arrival

TOA Time-of-Arrival

TSCH Time-Slotted Channel Hopping

TSR Time-Switching based Relay

TKL Token Length

TF Traffic class and Flow label

TIM Traffic Indication Map

TCP Transmission Control Protocol

TXOP Transmission Opportunity

TLS Transport Layer Security

TN True Negative

TP True Positive

T Type

UDI Uplink Data Indication

UDP User Datagram Protocol

Ver Version

VM Virtual Machine

Wi-Fi Wireless Fidelity

WPAN Wireless Personal Area Network

WWW World Wide Web

Symbol Description

$h(x)$	Activation function	d	Distance
θ	Angle in polar coordinate	D^k	Distortion
ψ_i	Angle of arrival	λ_e	Eigenvalue
λ_a	Arrival rate	a, b	Elliptic curve parameters
W	Bandwidth for binary baseband	κ	Energy conversion efficiency
$b^i(A_j)$	Belief	E	Energy expenditure
b_k	Bits	A, B, C	Events of Bayes' theorem
B_i^k	Boundary region at kth iteration for ith cluster	$\mathrm{FIM}(\phi)$	Fisher Information matrix
CO	Carbon monoxide	V_{avg}	Flow velocity
w_c	Carrier frequency	b_E	Fraction of power that relay harvest
$\Delta u(k)$	Change of control input		
e	Channel gain between relay and destination	a_E	Fraction of time for energy harvesting
h^E	Channel gain for desired signal	f	Frequency
		η	Gaussian noise
g^E	Channel gain for interfering signal	g	Generator of Elliptic curve
		EH_R	Harvested energy at relay
CH_i	Cluster head	L_{header}	Header size
s	Complex variable of Laplace transform	H_i	Hypothesis
		$\mathbf{I}$	Identity matrix
k_i	Confidence parameter	η_l	Learning rate
ϵ	Constant	L_s	Length of sequence
$\mathbf{C_1}, \mathbf{c_2}$	Constraints of quadprog	M_a	M-ary
t	Continuous time	$\mathbf{A}, \mathbf{b}$	Matrices of constraint of quadratic optimization problem
$u(t)$	Control input		
β_j	Convergence parameter		
$H(p,q)$	Cross-entropy	$\mathbf{P}, \mathbf{q}$	Matrices of quadprog
$\mathbf{C}(\phi)$	Covariance matrix of RSS	$\mathbf{A}, \mathbf{B}$	Matrices parameters of derivative of state in a state-space model
$\tilde{R}_{y_1,y_2}$	Cross correlation		
A_{cross}	Cross-sectional area		
n_r, g	Cyclic group of Elliptic curve	$\mathbf{C}, \mathbf{D}$	Matrices parameters of output of state in a state-space model
k	Discrete time	x^{max}	Maximum value of variable

	of a quadratic optimization problem	a_l, b_l	Parameters of a linear regression model
$\mu(\phi)$	Mean matrix of RSS	α	Path loss exponent
m	Metric in task offload	L_{data}	Payload size
$CW_{\min}$	Minimum contention window size	$Pl(T_i)$	Plausibility
		$p(n)$	PN sequence
$x^{\min}$	Minimum value of variable of quadratic optimization problem	$\mathbf{W_i}$	Positive semi definite matrix
k_n	Nearest neighbors in kNN	θ_p	Predicted control input and plant output
M_d	Network dimensions	N_p	Prediction horizon
NO_2	Nitric dioxide	p_r	Prime number of an elliptic curve
$\rho(x,y)$	Nodes distribution		
n_b	Number of bits of code	p	Probability
k_b	Number of bits of data	P_d	Probability of detection
l	Number of bits of message in clustering	P_e	Probability of error
		P_f	Probability of false alarm
L_c	Number of chips per information bit	P_s	Probability of successful transmission
K	Number of cluster	r	Radius of a circled cluster
I	Number of interfering sources	R	Rate
		y	Received signal
M	Number of measurements	r_{priv}	Receiver private key
N	Number of nodes	r_{pub}	Receiver public key
o	Number of ones in observations	r_{key}	Receiver secret key
		h	Sampling instant
N_{preamble}	Number of preamble symbols	s_{priv}	Sender private key
		s_{pub}	Sender public key
M_s	Number of sensors in Dempster-Shafer fusion	s_{key}	Sender secret key
		s^E	Signal
S	Number of successful transmission per frame time	P	Signal power
		sl	Slack variable
N_{symbol}	Number of symbols	$\theta_{a \text{ or } d}$	Slope in ECC
G	Number of transmission per frame time	N_{RAW}	Slot number in RAW
		v	Speed of signal
O_p	Offload percentage	SO_2	Sulphur dioxide
$F(x)$	Output function in learning	$\lambda_{c \text{ or } d}$	Threshold for detection scheme
Q_i	Output of a flip flop in PN sequence generator		
		T	Time duration
O_3	Ozone	τ	Time lag
α^f, β_f	Parameters of the Friss transmission model	D	Total number of shift registers
λ, μ	Parameters of the Lagrange function	$(.)^T$	Transpose of a matrix
		(x, y)	Two dimensional

coordinates of an unknown node

(x_i, y_i) Two dimensional coordinates of an anchor node

σ^2 Variance of Gaussian noise

$\mathbf{e}$ Vector of all ones

w_i Weight

Chapter 1

Things and Internet

1.1 Introduction

We first give an overview of an Internet of Things (IoT) architecture before getting into the intricacies of an IoT network. There are four layers in a general IoT architecture. They are things layer, network layer, middleware services, and application layer in a 4-stage IoT architecture as shown in Figure 1.1. In the things layer, the sensors collect data from an event and the actuators take mechanical actions based on the decision made. At the network layer, gateways and IoT devices form a larger network for sending data or decisions from one IoT device to other. They communicate and notify among themselves using the IoT communication protocols . The data is analyzed further using things data analytics in middleware services.

In addition to collecting data from things, we also need the location of the IoT devices. The Global Positioning System (GPS) fails in an indoor or an underground scenario because of the unavailability of satellite signals. Further, the energy consumption of GPS is high. Therefore, we utilize a localization algorithm for estimating the location of a device. Since we know that there are resource-constrained devices in the IoT networks, the computation is not always achievable on the IoT devices. To facilitate the distributed storage and computing capabilities closer to the IoT devices and gateways, we leverage a concept of fog computing paradigm. Moreover, an energy harvesting technique is leveraged to harvest energy from mechanical energy, wind energy, water current, or electromagnetic waves amongst others. A low complexity constrained application protocol and message queue telemetry transport is used at the application layer for providing user interface and supporting services to the users. Finally, the privacy and security in the IoT network are achieved using things data anonymization, elliptic curve cryptography, and blockchain technology.

DOI: 10.1201/9781003225584-1

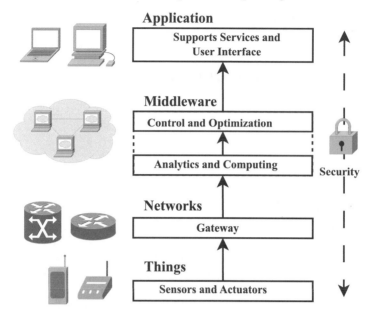

FIGURE 1.1: 4-stage architecture of IoT

1.2   Things

Thing is a physical smart object which has a sensor, unique identity over the networks, microcontroller for data processing and filtering, and transceiver for transmitting and receiving purposes. The sensor is a device that senses some physical phenomena such as temperature, humidity, light, heat, pressure, chemical substances amongst others, and converts to some meaningful output. Note that the transducer converts the sensed physical input to an electric one for an electrical transducer. Further, an actuator does some control action by converting electrical signals to some mechanical motions. The simplest example of an actuator is the opening and closing of a door or an air conditioner based on the temperature of a room. Therefore, the things must have *Sensing, Actuating, and Unique Addressing* characteristics in the IoT network. We discuss different types of sensors next.

1.2.1   Temperature Sensor

The amount of heat (Joule) of an object cannot be measured. However, the change of heat content as a result of a temperature change can be measured. Temperature sensor converts the temperature of a body, home, plant, soil, or air amongst others to an electrical signal. Let us briefly discuss different types of temperature sensors.

Thermocouple: Two dissimilar conductors in contact (junction) give rise to small contact potential and change as temperature varies. Voltage is generated as a result of a difference in temperature of hot and cold junctions because of the thermoelectric Seebeck effect. We assume the temperature of the cold junction known for calculation purposes. Therefore, we do not require an external current source. The range of temperature that can be measured by it is $-260°$ C to $2300°$ C.

Resistance Temperature Detector (RTD): The resistance changes as a function of temperature linearly. RTD is a passive element, therefore, an external electric current is applied to it. The voltage is generated across terminals is an indication of temperature. It can measure temperature range from $-200°$ C to $600°$ C.

Thermistor: This is a temperature-dependent resistance. In negative (or positive) temperature coefficient, resistance decreases (or increases) at temperature increases. In thermistor, the range is $-100°$ C to $500°$ C.

Semiconductor Temperature Sensor: The principle is that the voltage across the PN junction is a function of temperature. It has low cost, small size, and linear characteristics, however, range $-55°$ C to $200°$ C is limited. In short, the thermocouple has high sensitivity, RTD is more accurate and a semiconductor sensor is used for measuring the temperature of electronics products.

1.2.2 Pressure Sensor

We measure pressure of a gas or liquid. Pressure is a force per unit area which is equal to Pascal $= \frac{N}{m^2}$ or Bar. The capacitance or Ohmic resistance of a strain gauge or piezoelectric element changes as a function of applied pressure.

Piezoelectric Pressure Sensor: The charges are produced when the pressure is applied and in turn generate the electric signal. The original shape is deformed by applying force. This is suitable for dynamic pressure measurements. The applications are notifying the user when the air pressure of a tire becomes low, and weather forecasting by measuring air pressure to name a few.

1.2.3 Proximity Sensor

Proximity sensor is used for object detection and distance estimation between a sensor and an object using electromagnetic field, light, or sound signals without any physical contact. The absence of physical contact increases the durability of the proximity sensor. Inductive, capacitive, and infrared sensors are examples of a proximity sensor.

Inductive sensor detects the metallic object using an electromagnetic field which is produced by passing an alternating current to the coil. Eddy current generates and inductance changes in the presence of an object.

Capacitive sensor detects both metallic and non-metallic objects using electrostatic field. When an object comes closer to the sensing area, the capacitance increases. In parallel plate capacitor, the capacitance is given by

$$\text{Capacitance} = \frac{\text{Permittivity} \times \text{Area}}{\text{PS}} \tag{1.1}$$

where PS is the plate separation.

Ultrasonic sensor detects the object within its vicinity using round-trip time of sound signals and its speed as

$$\text{distance} = \frac{\text{round-trip time} \times \text{speed}}{2} \tag{1.2}$$

Infrared (IR) Sensor is similar to an ultrasound sensor, however, it uses an infrared signal. This uses an IR Light-Emitting Diode (LED) for emitting and a light detector for detecting reflecting signals. The applications of inductive, capacitive, ultrasonic, and IR sensors are in smart parking, smart device screen, robotics, and TV remote control respectively.

1.2.4 Air Quality (Gas) Sensor

This measures particulate matter with a diameter of less than and equal to 2.5 microns (PM 2.5), the gas emitted by volatile organic compounds, carbon monoxide, carbon dioxide, ozone, sulfur dioxide, and nitrous oxide.

1.2.5 Humidity Sensor (or Hygrometer)

Humidity sensor measures the amount of water vapor in the air (gas). The electrical permittivity of the dielectric material between two electrodes changes with a change in humidity. Note that the moisture is the water content present in solid and liquid.

1.2.6 Level Sensor

Level sensor measures the level of fluid using a non-contact ultrasonic sensor. It is similar to measuring the distance based on the round trip time between transmitted and reflected signals from the surface of the liquid. The maximum range that can be measured is about 4 m to 8 m. The applications of level sensors are for water-level, tank-level, or any other liquid.

1.2.7 Flow Sensor

Flow sensor measures the rate of fluid in a pipe in liters per hour or a minute or cubic meter based on the Hall effect. There is a valve through which water passes. The rotor in the valve rotates at a different rate of flow and indicates the speed in terms of the pulse signal. A potential difference that is transverse to the electric current is created in the conductor because of the rotation of the rotor which has the magnet. The induced voltage is measured by a Hall effect sensor. The flow rate, FR, is given by

$$\text{FR} = V_{\text{avg}} A_{\text{cross}} \tag{1.3}$$

where V_{avg} (m/s) and A_{cross} (m^2) denote average velocity of the flow and known cross-sectional area of the pipe. The applications include flow of cold/warm/dirty water in water management, dairy industry, agriculture sector, and coffee machine.

1.2.8   Accelerometer

Acceleration is the rate of change of velocity of the object with respect to the time. An accelerometer is an electro-mechanical device that measures the acceleration of an object. The mass on a spring is displaced with a rate equal to the sensed acceleration of the object. In a piezoelectric accelerometer, the crystal generates a voltage equivalent to the velocity and orientation of the object by applying stress. The use cases are in the inertial navigation system to measure position, orientation, and velocity of an object in motion; to measure vibration is machine/structure of building/bridge and health monitoring.

1.2.9   Imaging sensor

In an image sensor, the photons of a small portion of an image are collected and stored as electrons. These charges need to be read. The image sensor is built using either charge-coupled device (CCD), analog in nature, or complementary metal-oxide-semiconductor (CMOS), which is digital in nature technology. CCD is a collection of capacitors and each capacitor transfers the content to the neighboring capacitors. The content of the last capacitor is fed to the amplifier. Notably, each capacitor carries an electric charge related to the pixel's light intensity. In CMOS, there are CMOS transistors and photodiode for each pixel. Pixel signals are amplified individually. The CMOS image sensor has a higher speed and smaller power consumption and cost than that of a CCD image sensor. The application is in a digital camera and medical imaging.

1.2.10   Characteristics of Sensors

The accuracy, precision, sensitivity, threshold, and resolution are the important characteristics of sensors in measurement. The accuracy is measured by how close the measured value is to the true value. The higher the closeness, the higher the accuracy. On the other hand, precision deals with repeatability and reproducibility where the same measured value repeats if the measuring conditions do not change. For example, if the actual temperature is 98 degrees Celsius and multiple measurements are closer to 98 degrees Celsius, then it is both accurate and precise. However, all measurements are closer to say 95 degrees Celsius then the sensor has low accuracy and high precision. Finally, if measurements are scattered say between 95 and 98 degrees Celsius, then the sensor is both inaccurate and has low precision. In short, the standard deviation (drift) of measurements is small for high precision.

The sensitivity is defined as the ratio of change of output to the change in input. The threshold is the minimum input for which the output can be detected. The resolution is defined as the smallest change in the input for which the output can be detected. The sensitivity and resolution should be high.

The hysteresis is because of the reluctance of a material. We have different measurements at the same actual value because of different directions of measurements, say, increasing and decreasing actual measurements. This is not desirable. There are other characteristics in instrumentation and measurements.

1.2.11   Actuators

The sensor senses the physical phenomena and the actuator takes some mechanical action. The actuator converts some form of energy into motion such as linear, rotary, and oscillatory. The screw is a simple example of a mechanical linear actuator.

Electric Actuator: Electric actuator converts electrical energy of Alternating Current (AC) or Direct Current (DC) form into kinetic energy of mechanical motion. The simple examples of the electric actuator are DC and AC motors, and solenoids for an electric actuator.

Pneumatic Actuator: Pneumatic actuator uses compressed air at high pressure and convert this energy into motion. The simple pneumatic actuator is an air brake.

Hydraulic Actuator: Hydraulic actuator uses the liquid for generating motion. A cylinder or fluid-based motor uses the power of hydraulics to generate mechanical action. An example of a hydraulic actuator is hydraulic cranes or jacks.

Thermal Actuator: Thermal actuator converts thermal energy into kinetic energy. An example of a thermal actuator is a valve. This opens and closes based on a threshold temperature in temperature control.

1.3   Internet

Open System Interconnection (OSI) model was developed by International Organization for Standardization (ISO) in 1984. This standardizes data transfer from one open computer to another open computer in a computer network regardless of underlying software and hardware architectures.

Let us define service and protocol in a layered architecture. The service is a set of operations that a layer renders to the layer above it. The protocol is a set of rules and conventions that allow two or more entities to interact within a layer. The protocol must not be ambiguous and implements the service.

The OSI has seven layers, namely, Physical, Data Link, Network, Transport, Session, Presentation, and Application. On sending side, the data goes from the top layer to the bottom layer, while on receiving side, it goes from the bottom to the top layer in opposite direction.

1.3.1   OSI Model

Let us consider an analogy of sending a letter through post or courier. At higher layers of OSI model, the sender writes a letter, puts it in an envelope, mentions sender and receiver addresses, drops it in a letterbox. In the middle layers, the letter goes from the letterbox to the post office. At lower layers, the post office hand-overs the letter to a van (carrier) to carry it to the city of destination.

The letter arrives at the post office of the destination. At the lower layers of the receiver side, the post office receives the letter from the carrier. In the middle layers, the letter goes from the post office to the person's letterbox. At higher layers, the letter is opened from the envelope and read by the receiver.

The first layer for the sender is an application layer, while the receiver is the physical layer. The top three layers mainly deal with software, the middle one connects higher and lower layers, and the bottom three layers mainly deal with hardware. Generally, computer science or information technology people work with higher layers. The electrical and electronics people generally deal with lower layers. The seven layers of the OSI model for sender and receiver sides are shown in Figure 1.2. At the sender side top to bottom movement, while bottom to top on the receiver side. We discuss each layer starting from the bottom-most layer next.

Physical Layer: The physical layer converts the frames which is the sequence of 1s (ones) and 0s (zeros) from the data link layer and encodes them into a signal suitable for transmission media. This provides an electrical and mechanical interface between the device and media. The layer generates different signals based on the types of transmission media. Those are electrical on-off signal, light signal, and radio signal for copper/LAN wires, fiber-optic cable, and air, respectively.

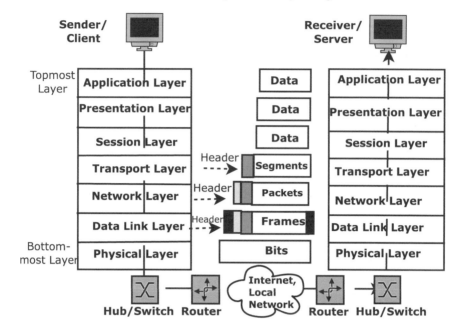

FIGURE 1.2: End-to-end perspective of OSI Model

Data or transmission rate is the number of bits per second which is decided by the physical layer. The source and destination need to be synchronized at the bit level. The connections of devices can be point-to-point and multipoint communications. This leads to different topologies of the network such as star, ring, and mesh. Transmissions can proceed in

- *Simplex*: only one device can send and the other can receive and their roles cannot be interchanged.

- *Half-duplex*: both devices can send and receive, but not at the same time.

- *Full-duplex*: both devices can send and receive at a time.

Data Link Layer: The packet is received at the data link layer from the network layer. The packet is broken into smaller units called frames. The layer uses physical address such as Media Access Control (MAC) address for *hop to hop delivery* among different systems on the same network/LAN (Local Area Network). Therefore, a packet together with MAC addresses of source and destination form a frame. Notably, media implies physical link herein not audio, video, and animation. *Media access control* refers to sending (or receiving) the frames to (or from) the media. Several devices share the same media and it can lead to a collision in case of simultaneous access of media by

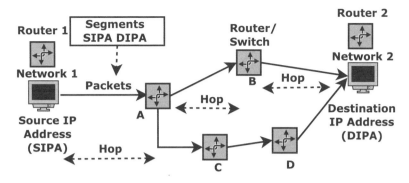

FIGURE 1.3: Interconnection of various devices

different devices. Carrier Sense Multiple Access (CSMA) scheme ensures that media is free before transmission to avoid a collision.

Example: In Figure 1.3, data link layer at the source sends the frames to router A. The router A is the destination address in the first hop. Similarly, the data link layer of A (source for the second hop) sends the frame to Router B (destination for the second hop). The header changes for each hop because of a change in source and destination. This process repeats until it arrives at the final destination. The layer is responsible for error control, flow control, and access control. The protocol is Ethernet for LAN at this layer.

MAC Address: MAC address is a physical address which is a 12 digits hexadecimal number of Network Interface Card (NIC) of the computer or laptop. This address is also called hardware address or Burnt-In Address (BIA) for Cisco systems. The address is globally unique because the first 6 hexadecimal digits are provided by Organization Unique Identifier (OUI) which is unique for each organization. The rest 6 hexadecimal digits are organization-specific serial number, which is decided locally by the organization.

Example of MAC Address: For instance, assign serial number one to the first system, two to the second system, and so on. The example of MAC address is shown in Figure 1.4. If organization-specific serial numbers are exhausted, then the organization needs to get a new OUI from IANA (Internet Assigned Number Authority). A computer has several MAC addresses as many as the number of NICs of Ethernet, WiFi, and Bluetooth.

The least significant bit of the first byte is 0 for unicast (frames are sent to a specific device or NIC) and 1 for multicast (frames are sent to a group of devices in a LAN). The MAC address of the source device is always set to unicast. In a broadcast, frames are sent to all devices on the LAN. The broadcast address has all ones in all bits of the destination address, that is, FFFF FFFF FFFF. In error control, the layer uses Cyclic Redundancy Check (CRC) to detect an error. The bits can be corrupted while transmission from the source to the destination.

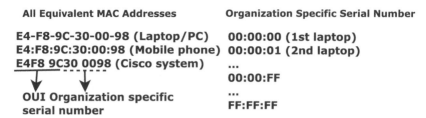

All Equivalent MAC Addresses	Organization Specific Serial Number
E4-F8-9C-30-00-98 (Laptop/PC)	00:00:00 (1st laptop)
E4:F8:9C:30:00:98 (Mobile phone)	00:00:01 (2nd laptop)
E4F8 9C30 0098 (Cisco system)	...
	00:00:FF
OUI Organization specific serial number	...
	FF:FF:FF

FIGURE 1.4: MAC address example

Example of CRC Encoder: Let k_b (= 4) and n_b (= 6) be the number of bits of data and code, respectively. Therefore, we append $n_b - k_b$ (= 2) bits zeros at the end of the data initially. The highest power of the generator polynomial is also $n_b - k_b$ (= 2), however, the number of bits in it is $n_b - k_b + 1$ (= 3). Say, $x^2 + 1 \equiv 101$ (coefficients of different powers of x in sequence) and data $x^3 + x^2 + 1 \equiv 1101$ in Figure 1.5(a). The number of bits that we bring from the original dividend is equal to the number of leftmost zeros in the dividend at any step. There is no use of quotient and the remainder is the redundant bits that need to be added at the end of the original data. In Figure 1.5(a), no further division is possible at the end and the remainder is 10. Therefore, the codeword is 1101 10.

Let us discuss Modulo-2 arithmetic for CRC encoding and decoding. The additions are $0 + 0 = 0$, $0 + 1 = 1$, $1 + 0 = 1$, $1 + 1 = 0$. The subtractions are $0 - 0 = 0$, $0 - 1 = 1$, $1 - 0 = 1$, $1 - 1 = 0$. Note that the results for addition and subtraction are the same. The addition or subtraction is like a XOR operation. When both bits are the same the result is 0, otherwise 1. Here, modulus is 2, therefore, only two bits 0 and 1 are allowed.

Example of CRC Decoder: It is assumed that transmitter and receiver know the same generator polynomial. The steps for CRC encoder and CRC decoder are similar as shown in Figure 1.5(b)–(c). In the decoder, the modulo-2 division is carried out using generator polynomial and received data. If the remainder is 0 then bits of transmitted are not corrupted in Figure 1.5(b). Otherwise, 4-bits data is corrupted as shown in Figure 1.5(c) and discarded. It can detect single-bit error and burst error of length equal to a polynomial degree.

Network Layer: The layer is responsible for the delivery of packets from source to destination across different networks. The network layer does *logical addressing* and *routing*. The segments received from the transport layer is broken into smaller data units called packets (or IP datagrams). This contains source (SIPA) and destination addresses (DIPA) as shown in Figure 1.3.

In logical addressing (IP addressing), every computer in the network has a unique IP address so that the packet arrives at the correct destination. Routing protocols determine the best route or path (through B) for forwarding packets from source to destination via router or switch. When the packet arrives at A from the source, router A uses a routing table to send it to the next router

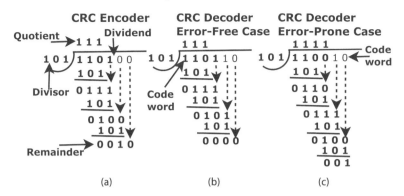

FIGURE 1.5: Cyclic redundancy check

B. Further, B sends that to the final destination. The protocols of this layer are IPv4 and IPv6. We discuss the IP addressing in the IP addresses section.

Transport Layer: Transport layer is an end to end delivery of the message from source to destination. On the other hand, lower layers is for source to neighbor (hop). The layer is responsible for reliability of communications using *segmentation, reassembly, flow control, error control, and connection control.*

Segmentation and Reassembly: The data received from the session layer is broken into smaller units called segments. This is shown in Figure 1.6. Each segment has source and destination port numbers and sequence number. The port number directs each segment to the correct application. Segment number helps in the reassembly of the segments correctly at the receiver. Notably, the port number connects application and transport layers, while the protocol number connects TCP (Transmission Control Protocol) or UDP (User Datagram Protocol) and network layer.

Connection Controls: TCP and UDP are transport layer protocols. TCP is a connection-oriented transmission for Email, WWW and FTP services, while UDP is a connection-less transmission for online movies, and games to name a few. In TCP, a connection is established with the transport layer of the destination, segments are sent and then a connection is terminated. TCP provides acknowledgment and helpful for retransmission of lost data, while UDP does not, and hence, the UDP is faster than the TCP. Finally, the transport layer sends the segments underneath the network layer.

Error and Flow control: Error control deals with the arrival of segments at the receiver whether it is error-free or not. The error can happen because of damage, loss, or duplication of segments. In the flow control, rate of generation of data at the source is controlled according to the rate of absorption of data at the destination to avoid loss of segments.

Presentation Layer: *Presentation layer* is responsible for the syntax and semantics of the information transmitted. The layer does translation, encryption, and compression. Since the sender may use different data representations

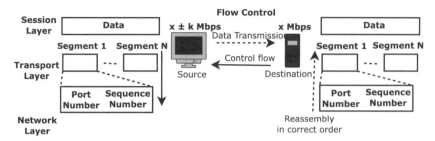

FIGURE 1.6: Segmentation, reassembly and flow control at transport layer

or encoding formats, the layer translates that to a standard encoding format to be used on the wire. The reverse operation is followed at the presentation layer at the receiver side.

Session layer: establishes and maintains connections between different systems at the sender and received sides. The layer is responsible for dialog control and synchronization. In dialog control, half-duplex (unidirectional communication at a time) or full-duplex mode (bidirectional communication at a time) is decided for the communication among devices.

In synchronization, checkpoints are added to a stream of data. For instance, if we have 100 bytes to be transmitted, then the checkpoints are added after every 10 bytes and acknowledgment is needed to ensure proper receipt. If some crash happens at byte number 26, then only bytes 21 to 26 need to be retransmitted.

Application Layer: The data is encapsulated as it moves down the layers by adding headers at each layer. The application layer provides an interface to the user for accessing the network and allows for email, remote file transfer, and remote desktop.

HyperText Transfer Protocol (HTTP) application layer protocol is used for World Wide Web. When a webpage is needed by the web browser (say, Mozilla or Chrome) which in turn sends the name of the webpage via HTTP to the server. Subsequently, the server sends back the webpage. Note that the web browser is not the application layer protocol. The other application layer protocols are FTP (File Transfer Protocol), SNMP (Simple Network Management Protocol), SMTP (Simple Mail Transfer Protocol), DNS (Domain Naming System), RDP (Remote Desktop Protocol), Telnet, and SSH (Secure Socket Shell).

1.3.2   OSI Model versus TCP/IP Model

On the sender side, the message comes top-to-down and gets encapsulated at each layer. The receiver does the reverse operation by moving up the layers toward the application layer (bottom-to-top) by decapsulating bits to frames, frames to packets, and packets to segments. The sender message

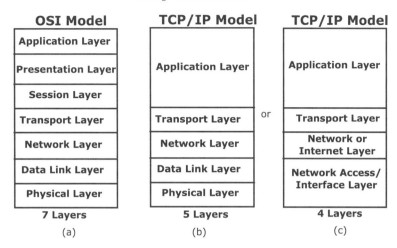

FIGURE 1.7: TCP/IP models

is then readable on the computer of the receiver. OSI model is a theoretical model of networking. However, it helps us in understanding the practical TCP/IP model.

OSI model and TCP/IP model are developed separately by ISO and Department of Defense of USA, respectively. TCP/IP model was already in the process of development at the time of publication of the OSI model. The number of layers in OSI model is seven as shown in Figure 1.7(a) while in TCP/IP model, it is four or five layers as shown in Figure 1.7(b) and 1.7(c). We start understanding the TCP/IP model by assuming four or five layers with the help of the theoretical OSI model.

TCP of the transport layer and IP of the network layer together facilitate communication in the TCP/IP model. Application, presentation, and session layers of the OSI model are viewed together as an application layer of the TCP/IP model. Functionalities of the layers in the TCP/IP model are similar to that of the OSI model. TCP provides sequencing and acknowledgment, while IP provides routing.

1.3.3 Devices at Different Layers

The repeaters regenerate the signal and hub is the central element of the star topology. The hub is a multi-ports repeater. The number of direct connections among N nodes is $\frac{N(N-1)}{2}$. On the other hand, using the hub-and-spoke model, the number of connections is reduced down to N. This is because each node is not directly connected to other nodes rather connected to the hub. These devices work on the physical layer as shown in Figure 1.8.

The bridge connects two hubs and forward the frame based on the forwarding table at each node. Switch is a device that creates temporary connections between two or more devices. The switch is a combination of hubs and bridges.

Layers	Devices
Application	Gateway
Transport	
Network	Router
Data Link	Bridge and Switch
Physical	Repeater and Hub

FIGURE 1.8: Devices at different layers

There are multiple ports of a switch. We can write devices in descending order of performance as a switch, bridge, and hub. The switch and bridge work on the data link layer. We use router and gateway at the network and higher layer, respectively. The router connects two or more different networks. The number of ports in a router is lower than that of the switch.

1.3.4   Circuit and Packet Switching

In a circuit switching, a dedicated connection is established for two communicating stations as shown in Figure 1.9(a). Circuit switching is used in telephone systems which is ideal for communications. In packet switching, a large message is broken into packets. The packets are numbered from 1 through 5 in Figure 1.9(b). Each packet can take different paths while reaching the destination. Each packet has a sequence number, source, and destination IP addresses. At the receiver, packets can be out of order and are reassembled at the destination that makes it more flexible.

Internet is based on packet switching of TCP/IP protocol. Note that packet switching has two further types, namely, the datagram approach and the virtual circuit approach. The virtual circuit is like circuit switching. However, it creates dedicated logical connections between source and destination and uses the concept of packets.

1.3.5   Some Protocols of TCP/IP Model

We define herein some of the important protocols of TCP/IP briefly. At network layer, we use *Internetworking Protocol (IP)* which is unreliable and connectionless. IP sends data in a packet called datagram. They can take different routes and can be out of order at the receiver. IP does not reorder. However, the IP provides the best effort services. That is, it tries its level best to provide service but does not provide any guarantee. *Address Resolution*

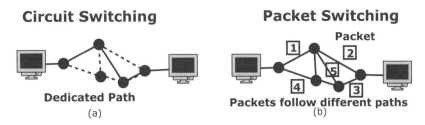

FIGURE 1.9: Circuit and Packet Switching

Protocol (ARP) identifies the physical address from logical (Internet) address. On a LAN, the device is identified by its physical address. On the contrary, *Reverse Address Resolution Protocol (RARP)* identifies the Internet address from physical address. This is used at the time of booting when a computer is connected to a network. In *Internet Control Message Protocol (ICMP)*, hosts and gateway send back the sender notification message such as error reporting. *Internet Group Message Protocol (IGMP)* sends the message to a group of recipients.

1.3.6   IPv4 Addresses

The addresses are categorized as physical (MAC) address and logical addresses. The logical address can be further divided into IP version 4 (IPv4) and IP version 6 (IPv6). These addresses again can be public or private. The IPv4 address consists of two parts, namely, network ID and host ID.

Subnet mask is used to separate IP address into network address and host address. The IPv4 address has 32 bits or 4 octets in total. In each octet, the value could be between 0 and 255 in decimal. The IP address is represented in a dotted-decimal format with 4 decimals for 4 different octets. There are five classes: Class *A*, Class *B*, Class *C*, Class *D*, and Class *E*. We use Class *A*, Class *B*, and Class *C* for large, medium, and small organizations, respectively. Class *D* is used in multicasting for communicating to a group of devices, while Class *E* for research purposes. We generally use a private IP and the provider uses a public IP.

Classes: The different types of classes in IPv4 address is shown in Figure 1.10. Theoretically, IP address 0.0.0.0 is for the network or host, itself. IP address 127.x.x.x belongs to Class A, however, 127.x.x.x is reserved for loopback IP addresses. This is used to check whether the NIC of the system is working fine or not while connecting to the Internet. If we ping 127.0.0.0 and get a reply, then the issue is not with the system but the outside network.

- *Class A*: The first bit of first octet is 0. The binary representation of first octet is 00000001 to 01111111 which is equal to 1 to 127 in decimal. Therefore, Class A IP address is 1.x.x.x to 127.x.x.x in decimal.

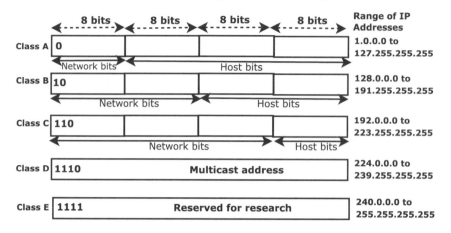

FIGURE 1.10: Types of classes

- *Class B*: The first two bits of the first octet is 10. The binary representation of the first octet is 10 000000 to 10 111111 which is equal to 128 to 191 in decimal. Therefore, Class B IP address is 128.0.x.x to 191.255.x.x in decimal.

- *Class C*: The first three bits of the first octet is 110. The binary representation of the first octet is 110 00000 to 110 11111 which is equal to 192 to 223 in decimal. Therefore, Class C IP address is 192.0.0.x to 223.255.255.x in decimal.

- *Class D*: The first four bits of first octet is 1110. The binary representation of the first octet is 1110 0000 to 1110 1111 which is equal to 224 to 239 in decimal. Therefore, the Class D IP address is 224.0.0.0 to 239.255.255.255 in decimal.

- *Class E*: The first four bits of first octet is 1111. The binary representation of the first octet is 1111 0000 to 1111 1111 which is equal to 240 to 255 in decimal. Therefore, the Class E IP address is 240.0.0.0 to 255.255.255.255 in decimal.

Subnet Mask: The network and host bits are represented by 1 and 0, respectively.

- *Class A*: The first one octet is of network and rest three octets are of host. Therefore, subnet mask for this class is 1111 1111.0000 0000.0000 0000.0000 0000 in binary, that is, 255.0.0.0 in decimal.

- *Class B*: The first two octets are of network and the rest two octets are of the host. Therefore, the subnet mask for this class is 1111 1111.1111 1111.0000 0000.0000 0000 in binary, that is, 255.255.0.0 in decimal.

- *Class C*: The first three octets are of network and the rest one octet is of the host. Therefore, the subnet mask for this class is 1111 1111.1111 1111.1111 1111.0000 0000 in binary, that is, 255.255.255.0 in decimal.

We purchase a particular network ID for connecting some number of hosts, not a full class. If we run short of it, we purchase one more network ID. We do not need to purchase the private IPs, which can be allocated may be on a serial number basis to the computers by the organization locally.

Number of Network IDs and Host IDs: The total number of hosts is equal to $2^{\text{host bits}}$. However, the actual number of hosts is equal to $2^{\text{host bits}} - 2$. We subtract 2 because we cannot use the first ID which is a network ID and the last ID which is a broadcast ID. For example, IP 130.5.10.15 belongs to class B. Therefore, the first 16 bits are of the network and the next 16 bits are of the host. In this example, the network ID is 130.5.0.0. The broadcast ID 130.5.255.255 cannot be used. The broadcast ID is used to send the message from one computer to all the computers on that LAN or network.

The number of usable hosts in class A, class B, and class C are $2^{24} - 2$ = 1,67,77,214, $2^{16} - 2 = 65534$, and $2^8 - 2 = 254$, respectively. Similarly, the number of networks for class A, class B, and class C are $2^7 = 128$, $2^{14} = 16384$, and $2^{21} = 20,97,152$, respectively. Therefore, class A supports a large number of hosts for a large organization, class B for a medium sized organization, and class C for a small number of hosts in a small organization.

Example: Identify the classes of the IPs: 110.10.20.30, 150.10.20.30, and 200.10.20.30, and find the network IDs, broadcast IDs, and the number of actual hosts for the given IP.

Solution: Based on the first octet, 110, 150, and 200 belong to class A, class B, and class C, respectively. The first one, two, and three octets are of network for class A, class B, and class C, respectively. Since the network bits are represented by bit 1, therefore, networks ids are 110.0.0.0, 150.10.0.0, and 200.10.20.0, respectively. The broadcast IDs are 110.255.255.255, 150.10.255.255, and 200.10.20.255, respectively. The number of actual hosts are $2^{24} - 2$, $2^{16} - 2$, and $2^8 - 2$, respectively.

Subnet: It is a network within the network or division of IP address. A network can connect several computers, say 254 computers in class C. However, if we connect only 10 computers, then $254 - 10 = 244$ IPs are wasted. The different departments or labs of an organization are divided internally. Notably, an outside world can see a single network.

First Approach: Make a large routing table of 254 entries in the main router. When some packets arrive, direct them to an appropriate subnet. This approach is highly complex if we use class A or B.

Second Approach: Say for class C, we have 24 bits for the network and 8 bits for the host. We can borrow some bits from the host to network. Let us consider the following example to illustrate it.

Example of Subnet: Consider a class C network ID 200.10.20.0/24 with subnet mask 255.255.255.0. Make different possible subnets for 40 hosts in each subnet.

Solution: For 40 hosts, $2^{\text{host bits}} - 2 \geq 40$ gives 6 bits for host and rest 26 bits for network. Write ID like 200.10.20.**00** 000000 in mixed decimal and binary notation. The bold digit represents the borrow bits for network. As network and host bits are represented by bit 1 and 0, respectively. We can rewrite 200.10.20.**11** 000000 in mixed decimal and binary notation which is equal to 200.10.20.192 in decimal notation. This is the last subnet. The following are the possible subnets for this example:

- **Subnet 1**: 200.10.20.0/26 with subnet mask 255.255.255.192

- **Subnet 2**: Go from right to left and find bit 1 and write corresponding decimal value as 200.10.20.64/26 by adding 64 in previous step subnet ID. This is because $2^{\text{host bits}} = 64$ for host bits = 6. Each subnet must connect 40 hosts which is less than or equal to 64 hosts.

- **Subnet 3**: 200.10.20.128/26 by adding 64 like previous step.

- **Subnet 4**: 200.10.20.192/26 by adding 64 like previous step.

We cannot get Subnet 5 because adding 64 makes 192 to 256 which is greater than 255. This is because the decimal value of each octet must be in the range of 0 to 255. We cannot also make the third octet from 20 to 21. The network changes as ID is of Class C.

Classless Interdomain Routing: Classful addressing, namely, class A, B, and C are not flexible. This is because the number of hosts in class B is too high which is equal to $2^{16} - 2 = 65534$ for most of the organization. On the contrary, the number of hosts in class C is too low which is equal to $2^8 - 2 = 254$. In Classless Interdomain Routing (CIDR) notation, IP address 200.10.20.0/20 means that there are 20 bits for the network and 12 bits (= total 32 bits − 20 bits) for the host. The network mask is equal to 255.255.1111 0000. 0000 0000 in mixed decimal and binary notation. This is simplified to 255.255.240.0 in decimal notation.

Supernet: This is used to aggregate routes to reduce the size of a routing table. For example, IP addresses 200.10.0.0 and 200.10.2.0 are aggregated by performing binary AND operation of these two addresses. In binary notation, the first and second IP addresses are:
11001000.00001010.00000000.00000000 and
11001000.00001010.00000010.00000000. The binary AND of these two addresses is 11001000.00001010.00000000.00000000. The result is finally given by 200.10.0.0 in decimal notation.

1.3.7 IPv6 Addresses

Let us first discuss the limitation of IPv4 addressing. IPv4 address is 32 bits long. Therefore, it can provide the addresses to $2^{32} = 429,49,67,296 \approx 4.3$ billion devices. However, in IoT networks, we have 20 to 50 billion devices. This motivates us to use IPv6 address which is 128 bits = 16 bytes long. This

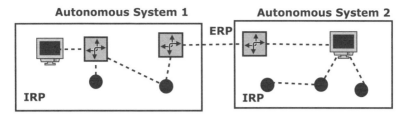

FIGURE 1.11: Autonomous systems

can provide $2^{128} = 3.4 \times 10^{38}$ unique addresses. We use hexadecimal colon notation and there are 8 sections. Each section is of length 2 bytes and requires 4 hexadecimal digits.

For example, ABCD:0034:12AB:4821:BAC2:0000:0000:FFFF. Since it is very long, the leading zeros can be discarded as ABCD:34:12AB:4821:BAC2:0:0:FFFF in simplified notation. Furthermore, consecutive zeros can be replaced with double semi-colon only once as ABCD:34:12AB:4821:BAC2::FFFF.

Note that we can express the address in binary form too as follows $(ABCD)_{16} = (1010\ 1011\ 1100\ 1101)_2$ and so on. Now, we can expand it to the original form by simply inserting an appropriate number of zeros. In the case of two or more sections having continuous zero, only one can be replaced with a double semi-colon. This is because there is an ambiguity to identify the number of sections of zeros at each place.

1.3.8 Routing at Network Layer

The router uses the routing table to send the IP packets from one hop to another. In the beginning, the entire route from source to destination is not known. Instead, the route is calculated after each hop. For IoT networks, we use *dynamic routing* in contrast to *static routing*. A static route in the network is precomputed manually beforehand, whereas, the path is automatically updated based on the speed or failure of the links in the case of dynamic routing.

Routing Information Protocol (RIP): The protocol is based on the distance-vector protocol. Distance vector is also known by other names such as Bellman-Ford or Ford-Fulkerson routing algorithm. The algorithm has a long convergence time or count-to-infinity problem. On the other hand, Open Shortest Path First (OSPF) protocol is based on link-state protocol. A route can have different metrics like delay, cost, and speed.

Interior and Exterior Routing Protocols: *Autonomous System* is a collection of networks under single administration having a common routing scheme. *Interior Routing Protocol (IRP)* is for routing within the autonomous system to exchange the information such OSPF routing protocol as shown in Figure 1.11. *Exterior Routing Protocol (ERP)* is for routing between

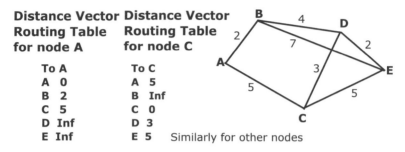

Distance Vector Routing Table for node A	Distance Vector Routing Table for node C
To A	To C
A 0	A 5
B 2	B Inf
C 5	C 0
D Inf	D 3
E Inf	E 5 Similarly for other nodes

FIGURE 1.12: Distance vector routing

autonomous systems to exchange the information between exterior routers. We use Border Gateway Protocol (BGP).

1.3.9   Distance Vector Routing

The distance vector consists of an array or table of distance and direction (node) to determine the route. Routers exchange routing tables with only immediate neighbors. This, in turn, propagated to the entire network. Initially, the cost is set to infinity if the node is not directly reachable.

After sharing of routing tables by, say, immediate neighbors A and C know about others, neighbors in Figure 1.12. Node A comes to know about node B, and node C comes to know about nodes D and E. The cost is updated then and the intermediate node is also updated.

Limitation of Distance Vector Routing: Let us consider nodes B, A, and C only with costs indicated in Figure 1.12. Assume that the link between B and A is down or failed.

Solution: The node C tells node A that it can reach to B with cost $2 + 5 = 7$. However, A does not know that the path of C is through itself. Therefore, A updates its routing table that it can reach to B via C with cost $5 + 7 = 12$. Subsequently, C updates that it can reach to B via A with cost $12 + 5 = 17$. This continues till infinity and is called a count-to-infinity or loop instability problem. The solution can be solved by setting infinity to a smaller number or split horizon or split horizon with poisoned reverse technique. In split horizon with poisoned reverse technique, if the neighbor is the next node in the direction of the shortest path, the minimum cost to the destination is set to infinity.

1.3.10   Link State Routing

Each node has the entire topology of the network, however, the routing table is different for each node. Let us consider an analogy for illustration purposes. Everyone has a map of the area, however, there is a different route for each person to reach the destination. The topology must be dynamic in the sense that the topology must be updated regularly if any node goes down or unreachable because of some reasons.

Initially, the complete topology is not known by each node. Each node shares partial information like the distances of its immediate neighbors with the rest of the nodes. In the end, all information is aggregated to get the entire topology which is shared among all the nodes like distance vector routing.

In the previous example, if A knows that it is connected to B and C with cost 2 and 5, respectively, then, B and C also come to know that costs involved for connecting with A are 2 and 5, respectively. This process is repeated.

The router after boots learn about the neighbor by sending a HELLO packet and other routers respond with its details. Then the cost is measured by sending the ECHO packet. It calculates the round-trip delay divided by 2. There are three steps in link-state routing for building routing tables.

- First, each node makes a link-state packet which consists of the node ID, list of links, sequence number, and age. The first two helps in building topology. The link-state packet is made periodically or when some events occur like node failure or nodes go down or come up.

- *Sequence number* helps in identifying new packets and discarding old packets at a particular node. There are some issues with a sequence number. First, we may run short of sequence numbers which can be solved by using 32 bits sequence numbers. It will take 136.2 years to wrap around for one link-state packet per second. This is calculated as 136.2 years $\times$ 365 days $\times$ 24 hours $\times$ 60 minutes $\times$ 60 seconds $= 4295203200 \approx 2^{32}$. Second, the sequence number starts from zero again if the router crashes. In this scenario, although the packet is new, however, it is rejected based on a duplicate sequence number (or duplicate packet). Third, if sequence number is changed from i to j ($j >> i$) because of some error, then all packets from $i + 1$ to j is rejected.

Remarks: The solution associated with the sequence number is addressed using *age*. Age is decremented once per second and if it hits zero, the packet is discarded. Second, those LSPs are sent to all the nodes not only to immediate neighbors. This is called *flooding*. In the previous step, we make a link-state packet periodically. The interval is chosen judiciously to avoid network congestion because of flooding. Say, we choose 1 hour or 2 hours.

Third, the topology is at each node after receipts of link step packets. Now, the Dijkstra algorithm is used to find the shortest route between any two nodes, and the best route is determined. In each routing table, the result of the Dijkstra algorithm is stored. Finally, we have the routing tables for each node like distance vector protocol. For N number of routers and K number of neighbors for each router, the memory requirement is NK.

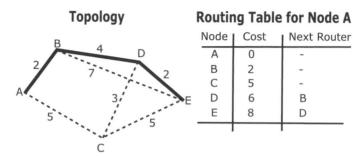

FIGURE 1.13: Topology for Dijkstra algorithm

1.3.11   Shortest Path Routing—Dijkstra Algorithm

The router represents a node and the edges connecting nodes represent a communication link. The weight over the edge represents metrics such as distance, latency, cost, and bandwidth amongst others. The number of hops can be a metric, however, the length of each hop can be different. We are interested in determining the shortest path or minimum metric path from the source to the destination.

We present herein the Dijkstra algorithm for computing the shortest path in an undirected graph. Dijkstra is read as DYKE-struh (Dutch name-Netherlands) and the algorithm was developed in the year 1959. The shortest path from node A to node B and node B to node A are the same for an undirected graph. Initially, nodes are assigned infinity weight because of unknown paths. The path is updated if we find a better path than the previous one. The weights on the path can be tentative or permanent. Once, it becomes permanent based on minimum metric criteria, then it does not change further.

Example of Dijkstra Algorithm: The idea of the Dijkstra Algorithm is as follows. We start from the source node and find the next closest node progressively. In the next iteration, find the minimum cost path via the new node of the previous iteration. The objective is to determine the shortest paths from the source node A to all other nodes in a topology of Figure 1.13.

The column of the Dijkstra algorithm table in Figure 1.14 represents the next node. The entry in the table shows the cost and the node through which we can reach. We can use the same table to find the shortest path between any two nodes even if the source and destination are changed later on. In the routing table of Figure 1.14, to go from node A to the rest of the nodes, node A to node A requires cost 0. Node A to node B and node C need costs 2 and 5, respectively. Since nodes D and E are not reachable from A, these are set to infinity initially.

After the first row, we choose cost 2 via node A to reach node B as this involves a minimum cost. This is shown in bold letter. Now, we find the shortest path through the new node B. In the second row, to reach node C, there is no path from node B to node C. We write the corresponding entry

Dijkstra Algorithm

Visited	A	B	C	D	E
A	0 via A	*2 via A*	5 via A	Inf	Inf
B			*5 via A*	6 via B	9 via B
C				~~8 via C~~ *6 via B*	~~10 via C~~ 9 via B
D					*8 via D*

FIGURE 1.14: Example of Dijkstra algorithm

from the first row. To reach node D from node B, cost 2 to reach node B from the first row plus cost 4 to reach from node B to D is needed. Similarly, to reach node E from node B, cost 2 to reach node B from the first row plus cost 7 to reach from node B to node E is needed. We choose cost 5 via node A to reach node C. This is shown in bold letter.

Next, we find the shortest path through the new node C. We need cost 8 to reach D via node C (5 from the previous step to reach node C plus cost 3 from C to node D). Similarly, to reach node E requires cost 10 via node C (5 from the previous step to reach node C plus cost 5 from node C to node E). However, these costs are more than the corresponding entry in the previous row and hence, they are discarded. Therefore, in the third row, we choose cost 6 via B to reach D. This is shown in bold letter.

Now, we find the shortest path through new node D. In fourth row, to reach node E from node D requires cost 8 via D (6 for reaching node D and 2 from node D to node E). The shortest path from node A to node E is written using back-propagating A—B—D—E. We use here 8 via D to reach node E, 6 via B to reach D and 2 via A to reach node B. Similarly, the shortest path from node A to node D is written using back-propagating A—B—D. We use here 6 via B to reach node D and 2 via A to reach node B.

Remarks: At every row of the table, we make one node permanent. We do this for all nodes. In case of a tie at any row, choose any node randomly.

1.3.12 Interior Gateway Routing Protocol

The oldest interior gateway routing protocol within an (intra) autonomous system is based on distance vector routing. An autonomous system is shown in Figure 1.15. Routing Information Protocol (RIP) is developed by Xerox network system. RIP uses *hop count* as a metric and it is measured from the source router to the destination subnet. The maximum hop count allowed is 15.

In distance vector routing, each router exchanges distance vector with neighboring routers. The distance vector is the current shortest path from that router to the subnet. Routing information is exchanged between routers every

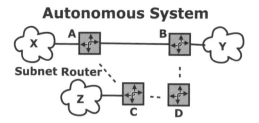

FIGURE 1.15: Autonomous system in RIP

Routing Table for Router A		
Destination	Cost	Next Router
X	1	-
~~Z~~	~~5 say~~	~~C~~
Z	4	B
Y	2	B

Using table of Router B,
second row is updated

Routing Table for Router B		
Destination	Cost	Next Router
X	2	A
Z	3 say	D
Y	1	-

FIGURE 1.16: Routing Table in RIP

30 seconds. The router does not listen to anything from the neighboring router once every 180 seconds in case of neighbor is down or failed. Subsequently, routing table is updated by sending advertisements to neighboring routers. A router can also send a RIP request message to know its neighbor's cost to the destination.

RIP Routing Table The RIP table consists of three columns. The first, second, and third columns have destination subnet, number of hops to destination subnet, and the next router on the shortest path toward destination subnet, respectively. This is shown in Figure 1.16. First, the routing table for router A is created, and then for router B. Next, when router A receives the advertisement from router B, router A comes to know the shorter path to destination subnet Z is via router D. Hence, the routing table for router A is updated by adding a 1 hop count via router B to subnet Z.

The limitation of RIP is as follows. It works well for a small system and also suffers from count-to-infinity problem and convergence. This motivates us to use OSPF which is based on link-state routing.

Open Shortest Path First: This is standardized by IETF in RFC 2328 for routing on the Internet. Different autonomous systems use different interior routing algorithms. Open Shortest Path First (OSPF) is an interior gateway routing protocol for within an (intra) autonomous system. It uses link-state routing for flooding the link state packets and Dijkstra's shortest path algorithm. Open in OSPF means that the routing protocol specification is publicly open in literature. The administrator calculates several metrics for the connection (edge) between two routers such as distance, delay, data rate,

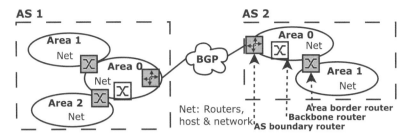

FIGURE 1.17: Illustration of OSPF

and inversely proportional to link capacity discourage traffic from a particular route. However, OSPF provides the mechanism to determine a minimum-cost path routing.

The router in OSPF broadcasts link-state information to all the routers in the Autonomous System (AS) periodically every 30 minutes or when the link goes down/up. This is unlike the distance vector where broadcasting is done for only immediate neighbors. OSPF also does load balancing between multiple paths. Exchange of information between OSPF routers is also secured. Novice researchers cannot inject false routing information. OSPF supports the hierarchical structure of an autonomous system for better management.

OSPF Terminologies The terminologies of OSPF are shown in Figure 1.17. *Area* is a generalized subnet which consists of networks, routers and hosts. The router in an area broadcasts link-state packets to other routers of that area. Each area runs its link-state routing using the shortest-path algorithm. It may be noted that the areas do not overlap, but some routers may not belong to any area. The network should be connected inside an area.

Area border router sends the packets to other areas. *Backbone router* is the router inside the primary area zero. The backbone area connects all the normal areas of an autonomous system. The traffic goes from one area to another area via the backbone area. The backbone area and normal areas act like hub and spokes, respectively, in a star topology. The packets are first sent to the area border router (intra-area routing) and then to the backbone router (inter-area routing) of the AS and finally to AS boundary router (inter-AS) for other ASes.

OSPF Links Transit networks carry data that neither originate nor terminate on the system attached to it as shown in Figure 1.18(a). *Stub network* is connected to a single router, that is, data either originate or terminate at the router. This is shown in Figure 1.18(b). To exchange information between routers, a *designated router* is elected with which other routers connect. This approach is efficient instead of sending between each pair of routers. In case of exigency, backup designated router and virtual link are used.

Each router floods link-state information (neighbors and costs) with a Hello message to all other routers in its area. The sequence number is used to keep track of the latest information. Each router creates a topology for its

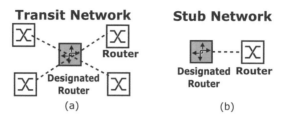

FIGURE 1.18: Transit and Stub networks of OSPF

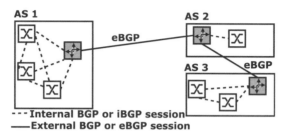

FIGURE 1.19: Illustration of BGP

area and then the Dijkstra algorithm is used to find the shortest path between the backbone router and other routers.

1.3.13   Exterior Gateway Routing Protocol

Border Gateway Protocol (BGP) is used as a routing protocol among multiple autonomous systems. BGP reliably communicates by establishing TCP connections. BGP is a distance-vector protocol, however, it is different from RIP as it considers only the cost to destination. BGP routing table consists of the exact path being used in addition to the cost to reach the destination.

The BGP is standardized in RFC 4271. In BGP, we choose a route based on the metric (cost) and local preference. In local preference, we have politics where some ASes may not send data through some ASes even though they are in the direction of the shortest path. ASes can charge for transit traffic from other ASes or can refuse also. BGP chooses the shortest path if the degree of local preferences for the two routes are similar. If both degrees of local preferences and costs are the same, then the route with the closest next-hop router is selected.

As shown in Figure 1.19, TCP connections inside an AS is called *internal BGP or iBGP session*. The TCP connection between two BGP is called *external BGP or eBGP session*. The traffic goes from source AS to destination AS via neighboring AS. AS 1 sends the reachability information to AS 2 through eBGP and vice versa. On similar lines, AS 2 and AS 3 do. Now, a gateway of AS 2 sends the reachability information of AS 1 to AS 3. The routing/forwarding table of AS 3 is updated with the reachability information

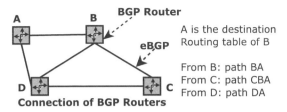

FIGURE 1.20: BGP stability

of AS 1. Thus, there are three steps in BGP, namely, *neighbor agreement, neighbor reachability, and network reachability.*

BGP Features: Autonomous system is known by globally unique Autonomous System Number (ASN) like IP address. This is provided by ICANN. *AS-Path* includes the list of ASes that are traversed for the route. When the advertisement goes from AS 1 to AS 3 via AS 2, AS-Path would be {AS 1, AS 2}. BGP does not suffer from count-to-infinity problem and hence prevent routing loops and instability. The router does not choose any route if it includes itself in the route. This is because AS path tells the exact ASes (BGP routers of those ASes) to be traversed. In Figure 1.20, suppose A is the destination BGP router and B chooses B-A path. Other paths are discarded those include B. Ties are resolved as mentioned before. Now, the A-B link fails. Then, B does not choose the CBA path as it includes B itself rather choose BDA.

1.3.14 Performance Metrics

The different types of delays are illustrated in Figure 1.21. The total delay (or latency) is defined as the amount of time required in a traversal of all packets from the source to the destination. This is given by

$$\text{Total delay} = \text{Processing time} + \text{Queuing time}$$
$$+ \text{Transmission time} + \text{Propagation time} \tag{1.4}$$

Let us define each of the delays below:

- *Processing Time*: This is the amount of time needed for examining the packet header, determining the next stop, and checking bit-level errors.

- *Queuing Time*: It is defined as the amount of waiting time needed before transmission. It depends on the number of packets that are already in the queue. If the queue is empty then queuing time is zero.

- *Transmission Time*: The amount of time required for transmitting all the packet's bits onto the communication link. This is given by

$$\text{Transmission time in second} = \frac{\text{Message size in bits}}{\text{Bandwidth in bits per second}} \tag{1.5}$$

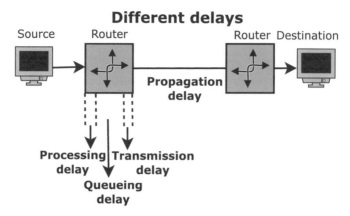

FIGURE 1.21: Types of delays

- *Propagation Time*: The amount of time required for bits to travel between the source and destination. It is given by

$$\text{Propagation Time} = \frac{\text{Distance}}{\text{Propagation speed}} \qquad (1.6)$$

The propagation speed of an electromagnetic signal in the air is 3×10^8 m/s. This speed is greater than the speed of cable which is two-third of the speed of light.

There are some important performance metrics, namely, Throughput, Bandwidth-delay Product and Packet loss for knowing the effectiveness of the network. *Throughput* is defined as the ratio of number of bits at the receiver and time elapsed. *Bandwidth-delay product* is the number of bits that can fit in the link. We can take an analogy of a pipe for understanding purpose. The bandwidth is the cross-section of a pipe, delay is length of the pipe and volume of the pipe is bandwidth-delay product as in Figure 1.22. The bandwidth-delay product is given by

$$2 \text{ bps} \times 3 \text{ second} = 6 \text{ bits} \qquad (1.7)$$

Further, the capacity of the buffer (queue) is finite. If the packet arrives and the queue is already full, the router drops the packet and this is called packet loss. The loss is proportional to traffic intensity.

Examples of Delay and Throughput:

1. Determine the transmission time and propagation time for a 10 kb message over a bandwidth of 100 Mbps. The distance between source and destination is 2000 km and propagation speed in cable is 2×10^8 m/s.

   - Transmission time $= \frac{10 \times 1024}{100 \times 10^6} = 0.0001024$ s $= 0.1024$ ms

Bandwidth-delay product

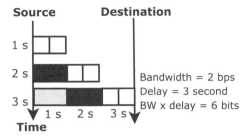

FIGURE 1.22: Bandwidth-delay product

FIGURE 1.23: Throughput of the network 1

- Propagation time $= \frac{2000 \times 1000}{2 \times 10^8} = 0.01$ s $= 10$ ms

2. We can send on an average 10,000 frames per minute with each frame is made of 6000 bits. Determine the throughput of this 5 Mbps bandwidth network.

- Throughput $= \frac{10,000 \times 6000}{60} = 1 \times 10^6$ bps $= 1$ Mbps which is less than theoretical 5 Mbps bandwidth network

Example of Throughput of Network: The overall throughput of a network is given by the transmission rate of a bottleneck link. This is given by the minimum of transmission rates of all links between the source and destination. In Figures 1.23 and 1.24, the throughput of those two networks are, respectively, given by

$$\text{Throughput}_1 = \min\{R_1, R_2\}$$

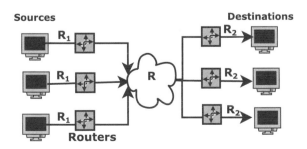

FIGURE 1.24: Throughput of the network 2

$$\text{Throughput}_2 = \min\{R_1, \frac{R}{3}, R_2\}$$

where R_1 and R_2 denote the rates of source-router and router-destination links, respectively. R is the transmission rate of the central link through which all three links from preceding routers go. The above expressions can be generalized for multiple routers between the source and the destination.

1.4 Summary

In this chapter, we discussed two main topics, namely, things and the Internet. The different types of sensors and characteristics are presented under things topic. Things collect data from the IoT environment and to further send it to other IoT devices, we need the Internet. The Internet is mainly needed for communications and notifications purposes. The layering concept of the TCP/IP model is also presented. In particular, switching, addressing, routing, and performance metrics are discussed in detail. We highlight the preference of IPv6 over IPv4 addressing scheme for an IoT network.

1.5 Exercises

1. Which sensor can be used in
   (a) touchscreen of a smart device and
   (b) object detection?

2. Consider a network of 4-nodes point-to-point. Determine the total number of connections required to allow each node to communicate with another. Draw some inferences out of it.

3. What is the difference between circuit and packet switching?

4. What is the parity bit for the bit sequence 0101101 if we use an odd parity checking scheme?

5. Create the code-word using cyclic redundancy check procedure and also verify the decoding procedure. Given the number of bits in the message, $k_b = 4$ bits, and the number of bits in the resultant frame, $n_b = 7$ bits. The generator polynomial is $x^3 + x^2 + 1$ and information polynomial is $x^3 + x^2 + x$.

6. Use the command prompt and know the IPv4 address, subnet mask, and type of IPV4 address. Then ping your IP address. Study the Time, TTL, bytes, request time-out fields of ping result.

7. Get all the MAC addresses of your system (laptop/desktop) and check which one is enabled.

8. Convert the IPv4 address from dotted-decimal notation 131.15.239.11 to binary notation.

9. Find the error in the IPv4 address:
   (a) 139.15.239
   (b) 131.15.239.11.120
   (c) 131.15.269.11
   (d) 131.015.239.11
   (e) 131.15.239.00001011.

10. What is the class of IPv4 address 224.0.0.6?

11. Determine Class, network ID, broadcast ID, and the number of actual hosts for IPv4 address 131.15.239.11.

12. Let us assign a subnet mask 255.255.224.0 of Class B IPv4 address for creating more subnets. Compute the number of actual hosts per subnet and the number of subnets.

13. What is the difference between Repeater, Hub, Bridge, Switch, and Router?

14. Write the broadcast IDs of each subnet in the example of the subnet of this chapter.

15. Which subnet does 200.10.20.82/26 and their corresponding broadcast ID?

16. Short ABCD:0000:FFFF:00CE:34AC:A000:0524:0000 IPv6 address.

17. Expand C::23:C2:A:0 IPv6 address into original form.

18. Why do we use different interior and exterior gateway routing protocols?

19. Convert the autonomous system of Figure 1.25 to a directed graph of autonomous system in OSPF protocol.

20. What is the ratio of transmission time to propagation time for a 40 kbyte message if the network bandwidth is 1 Gbps. Given that the distance between the sender and the receiver is 2,40,000 km and that signal travel at 2.4×10^8 m/s?

21. Determine the time the network takes for transfer of 10 kb in the "throughput of a network" example.

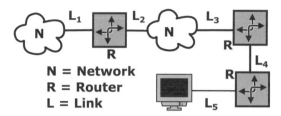

N = Network
R = Router
L = Link

FIGURE 1.25: Autonomous system for converting to a directed graph

22. In the previous question, if two parallel routes are having the same rate, what is the throughput of the network.

23. Find the shortest path from node A to node E using the Dijkstra algorithm in the following Figure 1.26.

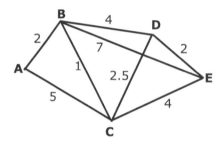

FIGURE 1.26: Topology to apply Dijkstra algorithm

24. Complete distance vector routing tables for the example of the chapter. Show how sharing routing tables with immediate neighbors help in knowing the entire network.

25. **Do It Yourself**: Study detailed electrical, electronics, and mechanical properties of various sensors and categorize them for different IoT projects.

26. **Do It Yourself**: Explore old Telegraph and Public Telephone Switched Networks (PSTN) and draw some motivations for today's IoT Networks.

Chapter 2

Standards and Protocols

2.1 Introduction

The protocol is a set of precise and unambiguous rules so that different devices in the IoT networks communicate seamlessly. We discuss herein protocols for different layers of a Transmission Control Protocol (TCP)/Internet Protocol (IP) model. There are two broad types of protocols: short-range (IEEE 802.11 and IEEE 802.15.4) and Long Range Wide Area Networks (LoRaWAN) protocols. In particular, modulation schemes, support of a large number of devices, and throughput for an IEEE 802.11 protocol are presented. The protocol is widely used in an indoor environment. There is a need to understand Pseudo-Noise (PN) sequence generation, its properties, and time-slotted channel hopping for an IEEE 802.15.4 protocol. The protocol is suitable for an interference-prone environment. Similarly, device class, link budget, data rate, time-of-air, and ALOHA scheme for LoRaWAN protocol are important for long-distance communication. Notably, the adaptive data rate is a key to LoRaWAN protocol for a harsh and/or large network. Finally, Constrained Application Protocol (CoAP) at the application layer augments Hypertext Transfer Protocol (HTTP) for an IoT network.

2.2 IEEE 802.11 Protocol

IEEE 802.11 protocol belongs to physical and MAC layers in OSI reference model. The different versions are a/g, n, ac, and ah of IEEE 802.11 approved or published in 1999/2003, 2009, 2014, and 2017, respectively. IEEE 802.11 Wireless Fidelity (Wi-Fi) is a Wireless LAN standard that operates at 2.4 GHz and 5 GHz frequency bands. However, IEEE 802.11 (a/g, n, and ac) suffers from high energy consumption, penetration loss, and short coverage. Next, an IEEE 802.11ah protocol operates at sub 1 GHz license-free bands (0.9 GHz) and useful when we have available narrow bandwidth. This version supports a

- large number of resource-constrained devices which is equal to 8191

DOI: 10.1201/9781003225584-2

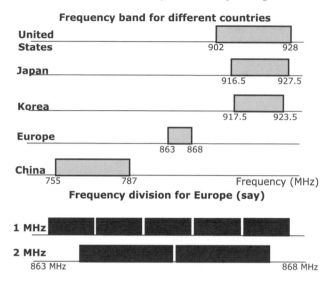

FIGURE 2.1: Channels of different countries

- large communication range of ~ 1 km at the expense of throughput

- infrequent short packet transmission with a data rate of ~ 100 kbps.

Hence, this protocol IEEE 802.11 is suitable for an IoT network.

2.2.1   Features

The features of IEEE 802.11 protocol are listed below.

- *Layers*: Amended Physical and MAC layers. Supports MCS (Modulation and Coding Scheme) index 0 to MCS index 10.

- *Channel bandwidth*: These are 1, 2, 4, 8, and 16 MHz. Different countries use different frequency bands based on the available spectrum. This leads to a different number of channels and channel sizes.

- *Antenna configuration*: 4 × 4 MIMO (Multiple Input Multiple Output) is used.

- *Modulation scheme*: Binary Phase Shift Keying (BPSK), Quadrature Phase Shift Keying (QPSK), and 16 Quadrature Amplitude Modulation (QAM), 64 QAM or 256 QAM is used.

- *Physical layer*: We use Orthogonal Frequency Division Multiplexing (OFDM) and multiple-users MIMO.

Frequency Band and Frequency Division: In the USA, all 1, 2, 4, 8, and 16 MHz channels in the range of 902 MHz to 928 MHz are available.

However, in Europe, only 1 and 2 MHz are present in the range of 863 MHz to 868 MHz as shown in Figure 2.1. Note that 1 MHz channel are merged to get higher bandwidth, say, 2 MHz. Similarly, in Japan, Korea, and China, the supported frequency ranges are 916.5 MHz to 927.5 MHz, 917.5 MHz to 923.5 MHz, and 755 MHz to 787 MHz, respectively. The selection of frequency band depends on the country.

2.2.2 Modulation Schemes

Let us first talk about motivation for using M-ary scheme. Higher level QAM (64-QAM and 256-QAM) are more bandwidth efficient. The bandwidth requirement reduces by the factor $\log_2 M_a$ for $M = M_a$. The bandwidth required is $\frac{W}{\log_2 M_a}$, where W bandwidth required for binary baseband transmission.

The probability of error depends on the distance between two constellations points. For maintaining the same distance between two constellation points as in the binary case, the M-ary scheme requires a larger power. Hence, the M-ary scheme needs a large Signal-to-Noise Ratio (SNR) but small bandwidth for the same bit rate. This is because an even bit is for $2T$ duration and an odd bit is also for $2T$ duration. Therefore, there are 2 bits for $2T$ duration. Hence, the bit rate is the same, that is, 1 bit for T duration like a binary scheme. It may be noted that the expansion in the time-domain is equivalent to compression in the frequency domain and vice-versa. For a noiseless scenario, the number of bits $N = \log_2 M_a$ can be increased indefinitely. However, if the two constellation points become closer for a noisy scenario, the detection performance degrades. The application is a digital voice channel that has limited bandwidth but a large SNR.

Quadrature Phase Shift Keying (QPSK): This is a form of Phase Shift Keying (PSK) where 2 bits are modulated at once. This makes 4 PSK, that is, four combinations of 0 and 1. We draw the constellation diagram and use Gray coding. The constellation diagram is a 2D representation (where axes denote the basis functions) of digitally modulated signals. In Gray coding, two adjacent symbols differ by 1 bit in the case of noise. We can also have other mappings where phase can be taken as $0°$, $90°$, $180°$, and $270°$ for different bit sequences.

Example of Even and Odd Sequences The data sequence is divided into even and odd sequences as shown in Figure 2.2. In even sequence, all even bits b_0, b_2, b_4, and b_6 of $b_k(t)$ are each for $2T$ duration. Similarly, in odd sequence, all odd bits b_1, b_3, b_5, and b_7 of $b_k(t)$ are each for $2T$ duration.

QPSK Modulator and Demodulator: QPSK modulator and demodulator are shown in Figure 2.3. The duration of each bit is $2T$, so, the rate of each sequence is $\frac{1}{2T}$. Hence, even and odd sequences together makes the bit rate of $\frac{1}{T}$. In QPSK modulator, the bit splitter decomposes data sequence into

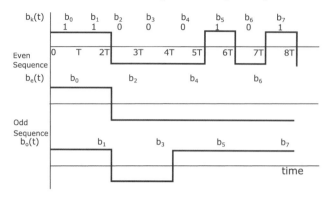

FIGURE 2.2: Even and odd sequences

even and odd sequences. Local oscillator generates the cosine and 90 degree phase shifted sine carrier frequency for modulation. Even and odd sequences modulate the cosine (in-phase) and sine carrier (quadrature), respectively. The QPSK modulated signal is

$$s(t) = b_e(t)\cos(\omega_c t) + b_o(t)\sin(\omega_c t) \qquad (2.1)$$

where $b \in \{0, 1\}$ or $\{-1, +1\}$ etc. We can map the four phases with our choice of bit sequence.

The modulated signal is transmitted over the channel. Similarly, in the QPSK demodulator, the local oscillator is used. Further, the integration is carried out for two-bit intervals, $T_s = 2T_b$, where T_s and T_b denote the symbol and bit duration, respectively. Finally, these are applied to a detection block followed by a bit combining block which is carried out using a multiplexing circuit. The detection block decides in the favor of one if the received signals is greater than zero, otherwise, zero.

Phase Change Diagram in QPSK: The constellation diagram for QPSK scheme is shown in Figure 2.4. There is a large phase shift in this case. The minimum phase change after every $2T$ interval is $90°$ when the symbol 00 becomes symbol 01 or 10. The maximum phase change is $180°$ when the symbol, say, 00 becomes symbol 11 as shown in Figure 2.5.

Offset-QPSK: In Offset-QPSK (QQPSK), we shift or stagger the waveform (by T) so that both the even and odd bits do not change simultaneously as shown in Figure 2.6. This is observed in QPSK, say, at time $2T$ for the previous even-odd example. This rules out the phase shift of $180°$, however, $\pm90°$ phase shift is still present. At any integer multiple of T, either even or odd sequence changes not both.

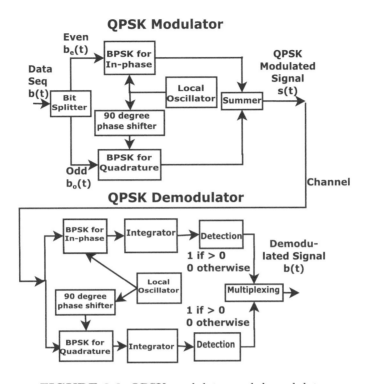

FIGURE 2.3: QPSK modulator and demodulator

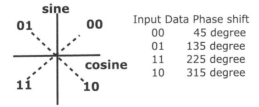

Input Data	Phase shift
00	45 degree
01	135 degree
11	225 degree
10	315 degree

FIGURE 2.4: Constellation diagram

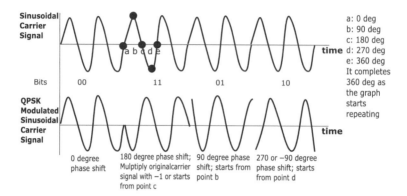

FIGURE 2.5: QPSK phase change

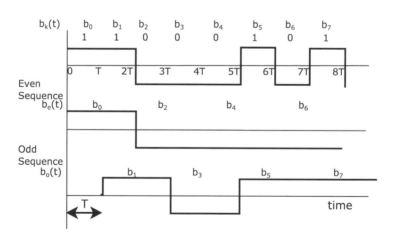

FIGURE 2.6: Even and odd decomposition of OQPSK

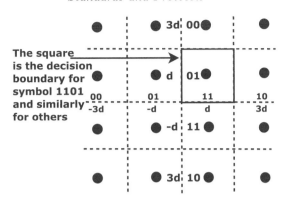

FIGURE 2.7: Constellation of QAM scheme

Quadrature Amplitude Modulation: A digital Quadrature Amplitude Modulation (QAM) is denoted by 16-QAM, or 64-QAM (say) where 16 or 64 symbols are used. This is also called QASK (Quadrature Amplitude Shift Keying). We also have QAM or specifically Analog QAM. The phases are different for different signals in BPSK, QPSK, and M-ary PSK. However, the amplitude remains the same. In the presence of noise, we distinguish different signals based on the minimum distance between constellation points as shown in Figure 2.7. Here, in digital QAM, signals differ both in amplitude and phase for improving the noise immunity, that is, amplitude and shift keying.

A symbol consists of 4 bits, that is, $2^4 = 16$ symbols. We use Gray coding and 4-PAM (Pulse Amplitude Modulation) along I and 4-PAM along Q. Two bits are chosen for four levels (00, 01, 11, and 10) each along I and Q. The corresponding mapping to distances is $3d$, d, $-d$, and $3d$ for levels 00, 01, 11, and 10, respectively along Q. Similarly, we can do the mapping along I and form a square decision boundary for, say, one symbol 1101. One of the possible constellation diagrams is shown in Figure 2.7. The points are symmetrical about the origin in the signal space to simplify the hardware design of the system and keeps minimum energy per signal.

Average Energy of Signal and Modulator: If all 16 symbols are equally likely, then the average energy of a signal is

$$E_s = \frac{1}{16} \times 4[(d^2 + d^2) + (d^2 + 9d^2) + (9d^2 + 9d^2) + (9d^2 + d^2)]$$
$$= 10d^2 \qquad (2.2)$$

Therefore, we get $d = \sqrt{0.1E_s}$. Hence, minimum distance between two constellation points is $2d = 2\sqrt{0.1E_s}$. For 4 bits-symbol, E_s is equal to $4E_b$, where E_s and E_b denote the normalized symbol and bit energy, respectively. Hence, minimum distance is equal to $2\sqrt{0.4E_b}$ which is less than QPSK, but more than 16-QPSK. This can be also observed by looking at the

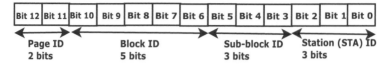

FIGURE 2.8: Structure of AID

constellation diagrams. That is, it has lower error rate than 16-QPSK but larger than QPSK.

In QAM, two quadrature carriers of the same frequency are independently amplitudes modulated by discrete amplitudes k_1 and k_2. The transmitted signal is

$$k_1 \cos(\omega_c t) - k_2 \sin(\omega_c t) \qquad (2.3)$$

where k_1 and $k_2 = \pm 1$ or ± 3. Similar to QPSK scheme, we can draw the block diagram representation for modulator and demodulator of QAM scheme.

2.2.3 Supporting a Large Number of Devices

We discuss the MAC layer of the IEEE 802.11 protocol herein. A unique Association Identifier (AID) is assigned by an Access Point (AP) to each client station. In the previous version, the number of stations that is can be associated is 2007 because of the limited length of Traffic Indication Map (TIM) bit map and Information Element (IE). Each bit denotes the corresponding station ID. For the IEEE 802.11ah version, we use hierarchical AID for supporting more stations as shown in Figure 2.8. There is a total of 13 bits. That is, $2^{13} - 1 = 8191$ number of stations can be supported. Note that AID 0 is for group addressed traffic, this is why we subtract one from the total number of stations (2^{13}).

AID Hierarchy: A page, block, sub-block and station ID consist of 2, 5, 3, and 3 bits respectively in Figure 2.8. We have $2^2 = 4$ pages, $2^5 = 32$ blocks, $2^3 = 8$ sub-blocks and $2^3 = 8$ stations. Each sub-block, block and page are associated with 8, 64 ($= 8 \times 8$), 2048 ($= 32 \times 8 \times 8$) stations, respectively. Hence, the total number of stations $= 4 \times 32 \times 8 \times 8 - 1$ is equal to 8291. We can refer to the group of stations by higher level IDs such as page ID, block ID, or sub-block ID instead of a group of an individual AID in Figure 2.9. We cluster the stations based on similar characteristics like location, battery level, and traffic pattern for better resource utilization.

Power Saving: There are two states in STA. In the awake state, the STA senses, transmits, and receives the signal all the time, while in the sleep state, the transceiver components are turned off and cannot sense the signals. AP buffers the packets if the STA is in a sleep state. Two power-saving mechanisms for STA are Non-TIM STA and TIM STA.

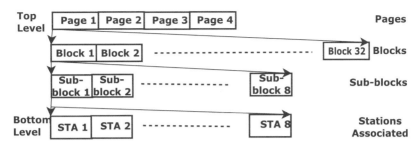

FIGURE 2.9: Terminologies in AID

- *TIM STA*: This receives the beacon frames having TIM IE broadcasted by AP periodically. It needs to wake up at regular intervals. The bit of TIM IE is set when the AP has buffered downlink packets for STA. When the station wakes up, it requests the AP via Power Saving (PS) Poll frame for delivery of the buffered packets.

- *Non-TIM STA*: The device does not receive the TIM IE broadcasted by AP and it does not wake up at the regular interval for receiving beacons by AP.

Example of RAW for TIM STA: Restricted Access Window (RAW) provides fair channel access to a large number of STAs for avoiding transmissions at the same time. AP defines RAW duration, T_{RAW} which is divided into slots of duration T_{slot}. STAs send or receive in the slot within the window only as informed by the AP.

Using above two information found from the beacon, we can calculate $N_{\text{RAW}} = \frac{T_{\text{RAW}}}{T_{\text{slot}}}$. The slot is numbered from 0 to $N_{\text{RAW}} - 1 = 3$ corresponding to AID 1 to 4 for $N_{\text{RAW}} = 4$. For index of STA, $i = 2$, $N_{\text{offset}} = 3$ then $(i + N_{\text{offset}}) \mod N_{\text{RAW}} = 1$. Hence, the given STA of index $= 2$ will use Slot 1.

Resource Allocation Frame: The protocol has scheduling information of all STAs at the beginning of each RAW. Using this, STA knows the time slot for contending for medium for Tx and Rx. The AP schedules uplink and downlink transmissions in the resource allocation frame after receiving two types of the poll, namely, normal PS and UDI PS (Uplink Data Indication). The field of UDI Poll is set to 1 for the station with only uplink data.

Short Header: Header in legacy 802.11 is 36 bytes plus 4 bytes for FCS and 100-byte data. The MAC header overhead is at least 36 %. The throughput of IEEE 802.11ah is low and it can be enhanced using a short header. The longer the header, the lower the throughput. This is because the size of the header is in the denominator of throughput expression.

For the short header, some information from Quality of Service (QoS) and High Throughput (HT) fields are moved to the Signal (SIG) field of PHY header. Duration and ID fields are removed as carrier sensing is not

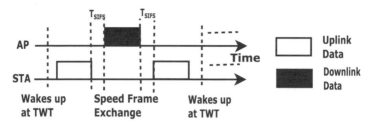

FIGURE 2.10: Speed frame exchange

supported in the short header. The short header is distinguished from the legacy MAC header by putting a new version in Frame Control (FC) field. The short header is at least 12 bytes shorter than the legacy 802.11 version. Similarly, ACK frame is replaced with NDP packet by removing MAC and Frame Check Sequence (FCS) fields and contain only PHY header.

Speed Frame Exchange: In legacy IEEE 802.11, STA contends for the medium, sends its frames, then waits for ACK from AP. AP contends for the medium as well and then sends ACK. Finally, STA sends ACK. Therefore, there are two-way acknowledgments. Note that, STA has to be awake while waiting for ACK from AP.

In speed frame exchange, STA wakes up, contends for the medium, sends the data frame to AP, and then AP immediately replies after Short Inter-Frame Space (SIFS) and allowing the STA to go for sleep within one Transmission Opportunity (TXOP) as shown in Figure 2.10. Note that, successful transmission from either transmitter or receiver side is notified using data frame instead of ACK or block ACK. The interval between each transmission is SIFS. This speeds up the exchange of frames between Tx and Rx as ACK overhead is eliminated. Throughput can be increased as the overhead is reduced. Power can be saved as the STA need not be awake for two-way ACK.

2.2.4   Throughput without Error

The throughput of the protocol is given by

$$\text{TP} = \frac{8 \times L_{\text{data}}}{T_{\text{DIFS}} + T_{\text{BO}} + T_{\text{data}} + T_{\text{SIFS}} + T_{\text{ACK}}}\text{Mbps} \qquad (2.4)$$

where L_{data} is the payload size in bytes. The denominator denotes the total duration in μs. T_{data} and T_{ACK} are the transmission time of a data frame and acknowledgment (ACK) frame, respectively. The denominator term is shown in Figure 2.11.

For SIFS interval = 160 μs and T_{slot} = 52 μs, the data interframe spacing (DIFS) interval = SIFS interval + $2T_{\text{slot}}$ = 160 + 2×52 = 264 μs. For packet error-free scenario during transmission, the backoff time can be taken from a uniform distribution (0, CW_{min}) with mean of $\frac{\text{CW}_{\text{min}}}{2}$, where CWmin is

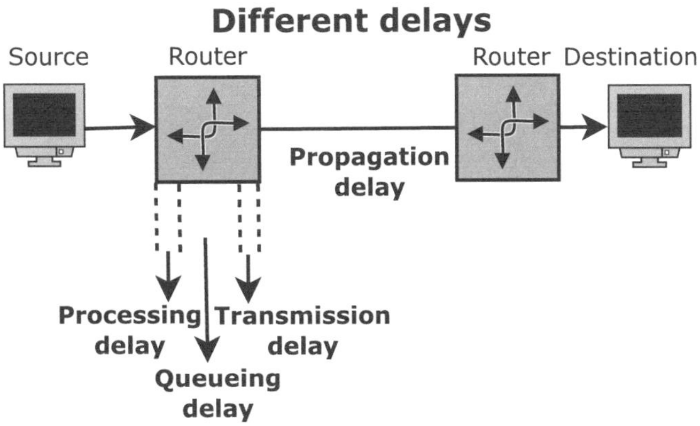

Different delays

Source   Router   Router Destination

Propagation delay

Processing delay   Transmission delay

Queueing delay

FIGURE 2.11: Timing diagram of data transmission

the minimum contention window size. The average $T_{\mathrm{BO}} = \frac{\mathrm{CWmin}}{2} T_{\mathrm{slot}}$, where CWmin $= 15$. The other parameters are

- $T_{\mathrm{data}} = T_{\mathrm{ph}} + T_{\mathrm{symbol}} N_{\mathrm{symbol}}$, where T_{ph} is duration for preamble and header equal to 560 μs.

- $T_{\mathrm{symbol}} = 40$ μs and N_{symbol} are the duration of a symbol and the number of symbols of the PSDU (PHY service data unit).

- $N_{\mathrm{symbol}} = \lceil \frac{14+8\times(L_{\mathrm{data}}+L_{\mathrm{header}})}{6} \rceil$, where $L_{\mathrm{header}} = 36$ bytes and 26 bytes for long and short headers, respectively. $\lceil . \rceil$ denotes the ceiling operator.

- L_{data} is the payload size can take $[12, 475]$ bytes and $[12, 485]$ bytes for longer and short header respectively. $L_{\mathrm{data}} + L_{\mathrm{header}} = 511$ bytes in IEEE 802.11ah at 1 MHz and MCS10.

- $T_{\mathrm{ACK}} = T_{\mathrm{ph}} + T_{\mathrm{symbol}} \lceil \frac{14+8\times(14)}{6} \rceil = T_{\mathrm{ph}} + 21 T_{\mathrm{symbol}}$.

Example of Throughput without Error: Determine the throughput with payload size 256 bytes in an error-free scenario.

- Here, $L_{\mathrm{data}} = 256$ bytes. Consider a long header with $L_{\mathrm{header}} = 36$ bytes

- $T_{\mathrm{BO}} = \frac{\mathrm{CWmin}}{2} T_{\mathrm{slot}} = \frac{15}{2} \times 52 = 390$ μs

- $T_{\mathrm{data}} = T_{\mathrm{ph}} + T_{\mathrm{symbol}} \lceil \frac{14+8\times(L_{\mathrm{data}}+L_{\mathrm{header}})}{6} \rceil$
  $= 560 + 40 \times \lceil \frac{14+8\times(256+36)}{6} \rceil$
  $= 560 + 40 \times \lceil 391.67 \rceil$
  $= 560 + 40 \times 392$
  $= 16240$ μs

- $T_{\mathrm{ACK}} = T_{\mathrm{ph}} + 21 T_{\mathrm{symbol}} = 560 + 21 \times 40 = 1400$ μs

- Hence, the throughput is

$$\text{TP} = \frac{8 \times L_{\text{data}}}{T_{\text{DIFS}} + T_{\text{BO}} + T_{\text{data}} + T_{\text{SIFS}} + T_{\text{ACK}}} \text{ Mbps}$$

$$= \frac{8 \times 256}{264 + 390 + 16240 + 160 + 1400} \text{ Mbps} \qquad (2.5)$$

$$= 0.110979 \text{ Mbps}$$

$$= 110.979 \text{ Kbps}$$

2.2.5   Throughput with Packet Error Rate (PER)

In the presence of error, we need to retransmit and back-off time increases exponentially. Multiply the numerator with $(1 - \text{PER})$ and recompute as $T_{\text{BO}} = \sum_{j=1}^{\infty} \gamma(j) T_{\text{bo}}(j)$. The average value of backoff interval

$$T_{\text{bo}}(j) = \begin{cases} \frac{(\text{CW}_{\min}+1) \times 2^{j-1}-1}{2} \times T_{\text{slot}}, & 1 \le j \le \text{threshold} \\ \frac{\text{CW}_{\max}}{2} \times T_{\text{slot}}, & j > \text{threshold} \end{cases} \qquad (2.6)$$

where threshold is the maximum number of backoff stages. We choose threshold = 6 because $\text{CW}_{\max} = 1023 \ge 2^6 \times \text{CW}_{\min} = 2^6 \times 15$ where $\text{CW}_{\min} = 15$. The iteration can be stopped until the convergence of $\beta = \gamma \times T_{\text{bo}}$ or $|\beta_j - \beta_{j+1}| \le 1$ μs. Typically, 6 to 10 iterations are sufficient for PER = 0.1 to 0.2

Let us denote $\alpha = (\text{CW}_{\min} + 1) \times 2^{j-1} - 1$. For $j = 1$, $\alpha = \text{CW}_{\min}$ which is the same as that of T_{BO} of error-free scenario. For $j = 2$, $\alpha = 2 \times \text{CW}_{\min} + 2 - 1$. For $j = 3$, $\alpha = 2^2 \times \text{CW}_{\min} + 2^2 - 1$. For $j = 4$, $\alpha = 2^3 \times \text{CW}_{\min} + 2^3 - 1$ and so on. Hence, T_{bo} is getting approximately doubled for each retransmission till $\text{CW}_{\max}$.

Example of Throughput with PER: The required number of packet retransmissions for successfully transmitting a packet is assumed to be geometrically distributed. Let PER be the retransmission probability. The retransmission is possibly because of collision and channel noise. Failure or retransmission with probability PER in $j - 1$ number of trials and success in the last trial with probability $(1 - \text{PER})$. Hence, $\gamma(j) = \text{PER}^{j-1} \times (1 - \text{PER})$.

Example: Determine the throughput with payload size 256 bytes in an error-prone scenario with PER = 0.1.

Solution: Re-computation of T_{BO} under PER

- Sum of the last column in Table 2.1, $T_{\text{BO}} = 441.97$.

- We can stop at $j = 6$ because $|\beta_j - \beta_{j+1}| \le 1$ μs. However, for PER = 0.5, we go to $j = 15$ for convergence.

TABLE 2.1: $\gamma(j)T_{\text{bo}}(j)$ for different iterations

j	$\mathbf{T_{bo}(j)}$	$\boldsymbol{\gamma(j)}$	$\boldsymbol{\gamma(j)T_{bo}(j)}$
1	390	9×10^{-1}	351.00
2	806	9×10^{-2}	72.54
3	1638	9×10^{-3}	14.74
4	3302	9×10^{-4}	2.97
5	6630	9×10^{-5}	0.60
6	13286	9×10^{-6}	0.12
7	26598	9×10^{-7}	0.24×10^{-1}
8	26598	9×10^{-8}	0.24×10^{-2}

We use all the values from the last example except new T_{BO} with PER = 0.1. Hence, the throughput is

$$
\begin{aligned}
\text{TP} &= \frac{8 \times L_{\text{data}} \times (1 - \text{PER})}{T_{\text{DIFS}} + T_{\text{BO}} + T_{\text{data}} + T_{\text{SIFS}} + T_{\text{ACK}}} \text{ Mbps} \\
&= \frac{8 \times 256 \times (1 - 0.1)}{264 + 441.97 + 16240 + 160 + 1400} \text{ Mbps} \\
&\approx 0.100 \text{ Mbps} \\
&= 100 \text{ Kbps}
\end{aligned}
\tag{2.7}
$$

2.2.6 Path Loss Models for IEEE 802.11ah

Outdoor path loss models are proposed by the IEEE TGah working group for 802.11ah sub 1 GHz. Macro deployment with AP antenna height of 15 m above the rooftop, the path loss model is given by

$$
\text{PL} = 8 + 36.7 \log_{10}(d) + 21 \log_{10}\left(\frac{f}{900\text{MHz}}\right)
\tag{2.8}
$$

where d is the distance between transmitter and receiver (m). Pico deployment with AP antenna height of 2 m above rooftop, the path loss is

$$
\text{PL} = 23.3 + 36.7 \log_{10}(d) + 21 \log_{10}\left(\frac{f}{900\text{MHz}}\right)
\tag{2.9}
$$

Another accurate path-loss model for indoor is two-slope with a breakpoint distance.

2.3 IEEE 802.15.4 Protocol

IEEE 802.15.4 protocol has a low data rate, low complexity, long battery life, and short-range communication. The typical data rate is 10 kbps to 1

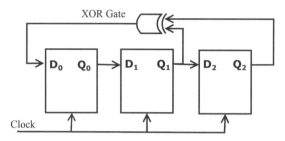

FIGURE 2.12: PN Sequence Generator

Mbps. The range of communication is tens of meters to 1 Km with IEEE 802.15.4 and 1 Km with IEEE 802.15.4g protocols. The protocol operates in the unlicensed international frequency band. This is meant for Wireless Personal Area Network (WPAN) which uses wearable devices. The protocol belongs to lower layers, that is, Media Access Control (MAC) or physical. This is the motivation for IEEE 802.15.4 protocol.

The physical layer defines transmission power, frequency band, coding, and modulation scheme. MAC layer defines medium access and flows control. The basic frame size is restricted to 127 bytes to minimize power consumption and probability of error. The size is 2047 bytes with IEEE 802.15.4g protocol. The protocol has increased the frame check sequence from 16 to 32 bits for better error protection.

2.3.1   Pseudo-Noise Sequence Generator

To understand the modulation scheme of the 802.15.4 protocol, we need the concept of the Pseudo-Noise (PN) sequence. The PN sequence is a binary sequence of 1s and 0s which is generated using sequential logic circuits with feedback from some stages. Although the sequence looks like a random binary noise sequence, it is deterministic. Some of its properties are the same as that of a random binary sequence. Here 3-stage shift register with D flip-flops acts as a delay element for the generation of the PN sequence. The PN sequence generator is shown in Figure 2.12. Each stage (Q_i) can have an output of 0 or 1. These three D flip-flops give $2^3 = 8$ outputs. These are also called states including state 000 of $Q_0 Q_1 Q_2$.

Example of PN Sequence Generation: We initialize with 111 states. However, initialization with 000 state is forbidden since flip-flop does not come out of this state. XOR operation which is $\oplus$ or modulo-2 adder of $Q_1 = 1$ and $Q_2 = 1$ of state 0 is 0. This is fed back to D_0 which in turn generates Q_0 of state 1. Q_1 and Q_2 of state 1 are, respectively, Q_0 and Q_1 of state 0. This process repeats. This is illustrated in Table 2.2. The PN sequence is output, Q_2, of flip-flop D_2. Let us now discuss some properties of the PN sequence.

TABLE 2.2: Output of flip-flops for different states

State	Q_0	Q_1	Q_2	Remarks
0	1	1	1	Initialization
1	0	1	1	$1 \oplus 1 = 0$
2	0	0	1	$1 \oplus 1 = 0$
3	1	0	0	$0 \oplus 1 = 1$
4	0	1	0	$0 \oplus 0 = 0$
5	1	0	1	$1 \oplus 0 = 1$
6	1	1	0	$0 \oplus 1 = 1$
7	1	1	1	$1 \oplus 0 = 1$, Starts repeating

Properties of PN Sequence:

1. *Maximum-length PN sequence*: A total of $2^D - 1$, where D is the total number of shift-registers. Here, $2^3 - 1 = 7$ states.

2. *Balance property*: The number of 1s and 0s are approximately the same. Precisely, the number of 1s = 4 is one more than the number of 0s = 3. This is because the total number of states is odd so, it cannot be exactly half. This is the noise-like properties as 1 and 0 are equiprobable.

3. *Correlation property*: The PN sequence which is the output of Q_2 is equal to 1 1 1 0 0 1 0. The length of sequence, L_s, is equal to 7. Then, the BPSK modulated PN sequence by mapping 1 to -1 and 0 to 1 is $p(n) = -1\ -1\ -1\ 1\ 1\ -1\ 1$. The auto-correlation is given by

$$\text{Auto-correlation} = \frac{1}{L_s} \sum_{n=0}^{L_s-1} p(n)p(n)$$
$$= \frac{(1+1+1+1+1+1+1)}{7} \quad (2.10)$$
$$= 1$$

The cross-correlation between any two sequences generated using different initial or different feedback connection for the same number of states or circularly shifted PN sequences ($p(n-l)$ and $p(n-k)$) is $-\frac{1}{L_s} = 0$ for $L_s \to \infty$. If $l = 0$ and $k = 1$, $p(n-1) = 1\ -1\ -1\ -1\ 1\ 1\ -1$. The cross-correlation is given by

$$\frac{1}{L_s} \sum_{n=0}^{L_s-1} p(n)p(n-1) = \frac{(-1+1+1-1+1-1-1)}{7}$$
$$= -\frac{1}{7} \quad (2.11)$$

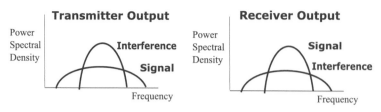

FIGURE 2.13: Power spectral density

4. *Run length property*: The string of identical bits is called run. The total number of runs is equal to $2^{D-1} = \frac{2^D}{2} = \frac{L_s+1}{2} = 2^2 = 4$. First run 1 1 1 is of length 3 with probability $\frac{1}{4}$. Second run 0 0 is of length 2 with probability $\frac{1}{4}$. Third and fourth runs 1 and 0, respectively, are of length 1 each with probability $\frac{2}{4} = \frac{1}{2}$.

2.3.2 Modulation Scheme

The modulation scheme uses Direct Sequence Spread Spectrum (DSSS) to code and transmit information. These are called modulation and transmission methods. DSSS provides reliability and security as IoT network is prone to noise and interferences. The modulation scheme is widely used in a military communication system. The power spectral density (PSD) is the distribution of power with frequency. The PSD of the transmitted wideband signal is spread out to resemble a noise-like signal as shown in Figure 2.13. Hence, this cannot be interfered and detected by the intruder. However, the power remains the same. Note that the spreading code is needed at the receiver to get back the encoded data.

Direct Sequence Spread Spectrum (DSSS): DSSS uses phase-shift keying modulation or its variant to encode information. Using a higher bit rate sequence, the original data sequence bandwidth is spread over a wider band. Pseudo-noise (PN) sequence is a higher bit rate sequence of 1s and 0s. PN sequence makes original data sequence to like a PN sequence noise, not a noise. This is shown in Figure 2.14. BPSK and Offset Quadrature PSK (OQPSK) modulation schemes are for 868/915 MHZ (20/40 kbps) and 2.4 GHz (250 kbps), respectively.

At the receiver side, the transmitted signal is despreaded with the same PN sequence to recover the original data sequence. For simple illustration purposes, channel noise, integrator, and sampler blocks in the receiver are not shown herein. Hence, we code the bit and spread the bandwidth of the original data sequence. Therefore, two objectives are fulfilled. Note that the Frequency Hopping Spread Spectrum (FHSS) uses the hopping concept to spread the original data sequence. This is another approach to carry out.

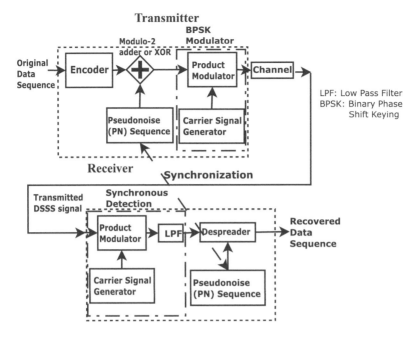

FIGURE 2.14: DSSS modulator and demodulator

General Modulation and Demodulation: Let $d(t)$ and $\cos(\omega_c t)$ be the data sequence and carrier signal with angular frequency ω_c to a modulator. In absence of other blocks, output of the modulator is

$$\text{Modulated signal} = d(t)\cos(\omega_c t) \tag{2.12}$$

Similarly, the output of demodulator is

$$d(t)\cos(\omega_c t)\cos(\omega_c t) = d(t)\left[\frac{1 + \cos(2\omega_c t)}{2}\right] \tag{2.13}$$

After passing this modulated signal through a Low-Pass Filter (LPF) with cut-off frequency ω_c, we get $\frac{d(t)}{2}$. The output can be further rescaled to get the original input. Notably, ω_c needs to be synchronized to both the transmitter and the receiver.

Example of BPSK Modulator: For one symbol, it has some fixed phase, while for other symbol phase difference is of 180 degree. Two symbols are used for binary scheme. The symbol and bit are the same for binary scheme. The BPSK modulated signal is

$$\begin{cases} A\cos(\omega_c t), \text{for symbol 1} \\ A\cos(\omega_c t + \pi) = -A\cos(\omega_c t), \text{for symbol 0} \end{cases} \tag{2.14}$$

where A and ω_c are the amplitude and frequency of the carrier.

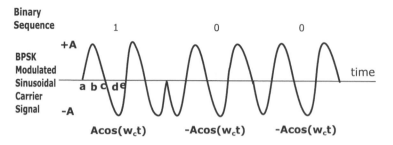

FIGURE 2.15: Binary phase shift keying

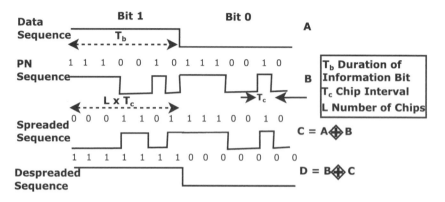

FIGURE 2.16: Spreaded and despreaded sequences

The amplitude remains constant for the modulated signal, only phase changes according to the data sequence as shown in Figure 2.15. If $\omega t = 0°$ for a, $90°$ for b, $180°$ for c and so on, then for symbol 0, the modulated signal will start from c. Otherwise, directly multiply -1 with $A\cos(\omega_c t)$ for showing the phase shift of $180°$.

Example of Spreader and Despreader: We know that the PN sequence has a higher bit rate. We use the Exclusive OR (XOR) operation to get spread sequence as shown in Figure 2.16. For example, the PN sequence is seven times shorter in duration in the figure. The duration in the time domain is inversely proportional to bandwidth in the frequency domain. Hence, the bandwidth of the spread signal is larger than the bandwidth of the original signal. On similar lines, despreading is carried out using the same PN sequence.

Example of Robustness in DSSS: Here, in Figure 2.16, $LT_c = T_b$. The processing gain which is the number of chips per information bit $L_c = \frac{T_b}{T_c} = \frac{f_c}{f_b}$ in terms of frequency. The probability of error is $P_e = \frac{1}{2}\mathrm{erfc}\left(\sqrt{2\frac{P_s}{P_j}\frac{T_b}{T_c}}\right)$, where erfc is the complementary error function. P_s and P_j are the power of desired signal and jamming signal, respectively. The larger the processing

TABLE 2.3: Frequency band and data rate for different countries

Frequency band	Country	Channel	Data Rate
868.3 MHz	ISM/Europe	1	20 kbps
902–928 MHz	ISM/America	10	40 kbps
2.4 GHz	ISM/Worldwide	16	250 kbps

gain $L_c = \frac{T_b}{T_c} = \frac{f_c}{f_b}$, the lower the P_e as the erfc is a monotonically decreasing function.

Let $P_s = 0.5$ mW, $P_j = 0.5$ W, $f_b = 50$ KHz, and $f_c = 50$ MHz. The processing gain $= \frac{50 \times 10^6}{50 \times 10^3} = 1000$. $P_e = 0.5\text{erfc}(\sqrt{2\frac{0.5 \times 10^{-3}}{0.5}1000}) = 0.5\text{erfc}(\sqrt{2})$ $= 0.5(1 - \text{erf}(\sqrt{2})) \approx 0.5(1 - 0.953) \approx 0.023$. We refer to table for erf(1.4) = 0.95229.

Channel, and Channel Access Scheme: The protocol operates in 3 frequency bands and 27 channels as shown in Table 2.3. We use Carrier Sense Multiple Access-Collision Avoidance (CSMA-CA) techniques. The protocol does carrier sense, that is, listen to the shared channel to check whether another node is sending or not. If the channel is not free, it waits for a random time and retries the transmission. It also waits for the acknowledgment to ensure successful packet delivery at the receiver. Thus, it is reliable for loss-prone environments having high noise and interference. This is because of acknowledgment of the successful transmission of the packets.

2.3.3   Topology

The topologies of IEEE 802.15.4 is shown in Figure 2.17. *Zigbee or PAN Coordinator* is the head coordinator who initiates, maintains, and controls the network. This acts as a gateway for connecting to other networks and is main powered. *Zigbee Router or Full Function Device (FFD)* acts as a router or at times PAN coordinator by relaying packets for extending the range. This is below the PAN coordinator in the hierarchy and allows communication with any device of the network. *Zigbee Device or Reduced Function Device (RFD)* is a very simple device that collects the data from things. This is the leaf node and battery-powered. RFD is below the FFD in the hierarchy.

Star Topology: Both FFDs and RFDs are directly connected to the PAN coordinator. There is a single PAN coordinator and there is no router. The number of FFDs and RFDs is greater than and equal to zero. Examples are personal area networks such as healthcare kits, toys, and computing systems.

Mesh Topology: The topology has one PAN coordinator and several FFDs and RFDs. Any device can be connected to any other device if they are in their coverage area. However, two RFDs cannot be connected. This is used for ad-hoc networks in wireless sensor networks.

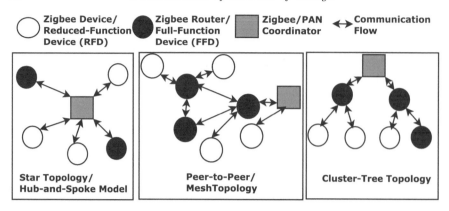

FIGURE 2.17: Topologies in IEEE 802.15.4

Cluster-Tree Topology: This is a special case of mesh topology with a single PAN coordinator. There is a parent (PAN coordinator/FFD) and children (FFD/RFD) paradigm in this topology. A cluster head is chosen and this broadcasts beacon frames to neighbors. The neighboring device requests the cluster head acting as a parent to join the network. Subsequently, this is added as a child node. Here, a large coverage area is achievable, however, it has high latency because of chained clusters.

2.3.4   Time-Slotted Channel Hopping

IEEE 802.15.4 Time-Slotted Channel Hopping (TSCH) ensures improved energy efficiency and reliability in communication. In *Time Slotted or Synchronization,* the time is sliced or slotted into equal length interval or slot. All devices are synchronized herein. The width of the slot can be chosen for the successful transmission of the frame and reception of acknowledgment and availability of BW and energy. The shorter the slot, the higher the chances of transmission. This, in turn, the higher the bandwidth requirement at the expense of increased energy expenditure.

Channel Hopping: If we change or hop the frequency, all messages between two nodes are unlikely to be lost. This is like the concept of diversity in wireless communication. On the contrary, using the same frequency for all the messages between two nodes may be disastrous, if the frequency is vulnerable.

Reliability in Communication: TSCH mitigates the effect of multipath fading and interference. TSCH is a 2D matrix that consists of time slots on one dimension and channel offsets on other dimensions. TSCH schedule is created for each node or complete network. Each node either transmits, receives, or sleeps in the given slot to the node. The element of the matrix is called a cell, an atomic unit, which has a unique channel offset and slot offset.

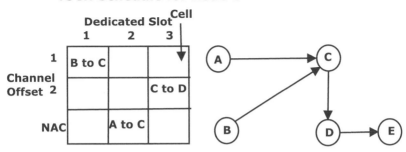

FIGURE 2.18: TSCH for node

The channel offset is mapped to a frequency. This is different for two consecutive transmissions between two nodes. The frequency is chosen based on the following:

$$\text{Frequency} = \text{Map}[(\text{ASN} + \text{CO}) \mod \text{NAC}] \qquad (2.15)$$

where Map is a bijective function which consists of lookup table. ASN, CO, and NAC denote, respectively, the Absolute Slot Number, Channel Offset and Number of Available Channels. Note that $\text{ASN} = 0$ when the network is created and incremented by 1 at each time-slot. Frequency is changed for two consecutive transmission between a pair of nodes. For example, between nodes A and C, we cannot use the same frequency f or channel offset CO for two consecutive slots T_1 and T_2.

Example of TSCH Schedule Matrix: For a particular node, a feasible schedule (not unique) is shown in Figure 2.18. Similarly, for a network, a feasible schedule (not unique) is illustrated in Figure 2.19. In a cell, only a single node transmits. That is, C to D and E to F of $(1, 1)$ cell and $(2, 1)$ cell are examples of collision-free communication. Also, A to D and C to D of $(5, 5)$ cells are allowed because of the slotted ALOHA or CSMA/CD scheme. That is, in a cell, multiple nodes can transmit assuming they are not nearby and hence, there is no interference.

Example of Infeasible TSCH Schedule Matrix: The half-duplex assumption is made herein for conflicting links of the IEEE 802.15.4e network. In the same time slot, the multiple nodes cannot transmit and receive. Also, it cannot receive from multiple nodes. In the same time slot, a common node in two or more links cannot be scheduled. This is illustrated in Figure 2.20. For example, B to C and D to E of $(1, 1)$ cell are interfering links and are not allowed. A to C and C to D of cells $(2, 3)$ and $(3, 3)$, respectively or A to C and B to C of cells $(2, 3)$ and $(3, 3)$, respectively are conflicting links. Hence, this is also not allowed assuming a half-duplex assumption.

Interfering link: Two nearby links use the same channel, which results in the lower Signal to Interference Plus Noise (SINR). This leads to unsuccessful

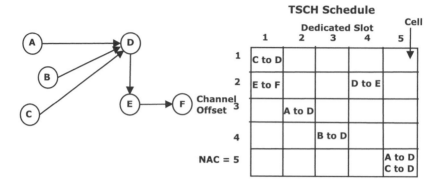

FIGURE 2.19: TSCH matrix

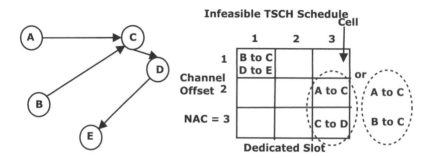

FIGURE 2.20: Example of infeasible TSCH matrix

transmission. If the same time slot is assigned, the interfering links should use different channels or schedule in different time slots. The same channel and same time slot can be used only by non-conflicting and non-interfering links for scheduling in parallel.

2.3.5   Blocking Techniques

The bad channel has poor performance in terms of reliability. The channel needs to be identified and blocked by a node. The blocked frequencies are removed which are generated using Equation. 2.15. A large number of blocked channels reduces the network capacity because the number of good channels decreases. Let us discuss two types of blocking, namely, local blocking and global blocking.

- *Local Blocking*: Each nodes pairs have a different list of good channels. The list is shared between child and parent nodes to maintain uniformity. There is some limitation such as collision might take place when two or more links use the same timeslot even with different channel offset. The computation of multiple channel offsets locally is difficult.

- *Global Blocking*: All the nodes have the same list of good channels. This has a suboptimal solution as the performance depends on the location of the links.

Example of Local Blocking Technique: Given the initial channel offsets of each node, Equation 2.15 is used to generate a channel. If a good channel is not generated using the first channel offset, use the second channel offset, and so on. If we still do not get a good channel, the packet transmission is delayed from the current time slot by the node. Notably, energy consumption increases as the radio of the receiver are on although the packet is not sent.

Let ASN $= 10$, CO $= \{2, 5\}$, and NAC $= 8$ then (ASN+CO) mod NAC $= \{4, 7\}$. If channel 4 generated using first channel offset is already blocked, then channel 7 (good channel) generated using second channel offset is considered for transmission.

Example of Global Blocking Technique: The advantage is that only one offset is needed herein. Once the channel is blocked, it is removed from the set and NAC has been decremented by 1. Equation. 2.15 then always gives a good channel.

Suppose that channels $\{2, 4, 5\}$ are blocked. Therefore, NAC $= 5$ because there are total eight channels and three blocked channels. The difference of 8 and 3 is 5. For ASN $= 10$ and CO $= 2$, (ASN+CO) mod NAC $= 2$. Therefore, the second element in good channel list $\{1, 3, 6, 7\}$ corresponds to channel 3.

2.4 LoRaWAN Protocol

Long Range Wide Area Networks (LoRaWAN) protocol is developed by French start-up company Cycleo and later acquired by Semtech corporation in years 2012–2015. LoRa technology uses an unlicensed ISM radio band. Anyone can use ISM (Industrial, Scientific, and Medical) band freely. However, the data rate is low and interferences exist as anyone can use these frequencies. The applications are microwaves, ovens, and medical equipment amongst others. LoRaWAN is used for low power, low data rate, and long-range communication. The usages are for low data rate applications such as sensor data, namely, temperature, the humidity not for audio or video message. The protocol bridges the gap between short-range wireless and cellular communication technologies.

Bluetooth, Wi-Fi, 3G/4G, and LoRA protocols, respectively, use transmit power of 2.5 mW, 80 mW, 500 mW (high), and 20 mW in Figure 2.21. The range of Low-Power Wide-Area Network (LPWAN) technology is larger than IEEE 802.15.4, Zigbee, Bluetooth, RFID and Wireless LAN protocols and comparable to cellular technology. However, the data rate is lower than wireless LAN and cellular technologies and comparable to IEEE 802.15.4, Zigbee,

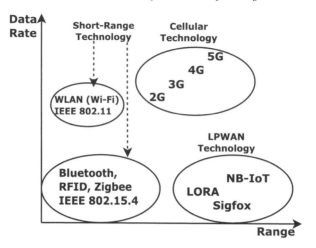

FIGURE 2.21: Need of LPWAN Technology

TABLE 2.4: Comparison of Link Layer Protocols

Parameter	ZigBee	WiFi	Bluetooth	LoRaWAN	Sigfox
Standard	IEEE 802.15.4	IEEE 802.11	IEEE 802.15.1, Bluetooth Special Interest Group (SIG)	LoRa alliance	Sigfox
Modulation	DSSS, QPSK	DSSS, OFDM	GFSK	CSS	BPSK
Frequency	ISM: 868 MHz, 2.4 GHz	ISM 2.4GHz, 5GHz	2.4GHz	Varies across countries	Varies across countries
Coverage	100m	100m	100m (depends on class and version)	10Km	40Km

Bluetooth, and RFID protocols. In Table 2.4, we use the following abbreviations. CSS is Chirp Spread Spectrum, DSSS is Direct Sequence Spread Spectrum, QPSK is Quadrature Phase Shift Keying, GFSK is Gaussian Frequency Shift Keying, BPSK is Binary Phase Shift Keying, OFDM is Orthogonal Frequency-Division Multiplexing. Table gives the overview of different technologies and here we focus on LoRaWAN protocol.

2.4.1 Architecture

The end node is battery powered while the gateway main powered. The node has a sensor, wireless transceiver, microcontroller, and printed antenna. Since the end node has a sensor, it becomes a reMOTE sensor or simply called mote in North America. Gateway is like an end node, however, it is connected to the Internet. It collects data from multiple end nodes and vice-versa as shown in Figure 2.22. The end node and gateway do bidirectional

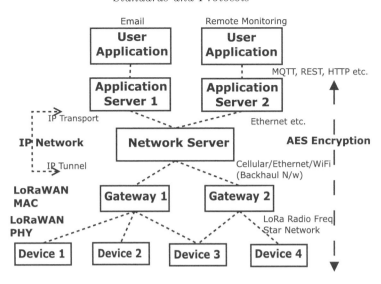

FIGURE 2.22: LoRaWAN architecture

communication in a star network topology. The center of the star would be the gateway while branches the end nodes. In a mesh topology, the nodes unnecessarily receive and transmit data to the other nodes.

The end node data is received by multiple gateways. The gateways send the data further to the network or data server via backhaul networks such as cellular, Ethernet, or Wi-Fi. The end node to gateway communication is through the LORA protocol. High capacity gateways employ adaptive data rates and multichannel multi-modem transceivers. Therefore, the gateway can use different spreading factors for different frequencies and listen to them simultaneously.

The network server manages the gateway, filtering of redundant data, performs security verification, scheduling of ACK through the optimal gateway, performs adaptive data rate control amongst others. In this architecture, for supporting mobility no handover mechanism is required from one gateway to another.

2.4.2 Device Class

There are three classes of LoRaWAN devices as shown in Figure 2.23. In *class A(ll)*, all device classes *B* and *C* can act like a class *A*. The device does bidirectional communication. It is battery-powered and the most energy-efficient. The device is the subset of other device classes supported by all LoRAWAN devices. The communication model used is uplink transmission by end node, then two receive windows open up after some delay for downlink communication.

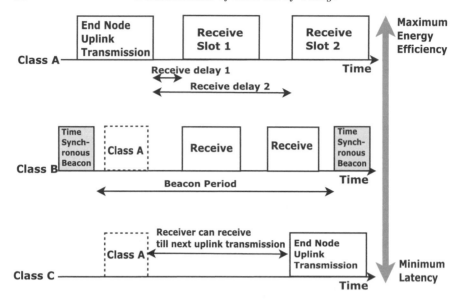

FIGURE 2.23: Device classes

In *class B(eacon)*, the features are bidirectional communication, having scheduled receive slots, and a battery-powered actuator. The end node receives a time-synchronized beacon for timing reference from the gateway so that the server or gateway knows when the end nodes listen on those extra receive slots or ping slots used to initiate a downlink communication. It is the same as class A and also opens up two receive slots at the scheduled time.

In *class C(ontinuous)*, the features are bidirectional communication, main powered actuator, least energy-efficient, and least latency. It is the same as class A but these devices listen continuously.

2.4.3   Radio Propagation

The signals from source to destination travel through the medium. The medium consists of obstacles such as tree, building, and hills amongst others. This causes reflection, refraction, and diffraction and incurs loss to the received signal strength. The free space loss is given by

$$\text{PL (in dB)} = 32.45 + 20 \log d + 20 \log f \qquad (2.16)$$

where f and d denote frequency (in MHz) and distance between the end node and gateway (in km).

Example: If $d = 100$ m and $f = 869$ MHz,

$$\text{PL} = 32.45 + 20 \log 0.1 + 20 \log 868 = 71.22 \text{ dB} \qquad (2.17)$$

TABLE 2.5: The values of SNR threshold for different SFs

SF	7	8	9	10	11	12
SNR$_{\text{threshold}}$ (dB)	−7.5	−10	−12.5	−15	−17.5	−20

2.4.4 Link Budget

Received Signal Strength Indicator (RSSI) is the sum of transmitted power, all gains, and losses. Receiver sensitivity is the minimum received power that a receiver can detect or demodulate. RSSI must be greater than receiver sensitivity for correct reception. For example, receiver sensitivity = −95 dBm. Receiver sensitivity should be as low as possible.

Link margin is the difference between RSSI and receiver sensitivity. For example, if RSSI = −70 dBm, then the link margin = −70 − (−95) = 25 dBm = 316 mW. LoRa protocol has a sensitivity of −148 dBm due to chirp spread spectrum modulation. SNR, the difference of RSSI and noise power in dB scale, varies between −20 dBm to +10 dBm. The maximum link budget is the difference between transmitted power and receiver sensitivity. For example, the maximum link budget is equal to 30 − (−148) = 178 dBm, if transmitted power is 30 dBm and receiver sensitivity, is −148 dBm.

SNR$_{\text{threshold}}$ is the minimum SNR required for proper demodulation of the signals at the receiver. The role of receiver sensitivity according to Semtech datasheet 1276 is illustrated in Table 2.5 for different Spreading Factor (SF).

$$\text{Receiver Sensitivity} = -174 + 10 \log \text{BW} + \text{NF} + \text{SNR}_{\text{threshold}} \qquad (2.18)$$

where BW is bandwidth in Hz, NF is noise figure (in dB) equal to 6 dB for SX1272/SX1276 and SNR$_{\text{threshold}}$ also in dB.

Example: For BW = 250 kHZ, the receiver sensitivity can be computed using Table 2.5 and Equation 2.18 as [−121.5, −124, −126.5, −129, −131.5, −134] dBm for SF = 7 to 12. Receiver sensitivity decreases with the increase of SF. If the distance between the LoRa end node and gateway increases, the SF must be also increased for lower receiver sensitivity in order to demodulate the signal properly.

2.4.5 Rate Definitions

The terminologies for LoRaWAN rate are listed below:

- Bandwidth (BW) is the number of cycler per second or Hertz. The bandwidth is equal to chip rate, R_c chips/sec.

- Chip duration is given by

$$T_c = \frac{1}{\text{BW}} = \frac{1}{R_c} \text{ second.} \tag{2.19}$$

- Spreading factor is the number of raw bits that are used for encoding a symbol. It varies from 7 to 12.

- Symbol represents one or more bits of data. It has 2^{SF} values.

- The symbol rate is given by

$$R_s = \frac{\text{BW}}{2^{\text{SF}}} = \frac{R_c}{2^{\text{SF}}} \text{ symbols/sec} \tag{2.20}$$

- The symbol duration is expressed as

$$T_s = \frac{1}{\text{symbol rate}} = \frac{2^{\text{SF}}}{\text{BW}} \text{ sec} \tag{2.21}$$

- The data rate or bit rate is the number of bits per symbol times symbol rate times code rate. This is given by

$$R_b = \text{SF} \times \frac{\text{BW}}{2^{\text{SF}}} \times \frac{4}{4 + \text{CR}} \tag{2.22}$$

Note that the code rate is the actual number of bits which carries information.

Example of Rate Calculations: Consider SF $= 7$ and BW $= 250$ kHZ. Determine all the parameters related to LoRaWAN rate.

Solution: The chip rate $=$ BW $= R_c = 250,000$ chips/sec and the chip duration is given by

$$T_c = \frac{1}{250,000} = 4\mu s \tag{2.23}$$

The symbol carries 7 raw bits of information. For example, with SF $= 7$, the symbol is 1001110 in binary. The corresponding decimal equivalent is 78. The symbol has any decimal value between 0 in decimal (binary equivalent 000000) and 127 in decimal (binary equivalent 1111111). Therefore, a total of 128 values. The symbol has $2^{\text{SF}} = 2^7 = 128$ chips. The symbol rate is given by

$$R_s = \frac{250,000}{2^7} = 1954 \text{ symbols/sec} \tag{2.24}$$

and the symbol duration is

$$T_s = \frac{2^7}{250,000} = 512 \ \mu s \tag{2.25}$$

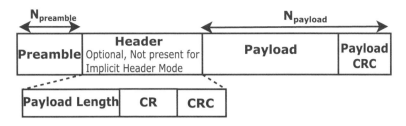

FIGURE 2.24: Explicit header structure

The data or bit rate for CR = 1 is

$$R_b = 7 \times \frac{250,000}{2^7} \times \frac{4}{4+1}$$
$$= 10937.5 \text{ bits/sec } \sim 11 \text{ kbps} \tag{2.26}$$

Remarks on LoRaWAN rate: We can conclude that the chip rate is greater than the symbol rate. As the BW increases, the symbol duration decreases as BW is in the denominator. As SF increases, the symbol duration also increases as 2^{SF} is in the numerator. As the BW increases, the data rate or bit rate also increases. As the SF increases, the data rate of bit rate decreases as 2^{SF} in the denominator is greater than SF in the numerator. If SF is increased by 1, then symbol duration gets doubled. The aforementioned insights are intuitive too.

2.4.6 Time of Air

The explicit header structure is shown in Figure 2.24. This consists of preamble, payload, and header (optional). Time of Air (ToA) is the packet transmission time. This is the amount of time needed for a data packet to travel from a transmitter to a receiver. The distance between the transmitter and the receiver is proportional to ToA. ToA is given by

$$\text{ToA} = T_{\text{preamble}} \text{ (in sec) } + T_{\text{payload}} \text{ (in sec)} \tag{2.27}$$

where $T_{\text{preamble}} = (N_{\text{preamble}} + 4.25)T_s$ with $T_s = \frac{2^{SF}}{BW}$. Further,

$$T_{\text{payload}} = N_{\text{payload}}T_s \tag{2.28}$$

where

$$N_{\text{payload}} = 8 + \max\left(\left\lceil \frac{8PL - 4SF + 28 + 16CRC - 20IH}{4(SF - 2DE)} \right\rceil (CR+4), 0\right) \tag{2.29}$$

Note that max and $\lceil . \rceil$ are the maximum and the celling operators, respectively N_{preamble} is 8 symbols for EU868. PL is Packet Length in the number of bytes. IH is an Implicit Header. This is 0 for header enabled for LoRaWAN and 1 otherwise. CRC is Cyclic Redundancy Check. This is 1 for an enabled case which is by default in LoRaWAN and 0 for a disabled case. CR is coding rate equal to $\{1, 2, 3, 4\}$. This is by default 1 for LoRaWAN. DE is data rate optimization and DE is 1 for low data rate for BW 125 kHz and SF $\geq$ 11.

Example of ToA: Consider SF = 7, BW = 250 kHZ, Payload = 10 bytes. Compute ToA.

Solution: T_s is computed as

$$
\begin{aligned}
T_s &= \frac{2^{\mathrm{SF}}}{\mathrm{BW}} \\
&= \frac{2^7}{250,000} = 0.512 \text{ ms}
\end{aligned}
\tag{2.30}
$$

Similarly, T_{preamble} is given by

$$
\begin{aligned}
T_{\mathrm{preamble}} &= (N_{\mathrm{preamble}} + 4.25)T_s \\
&= (8 + 4.25) \times 0.512 \text{ ms} = 6.272 \text{ ms}
\end{aligned}
\tag{2.31}
$$

Finally, N_{payload} is computed as

$$
\begin{aligned}
N_{\mathrm{payload}} &= 8 + \max\left(\left\lceil \frac{8\mathrm{PL} - 4\mathrm{SF} + 28 + 16\mathrm{CRC} - 20\mathrm{IH}}{4(\mathrm{SF} - 2\mathrm{DE})} \right\rceil (\mathrm{CR} + 4), 0\right) \\
&= 8 + \max\left(\left\lceil \frac{8 \times 10 - 4 \times 7 + 28 + 16 \times 1 - 20 \times 0}{4(7 - 2 \times 0)} \right\rceil (1 + 4), 0\right) \\
&= 8 + \max\left(\left\lceil \frac{96}{28} \right\rceil (5), 0\right) \\
&= 8 + \max(4 \times 5, 0) \\
&= 8 + 20 = 28.
\end{aligned}
\tag{2.32}
$$

Hence,

$$
\begin{aligned}
\mathrm{ToA} &= T_{\mathrm{preamble}} + T_{\mathrm{payload}} \\
&= T_{\mathrm{preamble}} + N_{\mathrm{payload}} T_s \\
&= 6.272 + 28 \times 0.512 = 20.608 \text{ ms}
\end{aligned}
\tag{2.33}
$$

If we increase SF, ToA also increases as 2^{SF} of T_s in the numerator is dominant than SF of numerator and denominator inside ceil operator. When the signal is weaker or interference is higher, LoRa end nodes use a higher SF. Also, if the distance between the LoRa end node and gateway is higher, we again use a higher SF.

Illustration of Coding Rate: In error correction, we add redundant bits to the transmitted data. This protects the original bits from channel error and restores them. The power consumption is proportional to the number of error correction bits. Coding efficiency is the proportion of bits that carries original information.

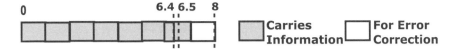

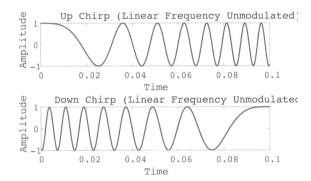

FIGURE 2.25: Illustration of coding rate

FIGURE 2.26: Frequency linearly increases and decreases with time

For LoRa, it is expressed as $\frac{4}{4+CR} = \{\frac{4}{5}, \frac{4}{6}, \frac{4}{7}, \frac{4}{8}\}$, where CR $= \{1, 2, 3, 4\}$. For example, SF $= 8$, that is, the number of transmitted bits is equal to 8 and CR is equal to $\frac{4}{5}$. The number of actual bits which carries information is $8 \times \frac{4}{5} = 6.4$ bits as in Figure 2.25.

2.4.7 Modulation

A signal is spread in the frequency domain in the spread spectrum technique. In chirp spread spectrum, the information is encoded by a wideband linear frequency chirp which acts as a carrier signal. Chirp is Compressed High Intensity Radar Pulse. The frequency increases and decreases linearly with time in up chirp and down chirp, respectively in Figure 2.26. This chirp acts as an unmodulated carrier signal and is used to modulate a message.

Examples of Chirp and Modulated Chirp: The up and down chirps are as the function of time in Figure 2.27. There is a center frequency and its swings are given by $f_{\text{high}} = f_{\text{center}} + 0.5\text{BW}$ and $f_{\text{low}} = f_{\text{center}} - 0.5\text{BW}$. Refer to Figure 1 and Equations 1 to 6 on Page 2 of Staniec 2018 et. al. for further readings. The data is encoded by an appropriate shift along the frequency axis using cyclic-shifted chirps. We consider SF equal to 8 and symbols out of 256 to be encoded by chirps are 00000000 in binary (in decimal 0), 10000000 in binary (in decimal 128), and 1001110 in binary (in decimal 78) as shown in Figure 2.28.

For decimal zero, the up chirp goes from f_{low} to f_{high}. For decimal 128, the chirp starts from the center frequency goes until f_{high}. Again it resumes

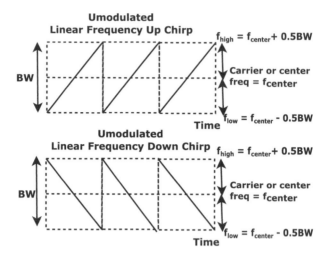

FIGURE 2.27: Up and down chirps

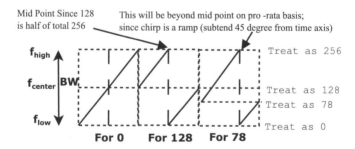

FIGURE 2.28: Illustration of modulated chirp

from 0 at the midpoint of the time interval and goes until center frequency. Note that the chirp starts from the midpoint of frequency and resumes from the midpoint of the time interval because 128 is half of the allowed decimal 256. Also, all segments of the chirp subtend an angle of 45 degrees from the time axis. On similar lines, we can draw the modulated chirp for decimal 78. Note the difference between chip and chirp. A symbol has 2^{SF} chips, while chirp is a ramp from low (or high) to high (or low) frequency.

2.4.8 Adaptive Data Rate

The end node requests the network server to compute the margin by setting a flag in the uplink message. In turn, the network server sends it back to the end node. Spreading factor, bandwidth and transmit power can be optimized by the network server. This is used by the end node. The margin is calculated by the network server and uses the most recent 10 to 20 uplink messages. The margin is calculated as

$$\text{margin} = \text{measured SNR} - \text{SNR Limit} \qquad (2.34)$$

For example, for SF12BW125 with SNR equal to 5 dB, the margin is 5 $- (-20) = 25$ dB, while the same for SF7BW125 is $5 - (-7.5) = 12.5$ dB. The use of SF12BW125 is a waste of ToA and energy. If SF increases, the ToA also increases. This leads to a decrease in data rate and an increase in battery power. The better the coverage the lower the SF. Therefore, the end node can use SF7 but it can be optimized further by reducing transmit power. Mobile end nodes are not mobile always. Thus, ADR can be set by the end node when it does not move.

2.4.9 Pure ALOHA—Access Protocol

ALOHA is a random access protocol for sending data from multiple end nodes over a shared medium. The protocol is developed by the University of Hawaii in early 1970. Pure ALOHA is simple in the sense that an end node can send the data whenever the node is ready like LoRaWAN device class A. This makes the architecture asynchronous and hence, energy-efficient. This is unlike a synchronous architecture where an end node needs to frequently wake up, check the message, and synchronize. However, pure ALOHA protocol suffers from collisions. Each end node sends two frames and finally, two frames survive as shown in black color in Figure 2.29.

The steps of a pure ALOHA protocol are listed in Algorithm 1. If the acknowledgment is received, then the frame transmission is successful. Otherwise, abort the transmission of the frame if the number of attempts exceeds the threshold. If the number of attempts is within the limit, then wait for some random time decided by binary exponential backoff algorithm. For this, a random number $[0, 2^{K_a} - 1]$ is chosen. The backoff time is given by the

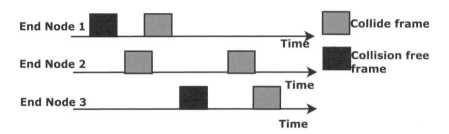

FIGURE 2.29: Pure ALOHA scheme

Algorithm 1: Algorithm for pure ALOHA scheme

Data: Frames to be sent and maximum number of allowed attempts K_a^{max}

Result: Success, Reattempt or Abort

1 Initialization: set an attempt index $K_a = 0$.;
2 Transmit the frame;
3 Wait for time out period which is equal to round-trip propagation delay $(2T_p)$;
4 **if** *ACK received* **then**
5   Successful transmission of frames;
6 **else**
7   Increment the attempt index to $K_a + 1$;
8   **if** *If the number of attempts exceeds maximum limit, that is, $K_a > K_a^{max}$* **then**
9   Frame is discarded and the transmission is stopped.
10   **else**
11   Run the backoff algorithm by choosing a random number between zero and $2^{K_a} - 1$;
12   Backoff time is the product of random number and frame time;
13   Wait for backoff time before next attempt;

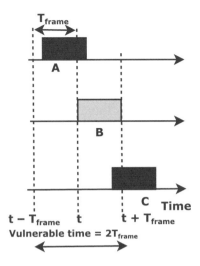

FIGURE 2.30: Vulnerable period for pure ALOHA scheme

product of the random number and average or peak frame transmission time. Finally, reattempt the transmission after the back-off time.

In pure ALOHA scheme, the frame can be sent anytime. Therefore, A and C can start sending anytime in $[t - T_{\text{frame}} \ \ t]$ and $[t \ \ t + T_{\text{frame}}]$, respectively as shown in Figure 2.30. This needs to be avoided for collision-free scenario. In other words, the tail end of A should not collide with the head end of B. Similarly, the tail end of B should not collide with head end of C. The vulnerable time is determined as $(t + T_{\text{frame}}) - (t - T_{\text{frame}}) = 2T_{\text{frame}}$.

Throughput Calculation for Pure ALOHA protocol: Let G and S be the total number of transmission per frame time and the number of successful transmission per frame time, respectively. The S is given by

$$S = GP_s \tag{2.35}$$

where P_s denotes the probability of successful transmission. Using Poisson distribution, the probability of successful transmission if there is no arrival ($n = 0$) in vulnerable time $2T_{\text{frame}}$ is computed.

$$P_0(2T_{\text{frame}}) = \frac{(\lambda_a 2T_{\text{frame}})^0 \exp(-\lambda_a 2T_{\text{frame}})}{0!} \tag{2.36}$$

where we set $t = 2T_{\text{frame}}$ and $n = 0$ in

$$P_n(t) = \frac{(\lambda_a t)^n \exp(-\lambda_a t)}{n!} \tag{2.37}$$

Therefore, the average number of successful transmissions is given by

$$P_0(2T_{\text{frame}}) = S = \exp(-2G) \tag{2.38}$$

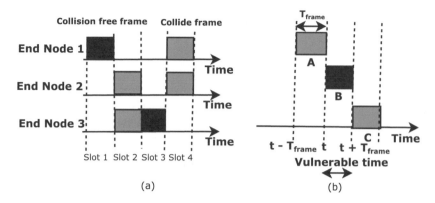

FIGURE 2.31: Slotted ALOHA scheme

where $\lambda_a = \frac{G}{T_{\text{frame}}}$ is the arrival rate. Notably, the maximum throughput is 18.4 % at $G = 0.5$.

2.4.10   Slotted ALOHA protocol

Slotted ALOHA as shown in Figure 2.31(a) is efficient than pure ALOHA. It has twice as much throughput as that of a pure ALOHA. The throughput is 0.368 at $G = 1$ as vulnerable time becomes half, T_{frame}. The end node can send a frame only at the beginning of the slot unlike pure ALOHA sends any time. If the frame misses the slot, then wait for the next slot. Here, collision happens when two nodes send frames in the same slot.

Since in the slotted ALOHA scheme, the frame can be sent only at the beginning of the slot, then the vulnerable time is equal to $[t\ t+T_{\text{frame}}]$ as shown in Figure 2.31(b). This needs to be avoided for the collision-free scenario. The comparison between pure and slotted is done in Figure 2.32. The slotted has higher throughput than pure and scaled ALOHA schemes.

Example 1: If the distance between end node and gateway is 9 km, determine the backoff time.

Solution: The maximum propagation time is

$$\frac{9 \times 10^3}{3 \times 10^8}\ \text{s} = 0.03\ \text{ms} \tag{2.39}$$

For $K = 2$, $R = \{0, 1, 2, 3\}$. Hence, $T_B = \{0, 0.03, 0.06, 0.09\}$ ms.

Example 2: Find vulnerable time for 10 bytes frame on a shared channel of 160 kbps.

Solution: The frame time is given by

$$T_{\text{frame}} = \frac{10 \times 8\,\text{bits}}{160 \times 10^3\,\text{bps}} = 0.5\ \text{ms}. \tag{2.40}$$

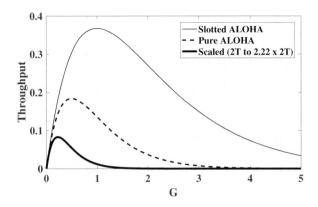

FIGURE 2.32: Comparison of pure and slotted ALOHA

The vulnerable duration is equal to 2×0.5 ms $= 1$ ms. No end node should send later than 0.5 ms before the intended end node starts sending and no end node should start sending in the next 0.5 ms duration.

Example 3: Find throughput for ALOHA in Example 2 if all end nodes renders 500 frames per second (fps).

Solution: Since $T_{\text{frame}} = 0.5$ ms and rendering rate 500 fps. G is equal to 0.25. This is because 1000 ms ($= 1$ s) is for 500 frames. Therefore, in 0.5 ms (per frame time), $\frac{500}{1000} \times 0.5 = 0.25$ frame.

S for pure and slotted ALOHA are $0.25 \exp(-2 \times 0.25) = 15.2\%$ and $0.25 \exp(-0.25) = 19.4\%$, respectively. The throughputs for pure and slotted ALOHA are, respectively, $0.152 \times 500 = 76$ and $0.194 \times 500 = 97$. Only these frames out of 500 survive.

2.4.11 Duty Cycle, Dwell and Hop Time, and Robustness

The maximum duty cycle is defined as the maximum fraction of time that a LoRa node operates. If the time of air is T_a and the duty cycle is 99%, then we need to wait for $0.99 \times T_a$ before sending the next signal. Since this protocol operates on an unlicensed band, we need to restrict the users to send maximum data and to not favor a particular user unlimited time. Next, the dwell time is the amount of time needed to transmit on a particular frequency. Hop time is the time needed to change a frequency to another frequency. Finally, for robustness purpose, the end node changes frequency in a pseudo-random fashion for every transmission. For example, in Europe, eight different frequencies are used in uplink.

2.5 6LowPAN Protocol

Link-layer IEEE 802.15.4 standard is widely used by wireless sensor networks. Wireless Personal Area Network (WPAN) has low-power, low data rate, low bandwidth, and low transmit power characteristics. IoT network needs to be connected to the Internet (IP Networks) for a wide coverage of sensed data.

6LowPAN (IPv6 over Low-Power Wireless Personal Area Networks) is introduced for carrying IPv6 packet over IEEE 802.15.4 networks as defined in RFC 6282. The maximum frame size for IEEE 802.15.4 and IPv6 are 127 and 2048 bytes, respectively. Therefore, we need an *adaptation layer* for compatibility. The adaptation layer gets added in between network layer and data link layer as it utilizes the existing TCP/IP layer architecture. Three main functions of the layer are *Header Compression and Decompression, Fragmentation and Reassembly, and Mesh Routing.*

2.5.1 6LowPAN Stack

We discuss each layer of 6LowPAN stack in bottom-up approach as shown in Figure 2.33 next.

- *Physical Layer* converts bits to signals and then transmitted.

- *Data Link Layer* is responsible for detection and correction of errors during transmission. MAC layer present in data link layer senses the medium for collision-free transmission of frames using CSMA/CA or CSMA/CD technique.

- *Network Layer* is responsible for routing of packets using IP. The IP provides addresses to the nodes.

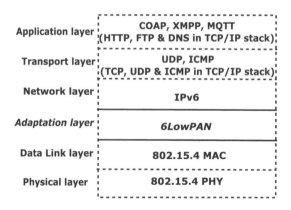

FIGURE 2.33: 6LoWPAN stack

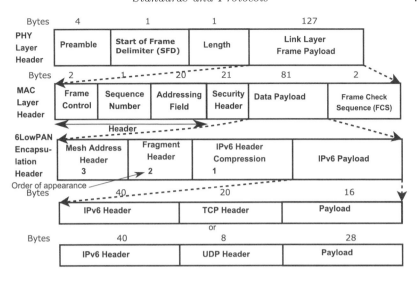

FIGURE 2.34: 6LowPAN Encapsulation Header

- *Transport Layer* is connection-based using TCP protocol or connection-less using UDP protocol. UDP has smaller header size and hence low complex than TCP.

- *Application Layer*: COnstrained Application Protocol (COAP), Extensible Messaging and Presence Protocol (XMPP) and MQTT (Message Queue Telemetry Support) are lightweight protocols for constrained nodes. These are chosen over Hypertext Transfer Protocol (HTTP) used in TCP/IP, Domain Naming System (DNS), File Transfer Protocol (FTP), and Simple Mail Transfer Protocol (SMTP).

2.5.2   6LowPAN Encapsulation Header

The 6LowPAN encapsulation header is shown in Figure 2.34. The *preamble* (4 bytes) synchronizes the sender and receiver for correct reception of the packet by receiver. *Start of Frame Delimiter (SFD)* (1 byte) indicates the receiver that the preamble ends and that the frame begins. The *length field* (1 byte) tells the receiver that how many bytes will follow. The maximum length of packet is 127 bytes. *Frame control* (2 bytes) contains the information about the frame being transmitted. The *sequence number* (1 byte) is sequence of transmitting packet. The acknowledgment and data packet carry same sequence number. *Addressing field* (20 bytes) provides addresses of the source and destination. *Security header* (21 bytes) is an optional security field. Finally, *frame check sequence* (2 bytes) and cyclic redundancy check (CRC) are used to check bit errors of the packets.

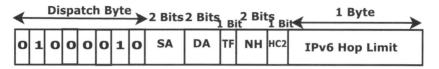

FIGURE 2.35: Header compression using HC1

The motivation for an adaptation layer is as follows: In the worst case, when the security header is present, the size of data payload is $127-(23+2)-21$ $= 81$ bytes in MAC layer header. In the subtraction, 127, 2, 1, 20, 21, and 2 are the length of link-layer frame payload, frame control, sequence number, addressing field, security header, and FCS, respectively in bytes. Finally, a very short payload of 16 bytes and 28 bytes left, respectively, after deduction of TCP and UDP transport layer headers. Hence, there is a need for an adaptation layer.

IPv6 Header Compression using HC1: *Stateless Header Compression* doesn't need information redundancy across layers. That is, there is no need for previous information from nodes exchanging compressed packets. IP header is suppressed and the IP address from the link-layer addresses is derived. *Header Compression (HC) 1* defined in RFC 4944 supports compression for link-local addresses not for global unicast and multicast addresses. 40 bytes IPv6 header is compressed to 2 to 3 bytes, namely, 1 byte for dispatch byte, 1 byte for HC1 byte, and 1 byte for hop limit field as shown in Figure 2.35.

The first two bits of dispatch byte are defined as follows: bits 00 for not a 6LowPAN frame, bits 01 for IPv6 addressing header, bits 10 for mesh header, bits 11 for fragmentation header. The last two bits of dispatch byte are defined as follows: bits 01 for uncompressed and bits 10 for compressed IPv6 header. In *Source Address (SA)* and *Destination Address (DA)*, first and third bits of Byte 2 are source and destination prefixes respectively. These are compressed and derived from link-layer address and 0 otherwise. The second and fourth bits of Byte 2 are source and destination interface IDs, respectively. These are compressed and derived from link-layer address and 0 otherwise. In *Traffic class and Flow label (TF)*, bit 1 is present if both are zero. In *Next Header (NH)*, bits 00, 01, 10, and 11 denote uncompressed header, packet uses UDP, TCP and ICMP, respectively. Finally, in *HC2*, bit 1 is used for compression of transport layer using HC2 and bit 0 if uncompressed.

IPv6 Header Compression using IPHC: Let us discuss IPv6 header compression using improved header compression (IPHC). In the case of link-local communication, 40 bytes IPv6 header can be compressed to 2 bytes in the best case. However, for routing over multiple IP hops, that can be compressed to 7 bytes. There is a context-based efficient compression technique for multicast and global IPv6 addresses in addition to link-local and unicast addresses. The prefixes of addresses are obtained from the network using a context-based approach.

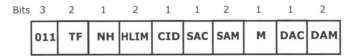

FIGURE 2.36: Improved Header Compression (IPHC)

First Fragment	5 bits	11 bits	16 bits
	11000	Datagram Size	Datagram Tag

Rest Fragments	5 bits	11 bits	16 bits	16 bits
	11100	Datagram Size	Datagram Tag	Datagram Offset

FIGURE 2.37: Fragment header

In Figure 2.36, bits 011 if we use IPHC, bit 0 for TF, and bit 1 for NH. Here, the next header is compressed using NHC. How the hop limit is compressed is shown in the HLIM field. This field is 00, 01, 10, and 11, for inline, 1, 64, 255, respectively. *CID* is Context Identifier Extension = 1. 8 bit CIE field follows after DAM (Destination Address Mode) field. *S/DAC* denotes Source/Destination Address Compression: whether the compression is stateless (bit 0) or context-based (bit 1). The field *M* is 1 if the destination address is multicast. *S/DAM* denotes source/destination address mode. This is used to know the number of bits or types of source/destination addresses.

Fragment Header: A large size payload of IPv6 cannot be transmitted over IEEE 802.15.4 networks. Therefore, we need fragmentation to fit transmission and reassembly operations into a single 802.15.4 frame. The size of the fragment is decided by the maximum frame size at the data link layer. Adaptation layer receives the packet from the network layer and fragments it in case the unfragmented payload is too large before sending it to the MAC layer.

Fragment header is shown in Figure 2.37. The first two bits are 11 for a fragment header. This is also mentioned in the first two bits of header compression. The third bit is an offset which is bit 0 for the first fragment and 1 for the rest fragments. The sizes of fragment headers for the first and rest fragments are 4 bytes and 5 bytes, respectively. The fourth and fifth bits are reserved for future use.

Datagram size is included in every fragment so that the receiver allocates a buffer in the case out of order arrival. If any fragment arrives at the receiver, it knows the total unfragmented size. That is why the original size is included with all fragments. With in-sequence arrival, including the original size with the first fragment is also sufficient. *Datagram tag* is a unique tag given to the set of fragments corresponding to the same IP packet. Finally, *datagram*

4 bits	4 bits	16 bits or 64 bits	16 bits or 64 bits
1 0 S D	**Hop Limit**	**Source Address**	**Destination Address**

FIGURE 2.38: Mesh addressing

offset is the position of fragment within the unfragmented payload from the beginning of the payload datagram.

Reassembly timer is used for reassembly at the adaptation layer of the receiver. A complete packet is sent to the upper layer. The maximum reassembly time is 60 seconds from the receipt of the first fragment. If only some fragments arrive, then all fragments are discarded.

Mesh Addressing Header: Routing is carried out by the network layer in TCP/IP protocol. However, routing is also done by adaptation layer in 6LowPAN. This is called mesh under routing. Mesh addressing header and mesh under routing are used to forward the 6LowPAN payload over multiple hops. The different fields of mesh addressing header are shown in Figure 2.38.

Hop limit is the maximum number of hops for forwarding the packets. The hop limit is decremented by one at each forwarding node. The packet is discarded if the hop limit hits zero. *Source and destination addresses* are identities of two ends, that is, sender and receiver, respectively. The first 2 bits are 10 as mentioned in the first two bits of header compression. *S/(or D) bit* is 1 (or 1) if we use 16 bits short address or 0 or (0) for 64 bits extended address of source and destination.

The mesh addressing header length is 5 bytes (= 4 bits + 4 bits + 16 bits + 16 bits) to 17 bytes (= 4 bits + 4 bits + 64 bits + 64 bits). We can use 64 bit address for source and 16 bits short address for broadcasting because of flexibility of S/D bits. For 4 bits hop limit field, the maximum hop limit is $2^4 = 16$, that is 0 to 15 hops.

Reassembly has been explained earlier. The fragments may come from different routes and these are reassembled by the adaptation layer. Even if one fragment is lost, all fragments need to be retransmitted. As per IEEE 802.15.4, the Reduced Function Device (RFD) sends all data to the Full Function Device (FFD). FFD can then perform mesh under routing. Mesh addressing header is not needed if source and destination are directly connected. The adaptation layer also does other functions such as neighbor discovery in addition to three main functions as mentioned.

2.5.3 Routing Protocol

IPv6 routing protocol for low power and lossy networks (RPL) is defined in RFC 6550. RPL utilizes a distance-vector routing protocol which is a distributed algorithm. The node shares a list of its distances with other nodes

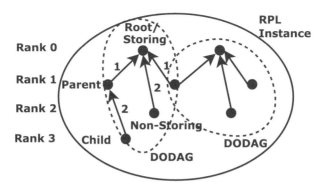

FIGURE 2.39: RPL Terminologies

to neighbors only. Then Bellman-Ford algorithm is used for creating routing tables. A list or array of distances is also called a vector.

In link-state routing protocol (LSRP), the node shares messages to all other nodes to learn the complete network and then uses the shortest path Dijkstra algorithm. A node has partial and full information of the network in distance vector and LSRP, respectively. Hence, LSRP consumes a large memory than the distance vector.

In RPL, routing is based on Destination Oriented Directed Acyclic Graph (DODAG) based on objective function and constraints. The objective function could be the shortest path from source to destination for minimization of energy and latency. The constraint supported by RPL could be excluding some battery-drained or failure nodes and then getting an alternate path dynamically called *DODAG version*.

RPL Terminologies: The following are the definitions of some important terms of RPL. This is also shown in Figure 2.39.

- *Root* is the destination node.

- *Rank* is the distance from the root node. Rank increases from the root to the leaf node.

- *Up (or Down)*: A directed edge toward (or away from) the root node.

- *Parent*: The edge points toward it.

- *Child*: The edge originates. A parent can have multiple children and similarly, a child can have multiple parents.

- *Directed acyclic graph (DAG)*: A graph that has no cycle like a spanning tree.

- *DODAG*: A special DAG with a single destination for all nodes. Each DODAG has an IPv6 128 bits ID.

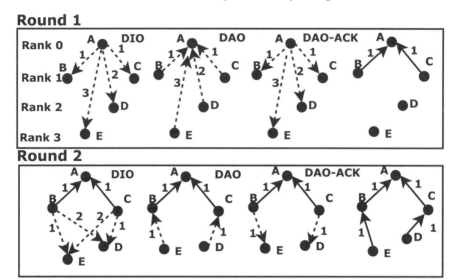

FIGURE 2.40: RPL example

- *RPL instance*: Since a node can be a member of different DODAGs each having a different objective, RPL instance is a set of DODAGs having different roots. Each RPL instance has a single objective then.

- *Storing node* has a complete routing table and knows how to go from one node to another.

- *Non-Storing node* has partial routing table for reaching to parent.

RPL Control Messages:

- DODAG Information Solicitation (DIS): This is a request for invitation. If a child wishes to join a DODAG in case no DIO is received.

- DODAG Information Object (DIO): This is an invitation. Multicasting of messages that allow the children to discover and choose the parent.

- DODAG Advertisement Object (DAO): This is a request to join. A child sends the request to the parent for joining DODAG.

- DAO Acknowledgment (DAO-ACK): This is a confirmation. The response can be yes or no from parent to child.

Example of RPL: In round 1, Let A be root node and it sends DIOs to nodes B, C D, and E in Figure 2.40. Then, nodes B, C, D, and E know the distances with respect to node A and send DAO request messages to node A for joining. The node A confirms the joining by DAO-ACK. Now nodes B and C are the nearest to node A having rank 1. In round 2, these nodes B and C

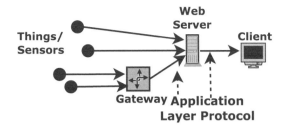

FIGURE 2.41: Application layer protocol

send DIOs to nodes D and E. The node D knows the distances with nodes B and C are 2 and 1, respectively. Similarly, the node E knows the distances with B and C are 1 and 2, respectively. The nodes E and D send the DAO to the nearest nodes B and C. Finally, nodes B and C reply with DAO-ACK to nodes E and D. Finally, DODAG is created now.

2.6 Application Protocols

The application protocol handles communications between things, sensors, or gateway and applications which use WWW. The web server uses application layer protocol as shown in Figure 2.41. That is, the data flow from sensor nodes, things, or gateway to applications, while control information like trigger or actuation in the opposite direction from the webserver to things.

2.6.1 Request-Response model

A client sends requests to a server. The server responds to the client as shown in Figure 2.42. Since each request-response is independent of others, this is also called a stateless communication model. The model is simple, however, there is a high coupling between client and server. This makes the request-response model complex for a large number of clients. The usage of the application protocol is in HTTP. In this case, the client is a web browser, and the application on the computer hosting a website is a server.

2.6.2 Publish Subscribe model

Similar to a request-response model, we have a publish-subscribe model. The publish-subscribe model allows for unidirectional communication between multiple subscribers (receiver of data) and a publisher (source of data) as shown in Figure 2.43. Here, the subscribers subscribe to some topics. Then

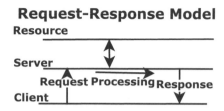

FIGURE 2.42: Request response model

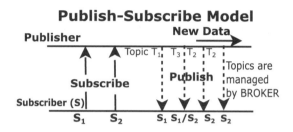

FIGURE 2.43: Publish subscribe model

publisher notifies and pushes new data to the subscriber in one-to-many. Any participant either can act as a publisher or subscriber.

The publisher is unaware of the subscribers. Therefore, there is a loose coupling between the subscriber and the publisher. This model is based on notifications of events from publisher to subscriber asynchronously and non-blocking mode. The meaning is that the subscriber does not wait while the publication of the message. There is also no need for client-to-server polling techniques. The protocol works well for a large number of subscribers in an IoT network. An example of this protocol is *Message Queue Telemetry Transport (MQTT)*.

2.6.3 Constrained Application Protocol

Constrained Application Protocol (CoAP) is standardized by IETF in RFC 7252. A light-weight CoAP is designed for constrained devices of IoT networks, in contrast to HTTP which has high complexity and high energy consumption. As we know, TCP is a connection-oriented protocol for high-reliability applications. This has high complexity. On the other hand, UDP is a connection-less protocol and the complexity is low. HTTP and CoAP use TCP and UDP as transport layer protocols, respectively.

CoAP is not a replacement for HTTP, rather a new design that has additional features. CoAP addresses the limitations of HTTP. CoAP uses a 4 bytes short fixed-length binary header that may be followed by compact binary options and a payload. CoAP supports the multicast IP destination address as

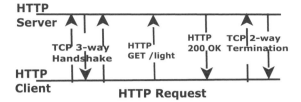

FIGURE 2.44: HTTP request

Abstract Layer of CoAP

Application
Request/Response
Message
UDP

FIGURE 2.45: Abstract layer of COAP

CoAP runs over UDP. HTTP is secured using Transport Layer Security (TLS) over TCP. CoAP uses Datagram Transport Layer Security (DTLS) over UDP.

HTTP and CoAP Abstract Layer: In HTTP, the number of messages exchanged between client and server for GET request is 7. That is 3 for TCP session plus 1 for HTTP request by client plus 1 for an HTTP response by server plus 2 for terminating TCP session as shown in Figure 2.44.

CoAP can be considered logically as a two-layer approach. Message layer deals with UDP and asynchronous nature of interaction and request/response interaction using method. There are four types of messages, namely, *confirmable, non-confirmable, acknowledgment, and reset*. Also, there are four methods in request/response layer, namely, *GET, PUT, POST, and DELETE*. The abstract layer of COAP is shown in Figure 2.45.

Unreliable and Reliable Transmission in CoAP: The two types of messages in CoAP are shown in Figure 2.46. *NON (non-confirmable message)* does not require reliability. For example, while sending each measurement from a sensor node, an acknowledgment is not sent back. For duplicate detection, the message ID (MID = 0xABCD) is still needed. In case the server cannot process NON-messages, they use RST (Reset).

CON (confirmable message) type provides reliability. Here the message is retransmitted after the default time-out and exponential back-off between retransmission till the receipt of ACK. In case the server cannot process the CON message, they use RST (Reset) instead of ACK. Note that, the message ID (MID = 0xWXYZ) should be the same for CON and ACK.

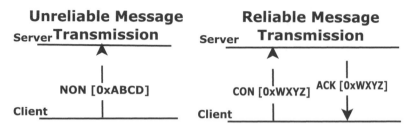

FIGURE 2.46: Confirmable and non-confirmable messages

Request/Response Models in CoAP: *Token* is used in order to match response and request. The token is different from the message ID. The token is a request ID. Every request should have a token even of zero length. A 2.05 (content) or 2.03 (valid) response code is part of the response in the success case. We get 2.05 and 2.03 from the message format to be discussed next.

If the response to a request by CON message is immediately ready, then the response is carried in ACK message. This is called *piggybacked response* as shown in Figure 2.47. Acknowledgment to piggybacked response is not sent assuming that the client requests again if the ACK carrying the piggybacked response is lost.

Separate Response in CON and NON in CoAP: Unlike piggybacked response, when the server is not ready, it sends an empty ACK to avoid further retransmission of request from the client as shown in Figure 2.48(a). Later, when the server becomes ready, it sends a new CON message which is acknowledged by the client. If a request is made using a NON-message, then the response is also in a separate NON-message in Figure 2.48(b). The server may also use a CON message. Note the importance of token in Figure 2.48(a).

Message Format in CoAP: The message header is fixed-size 4 bytes followed by message which consists of variable-length token value (0 to 8 bytes size), optional options and payload. This is shown in Figure 2.49. *Version (Ver)* field of CoAP is a version number which is of 2 bits. Here, bits 01 in binary is equivalent to 1 in decimal and other combinations are reserved for future use. *Type (T)* is made of 2 bits. The types of message are as follows: 0 for confirmable, 1 for non-confirmable, 2 for ACK and 3 for reset. *Token*

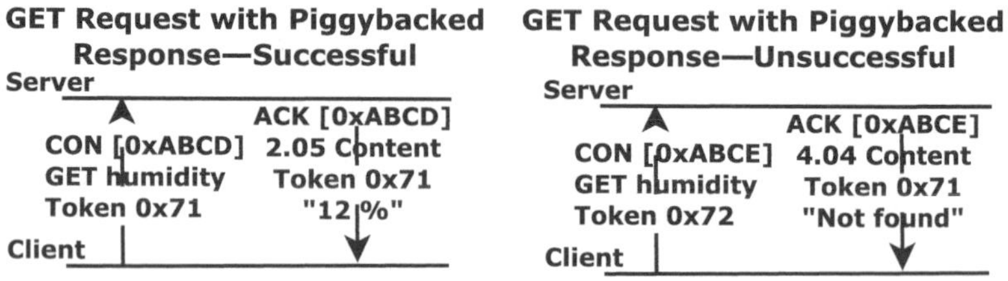

FIGURE 2.47: GET request with piggybacked response

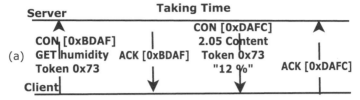

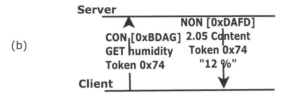

FIGURE 2.48: GET request with response

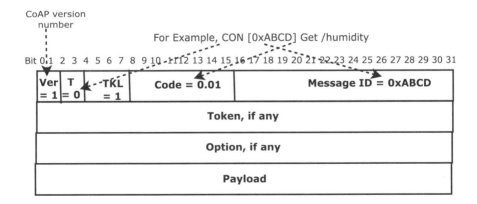

FIGURE 2.49: Message format

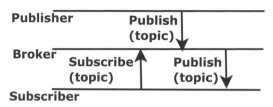

FIGURE 2.50: MQTT broker

Length (TKL) is of 4 bits. The size of variable-length token field is between 0 and 8 bytes. *CODE* is of 8 bits out of which 3 most significant bits for class (0 to 7 in decimal) and 5 least significant bits for code (00 to 31 in decimal) in the form x.yy. *Message ID* is of 8 bits for detecting message duplication, and to match ACK message with CON/NON message.

2.6.4   Message Queue Telemetry Transport

Message Queue Telemetry Transport (MQTT) TCP based application layer protocol is shown in Figure 2.50. The protocol is suitable for constrained devices. It provides high throughput and low latency than CoAP. It is designed by IBM, the latest version MQTT v3.1 adopted for IoT by the OASIS, supports multicast communication, and uses the publish-subscribe model as discussed before. Additionally, it uses hierarchical QoS as presented below:

- QoS Level 0: The sender tries *at most once* and the delivery is not guaranteed. The receiver does not send an acknowledgment. The message is neither stored nor re-transmitted. This is simple and has a low overhead. An example includes sensor sending measurements for a long time and some may be missed.

- QoS Level 1: The sender stores and retransmit multiple times till the receipt of the acknowledgment from the receiver, that is, *at-least once*. The delivery is guaranteed, however, duplicate message is possible.

- QoS Level 2: The message is delivered only once, that is *exactly once*. For example, billing system (invoice).

MQTT Wild Cards: *Topic* is a UTF-8 string that broker uses to filter messages for each subscriber. MQTT supports the hierarchical topic and uses forward-slash (/) like folders and files of a computer. For example, iot/sensor/light. Topics are case-sensitive and must have at least a character in the topic. *Wild card* is used by the subscriber, not the publisher.

- (+) Single level: This matches any string for a single topic level at the position in the topic filter (+). For example, topic filter iot/+/EEG publishes all the messages related to EEG signals for all different sensors of IoT. We get iot/sensor_libelium/EEG, iot/eHealthSens/EEG, iot/sensor5/EEG amongst others.

- (#) Multi-level: This matches any string for zero or multiple topic levels at the end of topic filter. For example, if we want to receive all the messages related to all the ehealthSens of IoT, we use topic filter iot/ehealthSens/#. We then receive iot/ehealthSens/EEG, iot/ehealthSens/ECG, iot/ehealthSens/EEG/singleChannel, iot/ehealthSens/EEG/singleChannel/5, iot/ehealthSens/battery amongst others.

2.6.5 Extensible Messaging and Presence Protocol

Extensible Messaging and Presence Protocol (XMPP) is standardized in RFC 6120 and 6121. The protocol is open source and the most common for IoT networks. It is a text-based protocol, instant messaging between person to person and TCP or HTTP based. It also supports bidirectional requests and the client-server or publish-subscribe model.

The protocol is highly secured. In MQTT and CoAP, TLS and DTLS encryptions are not built-in within the protocol, XMPP has built-in TLS mechanisms. It uses Extensible Markup Language (XML) text format for communication. The limitations are as follows: it does not provide QoS, the size of the message becomes large because of XML language, and inconvenient for networks with bandwidth constraints.

2.7 Summary

We need protocols for defining the rules to communicate among devices seamlessly. Several protocols such as IEEE 802.11 (wireless LAN), IEEE 802.15.4 (Zigbee), LoRaWAN, 6LowPAN, and application protocols are presented. We discussed the motivation, architecture, analysis, and use cases for different protocols of an IoT network. The theory of modulation and throughput are also briefed from a digital and wireless communications perspective. We highlight that all the protocols of traditional communication or computer network cannot be directly used in resource-constrained IoT networks.

2.8 Exercises

1. (a) At which layer, LoRa protocol work on?

   (b) If RSSI is -50 dBm and the receiver sensitivity is -90 dBm, what is the link margin?

   (c) If SF $= 7$, BW $= 125$ kHZ, and CR $= 1$, what is the data rate (kbps) approximately?

   (d) What is the actual number of bits which carry information for SF $= 10$ and CR $= 1$?

2. Consider a slotted ALOHA scheme. Derive the expression of the expected number of transmissions. Study the impact of G on the expected number of transmissions and draw some inferences.

3. How IEEE 802.11ah relay along with speed frame exchange can help in exchanging the information to a long-distance and reducing power consumption?

4. Determine the minimum and maximum throughput by considering L_{Data} $= 12$ Bytes and $L_{\text{Data}} = 475$ Bytes, respectively for IEEE 802.11ah standard. Comment on the throughput with increasing payload size.

5. Determine the throughput by considering $L_{\text{Data}} = 256$ Bytes for IEEE 802.11ah standard with PER $= 0.5$. Draw some inferences.

6. Can we estimate the distance between the transmitter and receiver using IEEE 802.11ah path loss models?

7. Consider a 4-stage linear feedback shift register, where XORed output of first and last stage is fed back to the input of the first stage. This is shown in Figure 2.51. Assume the initial state to be 0101 and generate the PN sequence.

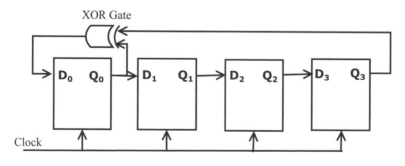

FIGURE 2.51: 4-stage PN sequence generator

8. Verify the properties of this PN sequence in Problem 7.

9. Identify the Star Topology and Peer-to-Peer Topology from the given Figure 2.52.

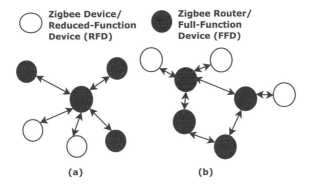

FIGURE 2.52: Topologies in IEEE 802.15.4

10. The channels are marked as 0, 1, 2, and 3, that is, NAC = 4 in IEEE 802.15.4-TSCH Networks. Given ASN = 5, CO = {1, 3} and channels 0 and 2 are blacklisted. Can we have an available channel? Make your observations.

11. How does Frequency Hopping Spread Spectrum (FHSS) reduce interference and jamming in the network?

12. Determine number of actual bits that carry information for SF = 8 and CR = {1, 2, 3, 4}. Comment on it.

13. What is the impact of SF, BW, and payload size on ToA?

14. A node X sends a frame via node Y to the final destination Z. List the link-layer addresses for each step.

15. Why do we compress using HC1 and HC2 bytes? In this case, HC2 bytes immediately follow HC1 byte and sits before the IP hop limit field.

16. For the given topology in Figure 2.53, find DODAG using RPL.

17. How does CoAP work with HTTP using a proxy intermediary in a smart home application?

18. Determine 4 bytes message header of CoAP for ACK [0xABCD] 2.5 content.

19. For a single level wild card of MQTT, if the subscriber uses topic filter iot/+/ECG, which among the following is (are) received: (a) iot/sensor1/abnormal, (b) cps/honywell/ECG,
(c) iot/sensorHoneywell/ECG, (d) iot/node/ECG?

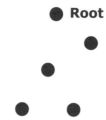

FIGURE 2.53: DODAG using RPL

20. For multi level wild card of MQTT, if the subscriber uses topic filter iot/ehealthSens/#, which among the following is (are) received: (a) iot/ehealthSens/link/2, (b) iot/libeliumSens/EEG, (c) iot/sensor1/ECG/1, (d) iot/ehealthSens1/battery?

21. **Do It Yourself**: Study AES encryption for a LoRaWAN protocol.

22. **Do It Yourself**: Explore Sigfox, Wireless Hart, and NB-IoT technologies and understand how those can be helpful for an IoT network.

Chapter 3

Clustering and Data Fusion

3.1 Introduction

The devices cannot directly communicate to a central node because of the limited communication range of IoT devices. Therefore, there is a motivation to partition the networks using an energy-efficient clustering technique. Then, devices in each of the partitioned or clustered areas can directly communicate to the head of the cluster. In this approach, a large IoT network is made for some application, say, for a smart city. The chapter presents two topics, namely, clustering and data fusion. The vector quantization for clustering of a network is briefed first. Subsequently, energy-efficient clustering for a resource-constrained IoT network is presented. Further, there are plenty of sensors, say, in smart city applications like temperature, humidity, pressure, gas, and noise level sensors to name a few. There are different sensors, which measure carbon monoxide, nitric dioxide, and ozone. The different sensors provide complementary information. In order to make a correct decision, the combined sensor data in a fusion technique is used. In particular, Bayesian data fusion, Dempster-Shafer's theory for data fusion, and decision fusion are presented herein.

3.2 Clustering Technique

Let us first discuss a basic clustering technique. We present herein Linde, Buzo, and Gray (LBG) algorithm—Generalized Llyod algorithm. The vector is a block of data. Here, N samples can be treated as a N dimensional vector. Quantization is a representation of a large infinite set of values with a smaller finite set. The application of this is for lossy compression.

For example, consider six finite levels in the range of 0 to 5 volt. Let us assign 3 V for 3.15 V, 4 V for 3.82 V, and so on. The assignment is carried out based on the nearest-neighbor criteria. Notably, we can-not recover original data or sample from the output of a quantizer. When we have a training

DOI: 10.1201/9781003225584-3

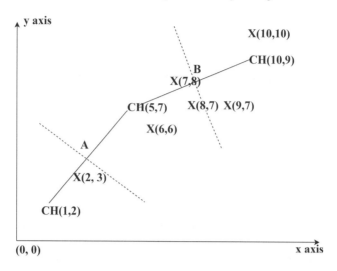

FIGURE 3.1: Initial cluster heads and measurements

or measurements set available, the algorithm looks very similar to k-means algorithm. The algorithm is listed below in Algorithm 3.2.1:

3.2.1   Algorithm for Clustering

1. Initial locations of cluster heads, $\text{CH}_i^{(0)}$ for $i = 1$ to M_n where i is index of CHs and (0) is zeroth iteration. The measurements to be clustered is denoted by X_n for $n = 1$ to N. Set $k = 0$ for zeroth iteration. $D^{(0)} = 0$ for initial distortion, Tolerance is ϵ which is a very small value.

2. Find boundary for regions $B_i^{(k)} = \{X_n : d(X_n, \text{CH}_i) < d(X_n, \text{CH}_j)$ for $j \neq i\}$ for $i = 1$ to M_n.

3. Compute squared residual between measurements and CHs.

4. If the fractional change in residual $\frac{D^{(k)} - D^{(k-1)}}{D^{(k)}} < \epsilon$ stop, otherwise, continue.

5. Set $k = k + 1$ and find new CHs. $\text{CH}_i^{(k)}$ for $i = 1$ to M_n that are centroid of each region. Repeat this process.

3.2.2   Example of Clustering

Let us initialize cluster heads (CHs) and measurements for clustering as x in Figure 3.1. Find boundary for partitioning the region.

Solution: The mid-point between two CHs is the perpendicular bisector joining CHs. The coordinates $A = (1 + \frac{5-1}{2}, 2 + \frac{7-2}{2}) = (3, 4.5)$, $B = (5 +$

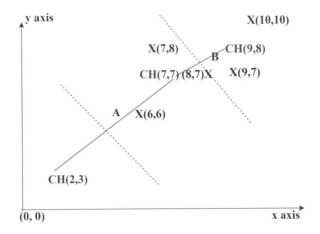

FIGURE 3.2: Cluster heads after first iteration

$\frac{10-5}{2}, 7 + \frac{9-7}{2}) = (7.5, 8)$. The squared distances or residuals are $(1 - 2)^2 + (2 - 3)^2 = 1^2 + 1^2 = 2$, $(5 - 6)^2 + (7 - 6)^2 = 1^2 + 1^2 = 2$, $(5 - 7)^2 + (7 - 8)^2 = 2^2 + 1^2 = 5$, $(10 - 8)^2 + (9 - 7)^2 = 2^2 + 2^2 = 8$, $(10 - 9)^2 + (9 - 7)^2 = 1^2 + 2^2 = 5$, $(10 - 10)^2 + (9 - 10)^2 = 0^2 + 1^2 = 1$. Therefore, the sum of residuals is 23. Note that we can take average residual also. $(8, 7)$ is closer to CH located at $(10, 9)$ than $(5, 7)$.

Let us do the next iteration. The new CHs are computed by taking centroid of measurements of each cluster. The first CH $= (\frac{2}{1}, \frac{3}{1}) = (2, 3)$, second CH $= (\frac{7+6}{2}, \frac{8+6}{2}) = (6.5, 7) \approx (7, 7)$, third CH $= (\frac{8+9+10}{3}, \frac{7+7+10}{3} = (9, 8)$. This is shown in Figure 3.2. Let us find now a new boundary region. $A = (2 + \frac{7-2}{2}, 3 + \frac{7-3}{2}) = (4.5, 5)$, $B = (7 + \frac{9-7}{2}, 7 + \frac{8-7}{2}) = (8, 7.5)$. The new squared residuals are $(2 - 2)^2 + (3 - 3)^2 = 0^2 + 0^2 = 0$, $(7 - 6)^2 + (7 - 6)^2 = 1^2 + 1^2 = 2$, $(7 - 8)^2 + (7 - 7)^2 = 1^2 + 0^2 = 1$, $(7 - 7)^2 + (7 - 8)^2 = 0^2 + 1^2 = 1$, $(9 - 10)^2 + (8 - 10)^2 = 1^2 + 2^2 = 5$, and $(9 - 9)^2 + (8 - 7)^2 = 0^2 + 1^2 = 1$. The sum of residuals is equal to 10. Note that $(8, 7)$ moves from region 3 to region 2.

Again, we determine the new CHs by computing the centroid of measurements of each cluster. The first CH $= (\frac{2}{1}, \frac{3}{1}) = (2, 3)$, second CH $= (\frac{6+7+8}{3}, \frac{6+8+7}{3}) = (7, 7)$, and third CH $= (\frac{9+10}{2}, \frac{7+10}{2} = (9.5, 8.5) \approx (9, 8)$ or $(10, 9)$. With third CH at $(9, 8)$, there is no change in residual. With third CH at $(10, 9)$, there is a little change in residual. We can stop now because the change in residual is insignificant.

3.2.3 Remarks on Clustering without Initialization

The algorithm is very simple and effective. The distortion does not increase from one iteration to the next. However, the optimal solution is not always

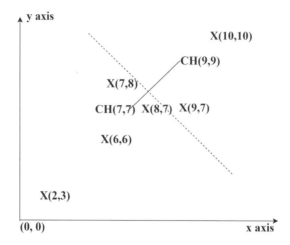

FIGURE 3.3: Cluster heads for initialization algorithm in first iteration

achievable. The convergence depends on initialization. We use the splitting technique for the same.

3.2.4   Algorithm for Initialization

1. *1 level*: Average of measurements.

2. *2 level*: CH from 1 level + second CH by adding a fixed perturbation ϵ. Use LBG algorithm to get 2-level vector quantizer. After convergence, get the final 2-level quantizer.

3. *4 levels*: 2 CHs from the previous level act as initial plus two more CHs obtained by adding ϵ. Use LBG algorithm until convergence.

We increase the number of levels by a factor of two until we get the required number of levels.

3.2.5   Example of Initialization

The 1 Level CH is $\left(\frac{2+6+7+8+9+10}{6}, \frac{3+6+8+7+7+10}{6}\right) \approx (7, 7)$ in Figure 3.3. Set $\epsilon = (2, 2)$. The initial 2 level CHs are then $(7, 7)$ and $(9, 9)$. The sum of squared residuals are $(7 - 2)^2 + (7 - 3)^2 = 5^2 + 4^2 = 41$, $(7 - 6)^2 + (7 - 6)^2 = 1^2 + 1^2 = 2$, $(7 - 7)^2 + (7 - 8)^2 = 0^2 + 1^2 = 1$, $(7 - 8)^2 + (7 - 7)^2 = 1^2 + 0^2 = 1$, $(9 - 9)^2 + (9 - 7)^2 = 0^2 + 2^2 = 4$, $(9 - 10)^2 + (9 - 10)^2 = 1^2 + 1^2 = 2$. The sum of residuals is equal to 51.

The first new CH $\left(\frac{2+6+7+8}{4}, \frac{3+6+8+7}{4}\right) = \left(\frac{23}{4}, \frac{24}{4}\right) = (5.75, 6) \approx (6, 7)$, second: $\left(\frac{9+10}{2}, \frac{7+10}{2}\right) = (9.5, 8.5) \approx (10, 9)$. The mid point is $(6+\frac{10-6}{2}, 7+\frac{9-7}{2})$ $= (8, 8)$ as shown in Figure 3.4. The sum of squared residuals are $(6 - 2)^2 +$

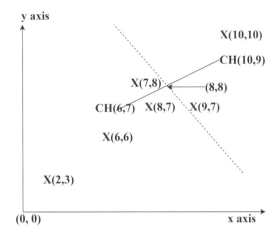

FIGURE 3.4: Cluster heads for initialization algorithm in second iteration

$(7-3)^2 = 4^2 + 4^2 = 32$, $(6-6)^2 + (7-6)^2 = 0^2 + 1^2 = 1$, $(6-8)^2 + (7-7)^2 = 2^2 + 0^2 = 4$, $(6-7)^2 + (7-8)^2 = 1^2 + 1^2 = 2$, $(10-9)^2 + (9-7)^2 = 1^2 + 2^2 = 5$ and $(10-10)^2 + (9-10)^2 = 0^2 + 1^2 = 1$. The sum of residuals is 45.

The new CHs are the same like previous iteration. The final 2 level CHs are $(6, 7)$ and $(10, 9)$. Now, initial 4 level CHs are $(6, 7) + (2, 2) = (8, 9)$, $(10, 9) + (2, 2) = (12, 11)$. This is shown in Figure 3.5. The first new CHs: $(\frac{2+6}{2}, \frac{3+6}{2})$ $= (4, 4.5) \approx (4, 5)$, second: $(\frac{7+8}{2}, \frac{8+7}{2}) = (7.5, 7.5) \approx (7, 7)$ or $(8, 8)$, third: $(\frac{9+10}{2}, \frac{7+10}{2}) = (9.5, 8.5) \approx (9, 8)$ or $(10, 9)$, fourth CH at $(12, 11)$. There is no measurement associated with fourth CH, therefore, discard this CH. Since, $(7, 8)$ and $(8, 7)$ are on boundary, we may take it in second region. Here, $(6, 6)$ is at the boundary. So, let us consider it to region 2. The sum of squared residual are $(4-2)^2 + (5-3)^2 = 2^2 + 2^2 = 8$, $(7-6)^2 + (7-6)^2 = 1^2 + 1^2 = 2$, $(7-8)^2 + (7-7)^2 = 1^2 + 0^2 = 1$, $(7-7)^2 + (7-8)^2 = 0^2 + 1^2 = 1$, $(9-9)^2 + (8-7)^2 = 0^2 + 1^2 = 1$, $(9-10)^2 + (8-10)^2 = 1^2 + 2^2 = 4$. The sum of residual is equal to 17.

The first new CH: $(\frac{2}{1}, \frac{3}{1}) = (2, 3)$, second: $(\frac{6+8+7}{3}, \frac{6+7+8}{3}) = (7, 7)$, and third: $(\frac{9+10}{2}, \frac{7+10}{2}) = (9.5, 8.5) \approx (9, 8)$ or $(10, 9)$. This is shown in Figure 3.6. There is no change in CHs and therefore, we stop here.

3.2.6 Remarks on Clustering with Initialization

- We add CHs from the previous level, therefore, CHs after splitting are at least as good as CHs before splitting.

- We can choose perturbation randomly. Here, we choose fixed for illustration purposes.

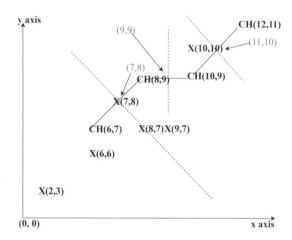

FIGURE 3.5: Cluster heads for initialization algorithm in third iteration

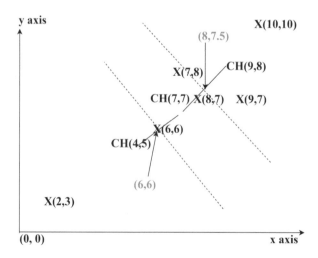

FIGURE 3.6: Cluster heads for initialization algorithm in fourth iteration

- The number of levels is not a power of two at the last level, we perturb only the required number of vectors. In Example 2, 1, 2, 2 + 1 = 3.

  Another example: 7 level vector quantizers. Generate vector quantizer 1—level then 2—level then 4—levels then perturb only 3 out of 4 vectors to get 7—level vector quantizer.

- Three vectors are chosen should be those with the largest number of training set vectors or the largest distortion.

- Hilbert chooses CHs randomly. This guarantees that there is at least one CH from the training set in each region.

3.3 Energy Efficient Clustering

We use energy-efficient clustering in order to increase the network lifetime of a clustered network. Sensors communicate via cluster head (CH) to the base station. Here, the network follows a decentralized architecture. Low-energy adaptive clustering hierarchy (LEACH) is an energy-efficient cluster-based protocol. We present herein the LEACH protocol of Heinzelman et al. (2002). The nearby nodes provide correlated data. We process and reduce the data locally and remove redundant data using the data aggregation technique. Therefore, we can use this protocol for a resource-constrained IoT network.

3.3.1 Radio Energy Dissipation Model

In an open environment, transmitted power is the function of squared distance (d^2) where d is the distance between the transmitter and the receiver. In a cluttered environment, transmitted power follows the d^α model. The α is a path loss exponent which varies approximately from 2 (open environment) to 5 (cluttered environment). For $d = 10$ m (say), to send the data in open environment, transmitted power is proportional to 10^2. In a cluttered environment, transmitted power is proportional to 10^5. The radio model for an open environment is given by

$$E_{\text{Tx}}(l, d) = lE_{\text{elec}} + l\varepsilon_{\text{oe}}d^2 \tag{3.1}$$

Similarly, the model for a cluttered environment is

$$E_{\text{Tx}}(l, d) = lE_{\text{elec}} + l\varepsilon_{\text{ce}}d^4 \tag{3.2}$$

where ε denotes the energy consumed by power amplifier of the transmitter for achieving acceptable SNR. ε_{oe} is used for an open environment and ε_{ce} for a cluttered environment. We assume herein $\alpha = 4$.

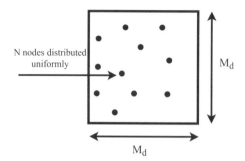

FIGURE 3.7: Uniformly distributed nodes

3.3.2   Radio Model for Receiver

Suppose that E_{elec} is the function of coding modulation, filtering, and spreading of the signal. Amplifier energy is $\varepsilon_{\text{oe}}d^2$ or $\varepsilon_{\text{ce}}d^4$ which is the function of distance and acceptable bit-error rate.

$$E_{\text{Rx}}(l,d) = lE_{\text{elec}} \qquad (3.3)$$

3.3.3   Optimal Number of Clusters

In a network of dimensions $M_d \times M_d$, N nodes are uniformly distributed as shown in Figure 3.7. Let K be the number of the clusters. The average number of nodes per cluster is given by

$$\frac{N}{K} = \underbrace{\frac{N}{K} - 1}_{\text{Number of non-cluster head nodes}} + \underbrace{1}_{\text{Number of cluster head node}} \qquad (3.4)$$

Energy Consumption by Cluster Head: Cluster head dissipates energy in order to receive signals from the nodes and aggregate the signals. Also, the cluster head transmits the aggregated signal to the base station. The energy is dissipated in this transmission too. We assume that the base station is placed far away from the nodes. Therefore, energy dissipation is according to cluttered environment model, that is, $\propto d^4$. The energy dissipated by the cluster head is given as

$$E_{\text{CH}} = \underbrace{lE_{\text{elec}}(\frac{N}{K} - 1)}_{\text{first term}} + \underbrace{lE_{\text{DA}}\frac{N}{K}}_{\text{second term}} + \underbrace{lE_{\text{elec}}}_{\text{third term}} + \underbrace{l\varepsilon_{\text{ce}}d_{\text{BS}}^4}_{\text{fourth term}} \qquad (3.5)$$

where the first term on right hand side is for receiving $l(\frac{N}{K} - 1)$ number of bits. The second term is to aggregate the received bits and its own bit $= l(\frac{N}{K} - 1) + l = l\frac{N}{K}$. The third term is for radio electronics of transmitter for compressed l

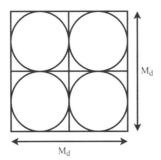

FIGURE 3.8: Computing expected energy

bits. Finally, the fourth term is for power amplifier of a transmitter to send l bits of compressed data over a distance d.

Energy Consumption by Non-cluster Head: We assume that the distance between CH and non-CH is small. Therefore, the power loss is proportional to d^2. Non-CH only transmits its data to the CH. The energy expended by the non-cluster head is given by

$$E_{\text{non-CH}} = lE_{\text{elec}} + l\varepsilon_{\text{oe}}d_{\text{CH}}^2 \tag{3.6}$$

Computation of Expected Energy: First, we find the expectation of the squared distance. Here, K is the number of clusters which is equal to four in Figure 3.8. The area occupied by each cluster is approximately $\frac{M_d^2}{K}$. The approximate area of a circle is given by

$$\frac{M_d^2}{K} = \pi r^2 \tag{3.7}$$

This can be written as

$$r = \frac{M_d}{\sqrt{\pi K}} \tag{3.8}$$

If X is a random variable, $E[X] = \int x f_X(x) dx$. Suppose that $f(x,y)$ denotes the node distribution. The expected squared distance is given by

$$E[d_{\text{CH}}^2] = \int_y \int_x (x^2 + y^2) \rho(x,y) dx dy \tag{3.9}$$

In two-dimensional coordinates system, the area in polar form as shown in Figure 3.9 is given by

$$\text{Area} = r dr d\theta \text{ and } x^2 + y^2 = r^2 \tag{3.10}$$

From Equation 3.9,

$$E[d_{\text{CH}}^2] = \int_r \int_\theta r^2 \rho(r,\theta) r dr d\theta \tag{3.11}$$

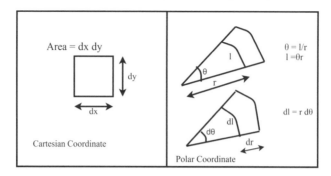

FIGURE 3.9: Cartesian to polar coordinates conversion

Let $f_X(x)$ be the probability density function. The nodes distribution is given by

$$\rho(r,\theta) = \frac{1}{\text{Area of each cluster}}$$

$$= \frac{\frac{1}{M_d^2}}{K} \tag{3.12}$$

$$= \frac{K}{M_d^2}$$

From Equation 3.11,

$$E[d_{\text{CH}}^2] = \int_\theta \int_r r^3 \frac{K}{M_d^2} dr d\theta$$

$$= \frac{K}{M_d^2} \int_\theta \int_r r^3 dr d\theta$$

$$= \frac{K}{M_d^2} \int_{\theta=0}^{2\pi} \frac{r^4}{4} \Big|_{r=0}^{r=\frac{M_d}{\sqrt{\pi K}}} d\theta \tag{3.13}$$

$$= \frac{K}{M_d^2} \left[\frac{\left(\frac{M_d}{\sqrt{\pi K}}\right)^4}{4} - 0 \right] \left[\theta \Big|_{\theta=0}^{2\pi} \right] \quad = \frac{K}{M_d^2} \frac{1}{4} \frac{M_d^4}{\pi^2 K^2} 2\pi$$

Hence,

$$E[d_{\text{CH}}^2] = \frac{M_d^2}{2\pi K} \tag{3.14}$$

Now, the total energy dissipated by non-cluster head using Equations 3.6 and 3.14 is

$$E_{\text{non-CH}} = l E_{\text{elec}} + l \varepsilon_{\text{oe}} \times \frac{M_d^2}{2\pi K} \tag{3.15}$$

The total energy dissipated by a cluster is

$$E_{\text{cluster}} = E_{\text{CH}} + \underbrace{\left(\frac{N}{K} - 1\right)}_{\text{Number of non-CHs}} E_{\text{non-CH}} \tag{3.16}$$

$$\approx E_{\text{CH}} + \frac{N}{K} E_{\text{non-CH}}$$

Therefore, the total energy for all clusters in a network using Equations 3.5, 3.15, and 3.16 is

$$\begin{aligned}
E_{\text{Total}} &= K E_{\text{cluster}} \\
&= K \left(E_{\text{CH}} + \frac{N}{K} E_{\text{non-CH}} \right) \\
&= K E_{\text{CH}} + N E_{\text{non-CH}} \\
&= l E_{\text{elec}} N + l E_{\text{DA}} N + l K \varepsilon_{\text{ce}} d_{\text{BS}}^4 + l N E_{\text{elec}} + l N \varepsilon_{\text{oe}} \frac{M_d^2}{2\pi K} \\
&= l \left(E_{\text{elec}} N + E_{\text{DA}} N + K \varepsilon_{\text{ce}} d_{\text{BS}}^4 + E_{\text{elec}} N + \varepsilon_{\text{oe}} \frac{M_d^2}{2\pi K} N \right)
\end{aligned} \tag{3.17}$$

where we use simplified form of Equation 3.5 as $E_{\text{CH}} = l E_{\text{elec}} \frac{N}{K} + l E_{\text{DA}} \frac{N}{K} + l \varepsilon_{\text{ce}} d_{\text{BS}}^4$.

In order to find the optimal number of clusters, we need to take partial derivative with respect to the number of clusters.

$$\frac{\mathrm{d} E_{\text{Total}}}{\mathrm{d} K} = 0 + 0 + \varepsilon_{\text{ce}} d_{\text{BS}}^4 + 0 + \varepsilon_{\text{oe}} N \frac{M_d^2}{2\pi} \times \frac{-1}{K^2} \tag{3.18}$$

Then, equate it to zero to get the optimal number of clusters as follows:

$$\begin{aligned}
\varepsilon_{\text{ce}} d_{\text{BS}}^4 &= \varepsilon_{\text{oe}} N \frac{M_d^2}{2\pi} \frac{1}{K^2} \\
K^2 &= \frac{N}{2\pi} \frac{\varepsilon_{\text{oe}}}{\varepsilon_{\text{ce}}} \frac{M_d^2}{d_{\text{BS}}^4}
\end{aligned} \tag{3.19}$$

Finally, the optimal number of clusters is given by

$$K_{\text{opt}} = \sqrt{\frac{N}{2\pi}} \sqrt{\frac{\varepsilon_{\text{oe}}}{\varepsilon_{\text{ce}}}} \frac{M_d}{d_{\text{BS}}^2} \tag{3.20}$$

where K_{opt} is the optimal number of clusters for minimal energy consumption. Therefore, the second-derivative of E_{Total} should be positive. We can ensure that by taking second-order derivative of Equation 3.18

$$\frac{\partial^2 E_{\text{Total}}}{\partial K_{\text{opt}}^2} = \varepsilon_{\text{oe}} N \frac{M_d^2}{2\pi} \times -1 \times \frac{-2}{K_{\text{opt}}^3} \tag{3.21}$$

As we know that

$$\frac{d}{dx}\left(\frac{1}{x^2}\right) = \frac{x^2 \times 0 - 1 \times 2x}{x^4} = \frac{-2}{x^3} \tag{3.22}$$

Hence,

$$\frac{\partial^2 E_{\text{Total}}}{\partial K_{\text{opt}}^2} = \varepsilon_{\text{oe}} N \frac{M_d^2}{\pi K_{\text{opt}}^3} > 0 \tag{3.23}$$

It must be noted that the individual term is positive and, therefore, the overall one is also positive.

3.3.4   Example of Optimal Number of Clusters

Given that, $E_{\text{elec}} = 100$ nJ/bit, $E_{\text{DA}} = 10$ nJ/bit/signal, $\varepsilon_{\text{oe}} = 20$ pJ/bit/m^2, $\varepsilon_{\text{ce}} = 0.0026$ pJ/bit/m^4, $M_d = 100$ m, $N = 100$, $l = \underbrace{200 \text{ bytes}}_{\text{data}} + \underbrace{25 \text{ bytes}}_{\text{header}}$. Determine the optimal number of clusters.

Solution: We obtain the optimal number of clusters using Equation 3.20

$$K_{\text{opt}} = \sqrt{\frac{100}{2\pi}} \sqrt{\frac{20}{0.0026}} \frac{100}{d_{\text{BS}}^2} \tag{3.24}$$

For $d_{\text{BS}} = 80$ m, $K_{\text{opt}} \approx 5$ and for $d_{\text{BS}} = 160$ m, $K_{\text{opt}} \approx 1$. All the given values are not needed in this question.

3.3.5   Example for Verification of K_{opt}

Compute the total energy consumption for a varying number of the clusters. Verify that K_{opt} calculated above indeed attains minimal average energy consumption.

Solution: Here, we use all the parameters which are given in previous example. Assume $d_{\text{BS}} = 80$ m and calculate E_{Total} for $K = 1$ to 8. We can find that E_{Total} is minimum for $K_{\text{opt}} = 5$ as expected.

3.3.6   Remarks on Energy Efficient Clustering

We do not calculate the expectation of d_{BS}^4 as this is the distance between CH and base station (outside) and nodes distribution does not depend on it.

3.4   Sensor Data Fusion

In the data fusion technique, we combine data of homogeneous or heterogeneous sensor data from IoT networks. Fused data provides complementary information than the individual sensor data. We estimate or predict some aspect of an observed event in the fusion process. The data fusion technique helps us in making more accurate decisions.

3.4.1 Motivation and Pointers for Data Fusion

We know that the communication range of IoT devices is limited. Hence, it provides data of its vicinity, that is, of neighboring sensors. There may be a loss of individual sensor data during data collection, communication, or reception. Further, some sensors may not provide a large number of observations or measurements due to their hardware specification. Hence, it limits the higher sampling rate. Finally, some sensors may not be accurate. This motivates us to study the data fusion technique.

Some of the pointers of the data fusion technique are as follows: first, there is no replacement for good sensor data. Even a sophisticated fusion algorithm cannot address the challenge if sensor data are not collected properly. Second, the error in one stage propagates to the next stage. We must do the best possible processing at every stage right from the data collection stage. Third, the results using fused data may not be better than the best sensor. Poor optimization of parameters such as weight during the fusion process may provide poor accuracy. Fourth, a fusion algorithm may not be universally accepted. An algorithm is chosen based on the characteristics of the data. Fifth, getting sufficient training data is not possible in a practical scenario. Hybrid algorithms that extract and use implicit and explicit features may help. Sixth, because of the dynamic fusion process, the refinement of the estimate does not end.

3.4.2 Fusion Architecture

There are three types of architecture of fusion, namely, centralized fusion, distributed fusion and hybrid fusion. *Centralized fusion* is used for homogeneous sensors. Temporal alignment and transformation of data are carried out appropriately herein. It uses estimation theory. *Distributed fusion* is used for heterogeneous sensors. Local decision is made or information is extracted by each sensor using estimation theory. Then it is fused. The fusion architecture is suitable for a large network. *Hybrid fusion* combines both centralized and distributed fusion methods. The distributed scheme is preferred to reduce computational overhead. The centralized scheme is used for high accuracy.

3.4.3 Bayesian Data Fusion

Let us discuss the Bayes theorem, probability density function, likelihood function, maximum likelihood estimate, and maximum a posteriori estimate briefly. These form the backbone for Bayesian data fusion.

Bayes' Theorem: From probability theory, the conditional probability of occurrence of an event A given that an event B has already occurred is

$$P(A|B) = \frac{P(A,B)}{P(B)} = \frac{\text{Probability of joint occurrence of events A and B}}{\text{Probabilty of occurrence of event B}}$$
(3.25)

We can then write

$$P(A,B) = P(A|B)P(B)$$
(3.26)

Since we know that

$$P(A,B) = P(B,A) = P(B|A)P(A)$$
(3.27)

Combining Equations 3.26 and 3.27,

$$P(A|B)P(B) = P(B|A)P(A)$$
(3.28)

Therefore, we can write

$$P(A|B) = \frac{P(B|A)P(A)}{P(B)}$$
(3.29)

For several events A_i

$$P(A|B) = \frac{P(B|A)P(A)}{\sum_i P(B|A_i)P(A_i)}$$
(3.30)

where $P(A)$ is the probability density function (PDF). The denominator term acts like a normalization factor.

Probability Density Function and Likelihood: Probability is likely of data given the parameters. In order to mathematically model the data, we describe the random data by its Probability Density Function (PDF), that is, $P(y[0], y[1], \ldots, y[N-1]; \theta)$. Note that θ is an unknown parameter of PDF. For example, for $N = 1$ sample and θ denotes mean, the PDF of data is

$$P(y[0]; \theta) = \frac{1}{\sqrt{2\pi\sigma^2}} \exp\left[-\frac{(y[0]-\theta)^2}{2\sigma^2}\right]$$
(3.31)

The PDF is viewed as a function of the unknown parameter with y fixed. *Likelihood function* deals with the probability of measurements y. The likelihood is a function of parameter given data is observed. In *Maximum Likelihood Estimate (MLE)*, we find θ such that $P(y = \text{data}|\theta)$ is maximum.

Maximum a Posteriori Estimate (MAP): Find θ such that $P(\theta|y = \text{data})$ is maximum. Here, y and θ denote the data or measurements and state or parameter, respectively. We use Bayes' theorem to compute posterior probability. $P(\theta|y)$ uses $p(\theta)$ and $P(y|\theta)$ where $P(\theta)$ is the prior probability and $P(y|\theta)$ is the observation probability.

$$P(y|\theta) = \frac{1}{\sqrt{2\pi\sigma_y^2}} \exp\left(-\frac{(y-\theta)^2}{2\sigma_y^2}\right)$$
(3.32)

In order to build the model, parameter θ is fixed and the distribution is then a function of y. When the observations are made during real-time testing, then the distribution is a function of θ. Let,

$$P(\theta) = \frac{1}{\sqrt{2\pi\sigma_\theta^2}} \exp\left(-\frac{(\theta - \theta_p)^2}{2\sigma_\theta^2}\right) \tag{3.33}$$

Using Bayes' theorem, we can write

$$P(\theta|y) = K\frac{1}{\sqrt{2\pi\sigma_y^2}} \exp\left(-\frac{(y - \theta)^2}{2\sigma_y^2}\right) \frac{1}{\sqrt{2\pi\sigma_\theta^2}} \exp\left(-\frac{(\theta - \theta_p)^2}{2\sigma_\theta^2}\right) \tag{3.34}$$

where K is a constant or normalization due to denominator term. Denote K' as $K \times \frac{1}{\sqrt{2\pi\sigma_y^2}} \times \frac{1}{\sqrt{2\pi\sigma_\theta^2}}$, we can write the expression as

$$P(\theta|y) = K' \exp\left[-\frac{(\sigma_y^2 + \sigma_\theta^2)\theta^2 - 2(y\sigma_\theta^2 + \theta_p\sigma_y^2)\theta + y^2\sigma_\theta^2 + \theta_p^2\sigma_y^2}{2\sigma_y^2\sigma_\theta^2}\right] \tag{3.35}$$

After simplifying the exponent, we can write

$$P(\theta|y) = K' \exp\left[-\frac{\theta^2 - \frac{2(y\sigma_\theta^2 + \theta_p\sigma_y^2)\theta}{(\sigma_y^2 + \sigma_\theta^2)} + \frac{y^2\sigma_\theta^2 + \theta_p^2\sigma_y^2}{(\sigma_y^2 + \sigma_\theta^2)}}{\frac{2\sigma_y^2\sigma_\theta^2}{(\sigma_y^2 + \sigma_\theta^2)}}\right] \tag{3.36}$$

Hence,

$$P(\theta|y) = K'' \exp\left[-\frac{(\theta - \hat{\theta})^2}{2\sigma^2}\right] \tag{3.37}$$

where $\sigma^2 = \frac{\sigma_y^2\sigma_\theta^2}{\sigma_y^2 + \sigma_\theta^2} = \frac{1}{\frac{1}{\sigma_y^2} + \frac{1}{\sigma_y^2}}$, $\hat{\theta} = \frac{\sigma_y^2\theta_p + \sigma_\theta^2 y}{\sigma_y^2 + \sigma_\theta^2}$ and

$$K'' = K' \exp\left[-\frac{\frac{y^2\sigma_\theta^2 + \theta_p^2\sigma_y^2}{\sigma_y^2 + \sigma_\theta^2}}{2\sigma^2} + \frac{\left(\frac{y\sigma_\theta^2 + \theta_p\sigma_y^2}{\sigma_y^2 + \sigma_\theta^2}\right)^2}{2\sigma^2}\right]$$

If measurements obtained from different sensors and sources are independent. We can write the following using Bayes' theorem:

$$P(\theta|Y^n) = \frac{P(\theta)\prod_{i=1}^{n} P(y_i|\theta)}{P(Y^n)} \tag{3.38}$$

Only states or parameters are common between the sources.

$$P(\theta|Y^n) = \frac{P(y_1, y_2, \ldots, y_n|\theta)P(\theta)}{P(y_1, y_2, \ldots, y_n)} \tag{3.39}$$

3.4.4   Fusion of Data from Two Sensors

Let x be the state which is the type of the target in this example. Identify the target type from current and previous measurements. Sensor 1 has new set Y_1^1 obtained from current measurement y_1^1 and old dataset Y_0^1. Note that the superscript and subscript denote the sensor index and measurement index, respectively. Similarly, Sensor 2 has Y_1^2 from y_1^2 and Y_0^2. Therefore, we can write the following

$$P(x|Y_1^1 Y_1^2) = P(x|y_1^1 y_1^2 Y_0^1 Y_0^2) \tag{3.40}$$

Using Bayes' rule

$$P(x|Y_1^1 Y_1^2) = \frac{P(y_1^1 y_1^2 |x, Y_0^1 Y_0^2) P(x|Y_0^1 Y_0^2)}{P(y_1^1 y_1^2 |Y_0^1 Y_0^2)} \tag{3.41}$$

Using independent assumption of sensor data,

$$P(x|Y_1^1 Y_1^2) = \frac{P(y_1^1 |x, Y_0^1) P(y_1^2 |x, Y_0^2) P(x|Y_0^1 Y_0^2)}{P(y_1^1 y_1^2 |Y_0^1 Y_0^2)} \tag{3.42}$$

Now, we know that

$$\begin{aligned} P(A, B, C) &= P(A|B, C) P(B, C) \\ &= P(A|B, C) P(B|C) P(C) \end{aligned} \tag{3.43}$$

Similarly,

$$\begin{aligned} P(B, A, C) &= P(B|A, C) P(A, C) \\ &= P(B|A, C) P(A|C) P(C) \end{aligned} \tag{3.44}$$

Since, $P(A, B, C) = P(B, A, C)$, we can write

$$P(A|B, C) P(B|C) P(C) = P(B|A, C) P(A|C) P(C) \tag{3.45}$$

Therefore,

$$P(A|B, C) = \frac{P(B|A, C) P(A|C)}{P(B|C)} \tag{3.46}$$

Here, $A = y_1^1$, $B = x$, $C = Y_0^1$. From Equation 3.42,

$$P(x|Y_1^1 Y_1^2) = \underbrace{\frac{P(x|y_1^1, Y_0^1) P(y_1^1 |Y_0^1)}{P(x|Y_0^1)}}_{\text{First term of numerator in RHS of Eq. 3.42}} \times \underbrace{\frac{P(x|y_1^2, Y_0^2) P(y_1^2 |Y_0^2)}{P(x|Y_0^2)}}_{\text{Similar to first}}$$

$$\times \underbrace{\frac{P(x|Y_0^1 Y_0^2)}{P(y_1^1 y_1^2 |Y_0^1 Y_0^2)}}_{\text{leftover term}} \tag{3.47}$$

Note that $P(x|y_1^1, Y_0^1) = P(x|y_1^1)$ and $P(x|y_1^2, Y_0^2) = P(x|y_1^2)$ because $P(\text{state}|\text{current}, \text{old}) = P(\text{state}|\text{current})$. The old measurement may not tell us anything about the state if we already know current measurement. The current measurement does not depend on old measurement because of uncorrelated property of white noise. Therefore, we can write $P(y_1|x_1, Y_0) = P(y_1|x_1)$. Hence, we can write finally,

$$P(x|Y_1^1 Y_1^2) = K_2 \frac{P(x|y_1^1)P(x|y_1^2)P(x|Y_0^1 Y_0^2)}{P(x|Y_0^1)P(x|Y_0^2)} \tag{3.48}$$

where $K_2 = \frac{P(y_1^1|Y_0^1)P(y_1^2|Y_0^2)}{P(y_1^1 y_1^2|Y_0^1 Y_0^2)}$

3.4.5 Fusion of Data from Three Sensors

On similar lines, we can write

$$P(x|Y_1^1 Y_1^2 Y_1^3) = K_3 \frac{P(x|y_1^1)P(x|y_1^2)P(x|y_1^3)P(x|Y_0^1 Y_0^2 Y_0^3)}{P(x|Y_0^1)P(x|Y_0^2)P(x|Y_0^3)} \tag{3.49}$$

where $K_3 = \frac{P(y_1^1|Y_0^1)P(y_1^2|Y_0^2)P(y_1^3|Y_0^3)}{P(y_1^1 y_1^2 y_1^3|Y_0^1 Y_0^2 Y_0^3)}$. Notably, the order of measurements for fusion does not matter.

Example of Fusion of Data from Two Sensors: Consider three targets T_1, T_2, and T_3 with two measurements and two sensors. We need to assume the posterior probabilities at zeroth iteration. Initialization is based on prior. Sensor 1 has $P(x = T_1|Y_0^1) = 0.5$, $P(x = T_2|Y_0^1) = 0.3$, and $P(x = T_3|Y_0^1) = 0.2$. Similarly, the sensor 2 has $P(x = T_1|Y_0^2) = 0.6$, $P(x = T_2|Y_0^2) = 0.2$, and $P(x = T_3|Y_0^2) = 0.2$.

Each sensor makes a local decision about the target based on measurements. At fusion center $P(x = T_1|Y_0^1 Y_0^2) = 0.6$, $P(x = T_2|Y_0^1 Y_0^2) = 0.3$, and $P(x = T_3|Y_0^1 Y_0^2) = 0.1$. For zeroth iteration, these are prior estimates. For next iteration, these are given from the current iteration. The updated posterior probabilities are $P(x = T_1|Y_1^1) = 0.7$, $P(x = T_2|Y_1^1) = 0.3$, and $P(x = T_3|Y_1^1) = 0.1$. Similarly, $P(x = T_1|Y_1^2) = 0.8$, $P(x = T_2|Y_1^2) = 0.1$, and $P(x = T_3|Y_1^2) = 0.2$.

Solution: We can compute the following

$$P(x = T_1|Y_1^1 Y_1^2) = K_2 \frac{0.7 \times 0.8 \times 0.6}{0.5 \times 0.6} = 1.12 K_2 \tag{3.50}$$

$$P(x = T_2|Y_1^1 Y_1^2) = K_2 \frac{0.3 \times 0.1 \times 0.3}{0.3 \times 0.2} = 0.15 K_2 \tag{3.51}$$

$$P(x = T_3|Y_1^1 Y_1^2) = K_2 \frac{0.1 \times 0.2 \times 0.1}{0.2 \times 0.2} = 0.05 K_2 \tag{3.52}$$

where K_2 is a normalization constant and sum of these three should be unity.

$$1.12 K_2 + 0.15 K_2 + 0.05 K_2 = 1 \tag{3.53}$$

This gives

$$K_2 = 0.7575 \qquad (3.54)$$

Final normalized probabilities are

$$P(x = T_1|Y_1^1 Y_1^2) = 1.12 \times 0.7575 = 0.85 \qquad (3.55)$$

$$P(x = T_2|Y_1^1 Y_1^2) = 0.15 \times 0.7575 = 0.11 \qquad (3.56)$$

$$P(x = T_3|Y_1^1 Y_1^2) = 0.05 \times 0.7575 = 0.04 \qquad (3.57)$$

Hence, the target is detected as Target 1 because of the highest probability using Bayesian data fusion.

3.5 Dempster-Shafer Theory for Data Fusion

In contrast to Bayesian method of fusion, we have an "unknown" state in the Dempster-Shafer method. The target is not of a certain type in an unknown state. We have a state of not being distinguishable between two similar targets. Dempster-Shafer's (DS) theory assigns initially belief in terms of mass. The mass could be a probability. For n number of targets, the total number of states is 2^n subsets possible. This is the power set. We assign masses to only useful states out of 2^n and add it up to unity.

3.5.1 Sensor Data Fusion of Two Sensors

These belief or masses are fused according to

$$
\begin{aligned}
b^{1,2}(A_3) &= \frac{\displaystyle\sum_{A_1 \cap A_2 = A_3} b^1(A_1) b^2(A_2)}{\displaystyle\sum_{A_1 \cap A_2 \neq \phi} b^1(A_1) b^2(A_2)} \\[2mm]
&= \frac{\displaystyle\sum_{A_1 \cap A_2 = A_3} b^1(A_1) b^2(A_2)}{1 - \displaystyle\sum_{A_1 \cap A_2 = \phi} b^1(A_1) b^2(A_2)}
\end{aligned}
\qquad (3.58)
$$

where b is the belief in terms of mass. Superscript 1, and 2 in b are sensor 1 and sensor 2, respectively. A_1, A_2, A_3 are the states. For instance, $T_1, T_2, T_3, (T_1, T_2), (T_1, T_2, T_3)$, that is, states need to be recognized.

3.5.2 Example of DS Theory

Let us understand the DS theory with an example. The initial beliefs are assigned to states as shown in Table 3.1. Note that the DS fused belief column is computed later using values of previous columns.

TABLE 3.1: Belief initialization

States in the power set	Sensor 1 (b^1)	Sensor 2 (b^2)	DS Fused belief
(T_1)	0.40	0.45	**0.455**
(T_2)	0.10	0.05	**0.075**
(T_3)	0.20	0.30	**0.357**
(T_2, T_3)	0.25	0.10	**0.103**
Unknown (T_1, T_2, T_3)	0.05	0.10	**0.009**
Total belief	1.00	1.00	1.00

The power set is 2^3 equal to 8 for 3 targets. The states are $\{(T_1), (T_2), (T_3), (T_1, T_2), (T_1, T_3), (T_2, T_3), (T_1, T_2, T_3), \phi$ that is, no target$\}$. Here, useful states are $\{(T_1), (T_2), (T_3), (T_2, T_3), (T_1, T_2, T_3)\}$.

Solution: We compute the fused belief for target T_1. Let us consider $A_3 = T_1$ and $A_1 \cap A_2 = A_3 = T_1$. For numerator term, we use Table 3.2. The sum of last column is 0.2425.

TABLE 3.2: Possible terms of the numerator for $A_3 = T_1$

A_1	A_2	$b^1(A_1)b^2(A_2)$	$b^1(A_1)b^2(A_2)$
(T_1)	(T_1)	0.40×0.45	0.1800
(T_1)	(T_1, T_2, T_3)	0.40×0.10	0.0400
(T_1, T_2, T_3)	(T_1)	0.05×0.45	0.0225

For denominator term, $A_1 \cap A_2 = \phi$. Table 3.3 is for denominator term. The sum of the last column is equal to 0.4675. Hence,

$$b^{1,2}(T_1) = \frac{0.2425}{1 - 0.4675} = 0.455 \tag{3.59}$$

Now consider $A_3 = T_2$ and $A_1 \cap A_2 = A_3 = T_2$. For numerator term, refer to Table 3.4. The sum of the last column is 0.04. For denominator, we already have this normalization factor. Hence,

$$b^{1,2}(T_2) = \frac{0.04}{1 - 0.4675} = 0.075. \tag{3.60}$$

Now consider $A_3 = T_3$ and $A_1 \cap A_2 = A_3 = T_3$. For numerator, refer to Table 3.5. The sum is equal to 0.19. Hence,

$$b^{1,2}(T_3) = \frac{0.19}{1 - 0.4675} = 0.357. \tag{3.61}$$

TABLE 3.3: Possible terms of denominator for $A_3 = T_1$

A_1	A_2	$b^1(A_1)b^2(A_2)$	$b^1(A_1)b^2(A_2)$
(T_1)	(T_2)	0.40×0.05	0.0200
(T_1)	(T_3)	0.40×0.30	0.1200
(T_1)	(T_2, T_3)	0.40×0.10	0.0400
(T_2)	(T_1)	0.10×0.45	0.0450
(T_2)	(T_3)	0.10×0.30	0.0300
(T_3)	(T_1)	0.20×0.45	0.0900
(T_3)	(T_2)	0.20×0.05	0.0100
(T_2, T_3)	(T_1)	0.25×0.45	0.1125

TABLE 3.4: Possible terms of numerator for $A_3 = T_2$

A_1	A_2	$b^1(A_1)b^2(A_2)$	$b^1(A_1)b^2(A_2)$
(T_2)	(T_2)	0.10×0.05	0.0050
(T_2)	(T_2, T_3)	0.10×0.10	0.0100
(T_2)	(T_1, T_2, T_3)	0.10×0.10	0.0100
(T_2, T_3)	(T_2)	0.25×0.05	0.0125
(T_1, T_2, T_3)	(T_2)	0.05×0.05	0.0025

Now consider $A_3 = (T_2, T_3)$ and $A_1 \cap A_2 = A_3 = (T_2, T_3)$. For numerator, refer to Table 3.6. The sum is equal to 0.055. Hence,

$$b^{1,2}(T_2, T_3) = \frac{0.055}{1 - 0.4675} = 0.103 \qquad (3.62)$$

Finally, consider $A_3 = (T_1, T_2, T_3)$ and $A_1 \cap A_2 = A_3 = (T_1, T_2, T_3)$. For numerator, refer to Table 3.7. The sum is equal to 0.005. Hence,

$$b^{1,2}(T_1, T_2, T_3) = \frac{0.005}{1 - 0.4675} = 0.009 \qquad (3.63)$$

3.5.3 Fusing Multiple Sensors

On similar lines, let us fuse more than two sensors now, that is, M_s number of sensors. The expression is given as

TABLE 3.5: Possible terms of numerator for $A_3 = T_3$

A_1	A_2	$b^1(A_1)b^2(A_2)$	$b^1(A_1)b^2(A_2)$
(T_3)	(T_3)	0.20×0.30	0.060
(T_3)	(T_2, T_3)	0.20×0.10	0.020
(T_3)	(T_1, T_2, T_3)	0.20×0.10	0.020
(T_2, T_3)	(T_3)	0.25×0.30	0.075
(T_1, T_2, T_3)	(T_3)	0.05×0.30	0.015

TABLE 3.6: Possible terms of numerator for $A_3 = (T_2, T_3)$

A_1	A_2	$b^1(A_1)b^2(A_2)$	$b^1(A_1)b^2(A_2)$
(T_2, T_3)	(T_2, T_3)	0.25×0.10	0.025
(T_2, T_3)	(T_1, T_2, T_3)	0.25×0.10	0.025
(T_1, T_2, T_3)	(T_2, T_3)	0.05×0.10	0.005

$$b^{1,2,3,\ldots,M_s}(A_{M_s+1}) = \frac{\displaystyle\sum_{A_1 \cap A_2 \cap A_3,\ldots,\cap A_{M_s}=A_{M_s+1}} b^1(A_1)b^2(A_2),\ldots,b^{M_s}(A_{M_s})}{\displaystyle\sum_{A_1 \cap A_2 \cap A_3,\ldots,\cap A_{M_s}\neq\phi} b^1(A_1)b^2(A_2),\ldots,b^{M_s}(A_{M_s})}$$

$$= \frac{\displaystyle\sum_{A_1 \cap A_2 \cap A_3,\ldots,\cap A_{M_s}=A_{M_s+1}} b^1(A_1)b^2(A_2),\ldots,b^{M_s}(A_{M_s})}{1 - \displaystyle\sum_{A_1 \cap A_2 \cap A_3,\ldots,\cap A_{M_s}=\phi} b^1(A_1)b^2(A_2),\ldots,b^{M_s}(A_{M_s})}$$

$$(3.64)$$

Notably, the order of measurements for fusion does not matter in this case too.

3.5.4 Support

Support is a loose lower limit to the uncertainty. It is the total mass of relevant states. This is given by

$$\text{Support}(A_1) = \sum_{A_2 \subseteq A_1} b(A_2) \qquad (3.65)$$

Example of Support: Consider $A_1 = (T_1)$. Therefore, only possibility for A_2 would be (T_1) such that $A_2 \subseteq A_1$. There is only one term, that is, $b(A_2)$. Support$(T_1) = b(T_1)$. Similarly for $A_1 = T_2$ and T_3. Support$(T_2) = b(T_2)$ and Support$(T_3) = b(T_3)$. Accordingly, let us fill up Table 3.8 for states T_1, T_2, and T_3.

Let $A_1 = (T_2, T_3)$ then $A_2 = (T_2), (T_3), (T_2, T_3)$. The support is given by

$$\text{Support}(T_2, T_3) = b(T_2) + b(T_3) + b(T_2, T_3) \qquad (3.66)$$

TABLE 3.7: Possible terms of numerator for (T_1, T_2, T_3)

A_1	A_2	$b^1(A_1)b^2(A_2)$	$b^1(A_1)b^2(A_2)$
(T_1, T_2, T_3)	(T_1, T_2, T_3)	0.05×0.10	0.005

TABLE 3.8: Support for different states

States	Sensor 1	Sensor 2	Fused belief
(T_1)	0.40	0.45	0.455
(T_2)	0.10	0.05	0.075
(T_3)	0.20	0.30	0.357
(T_2, T_3)	0.55	0.45	0.535
(T_1, T_2, T_3)	1	1	1

Let us calculate below for each sensor and fused one and fill up Table 3.8.

- For Sensor 1: $0.10 + 0.20 + 0.25 = 0.55$

- For Sensor 2: $0.05 + 0.30 + 0.10 = 0.45$

- For Fused: $0.075 + 0.357 + 0.103 = 0.535$

Finally, $A_1 = (T_1, T_2, T_3)$ then $A_2 = (T_1), (T_2), (T_3), (T_2, T_3), (T_1, T_2, T_3)$. The support is given by

$$\text{Support}(T_1, T_2, T_3) = b(T_1) + b(T_2) + b(T_3) + b(T_2, T_3) + b(T_1, T_2, T_3) \quad (3.67)$$

Let us calculate below for each sensor and fused one and fill up Table 3.8.

- For Sensor 1: $0.40 + 0.10 + 0.20 + 0.25 + 0.05 = 1.00$

- For Sensor 2: $0.45 + 0.05 + 0.30 + 0.10 + 0.10 = 1.00$

- For Fused: $0.455 + 0.075 + 0.357 + 0.103 + 0.009 = 1.00$

3.5.5 Plausibility

Plausibility is a loose upper limit to the uncertainty. It is the sum of belief of all states that do not contradict. This is given by

$$\text{Plausibility}(A_1) = 1 - \sum_{A_1 \cap A_2 = \phi} b(A_2) = \sum_{A_1 \cap A_2 \neq \phi} b(A_2) \quad (3.68)$$

Example of Plausibility: Consider $A_1 = (T_1)$, then $A_2 = (T_1), (T_1, T_2, T_3)$. The plausibility is given by

$$\text{Pl}(T_1) = b(T_1) + b(T_1, T_2, T_3) \quad (3.69)$$

Similarly, let $A_1 = T_2$, then $A_2 = (T_2)$, (T_2, T_3), (T_1, T_2, T_3). The plausibility is given by

$$Pl(T_2) = b(T_2) + b(T_2, T_3) + b(T_1, T_2, T_3) \qquad (3.70)$$

Let $A_1 = T_3$, then $A_2 = (T_3)$, (T_2, T_3), (T_1, T_2, T_3). The plausibility is given by

$$Pl(T_3) = b(T_3) + b(T_2, T_3) + b(T_1, T_2, T_3) \qquad (3.71)$$

Let $A_1 = (T_2, T_3)$, then $A_2 = (T_2)$, (T_3), (T_2, T_3), (T_1, T_2, T_3). Therefore, the plausibility is given by

$$Pl(T_2, T_3) = b(T_2) + b(T_3) + b(T_2, T_3) + b(T_1, T_2, T_3) \qquad (3.72)$$

Finally, $A_1 = (T_1, T_2, T_3)$, then $A_2 = (T_1)$, (T_2), (T_3), (T_2, T_3), (T_1, T_2, T_3). Therefore, the plausibility is given by

$$Pl(T_1, T_2, T_3) = b(T_1) + b(T_2) + b(T_3) + b(T_2, T_3) + b(T_1, T_2, T_3) \qquad (3.73)$$

TABLE 3.9: Plausibility for different states

States	Sensor 1	Sensor 2	Fused
(T_1)	0.45	0.55	0.464
(T_2)	0.40	0.25	0.187
(T_3)	0.50	0.50	0.469
(T_2, T_3)	0.60	0.55	0.544
(T_1, T_2, T_3)	1.00	1.00	1.00

Let us fill up the table as we now have expressions in Table 3.9. The loose uncertainty interval is given by [support, plausibility] in Table 3.10.

TABLE 3.10: Uncertainty interval for different states

States	Sensor 1	Sensor 2	Fused
(T_1)	[0.40, 0.45]	[0.45, 0.55]	[0.455, 0.464]
(T_2)	[0.10, 0.40]	[0.05, 0.25]	[0.075, 0.187]
(T_3)	[0.20, 0.50]	[0.30, 0.50]	[0.357, 0.469]
(T_2, T_3)	[0.55, 0.60]	[0.45, 0.55]	[0.535, 0.544]
(T_1, T_2, T_3)	[1.00, 1.00]	[1.00, 1.00]	[1.00, 1.00]

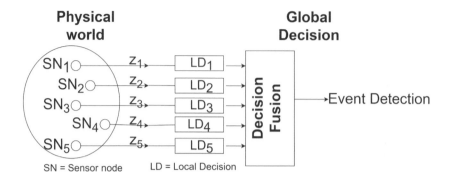

FIGURE 3.10: Global decision

3.6 Decision Fusion

We know that the applications of fusion are for signal detection, event detection, and target detection. Sensor nodes are randomly placed in the physical world. First, the local decisions are made and subsequently, the global decision is made in Figure 3.10. Centralized architecture sends all the data to a powerful central system for decision. In a distributed architecture, sensors collect data, process it locally, and transmit the local decisions to a central system for global decision. The distributed or decentralized is suited for IoT networks. Hybrid architecture combines both centralized and distributed schemes to achieve the trade-off between them.

3.6.1 Binary Signal Detection

We make the following assumptions: multiple observations are collected from each sensor node. There is no interference in communication. The observations are independent and identically distributed (IID). The order of observations does not matter. We ignore the spatial and temporal correlations among observations for the sake of simplicity.

Let H_1 be the hypothesis when an event occurs and the prior probability is $P(H = H_1) = p$ in Figure 3.11. This hypothesis is when the target is present. Similarly, H_0 is the hypothesis when an event does not occur and the prior probability is $P(H = H_0) = 1 - p$. This is when the target is absent. The received signal z_i for these two hypotheses are given by

$$H_0 : z_i = n_i \text{ (noise)}$$
$$H_1 : z_i = y_i + n_i \text{ (Target + noise)}$$

(3.74)

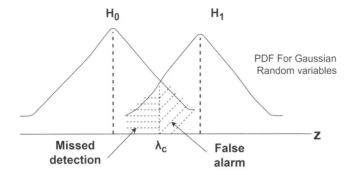

FIGURE 3.11: Probability density functions for two hypotheses

where y_i is the transmitted signal. Given y_1 is transmitted, if we make the decision in favour of H_0, this leads to incorrect decision. Similarly, y_0 is transmitted, if we make the decision in favour of H_1, this leads to incorrect decision.

Let N be the number of sensor nodes. M denotes the number of measurements received from each sensor node. z_i^j = jth measurement at ith sensor node, where $i = \{1, 2, ..., N\}$ and $j = \{1, 2, ..., M\}$. We assume that measurements have identical conditional probability, that is, $P(z_i^j = 1 | H_0) = p_0$ and $P(z_i^j = 1 | H_1) = p_1$. Hence, the probability of error

$$P_e = P(H_1|y_0)P(y_0) + P(H_0|y_1)P(y_1) \tag{3.75}$$

The goal is to minimize the probability of error (P_e).

Signal Model: Let the noise follows a Gaussian distribution with zero mean and unit variance, that is, $n_i, \sim \mathcal{N}(0, 1)$. y_i is the amplitude of the received signal and it decays with distance d_i according to

$$y_i^2 = \frac{P_0}{1 + \varepsilon d_i^\alpha} \tag{3.76}$$

where P_0 is the power emitted by the target or event at $d_i = 0$, α is the path loss exponent which varies from 2 to 5. ε is a large constant for fast decaying. d_i is the distance of the target with respect to ith sensor. Threshold is λ to make the local decision, $\in \{0, 1\}$, presence or absence of the target. We use an identical local decision rule by all the sensors.

3.6.2 Probabilities of Detection and False-Alarm

The probability of detection is given by

$$Pd_i = \frac{1}{\sqrt{2\pi}} \int_\lambda^\infty \exp\left(\frac{-(\gamma - y_i)^2}{2}\right) d\gamma$$

$$= Q\left(\lambda - \sqrt{\frac{P_0}{1 + \alpha d_i^\alpha}}\right) \tag{3.77}$$

The probability of false alarm is given by

$$Pf_i = \frac{1}{\sqrt{2\pi}} \int_\lambda^\infty \exp\left(\frac{-\gamma^2}{2}\right) d\gamma$$
$$= Q(\lambda) \tag{3.78}$$

where $Q(.)$ is the function given as

$$Q(x) = \frac{1}{\sqrt{2\pi}} \int_x^\infty \exp\left(\frac{-\gamma^2}{2}\right) d\gamma \tag{3.79}$$

3.6.3   Centralized Detection Scheme

At the global decision center, we have hypothesis as

$$\hat{H} = \begin{cases} H_1, & \text{if } o \geq \lambda_c \\ H_0, & \text{if } o < \lambda_c \end{cases} \tag{3.80}$$

where o_i is the number of 1s out of M observations at ith sensor node and $o = \sum_{i=1}^N o_i$ is the total number of 1s at the central system for the global decision. Note that, observation $\in \{0, 1\}$, therefore, it is described using a Binomial random variable.

A discrete random variable X is called a Binomial random variable with parameter (n, p), and the probability mass function is expressed as

$$P(X = k) = {}^nC_k p^k (1 - p)^{(n-k)} \tag{3.81}$$

where $k = \{0, 1, 2, \ldots, n\}$, $0 \leqslant p \leqslant 1$ and ${}^nC_k = \frac{n!}{k!(n-k)!}$ is called the Binomial coefficient.

Derivation of Threshold for Centralized Scheme: Using Bayes' rule, $P(A \mid B) = \frac{P(A \cap B)}{P(B)}$ and $P(B \mid A) = \frac{P(A \cap B)}{P(A)}$. As we know that, $P(A \cap B) = P(B \cap A)$, therefore, we can write

$$P(A|B) = \frac{P(B|A)P(A)}{P(B)} \tag{3.82}$$

where $P(B)$ is the normalization factor. Therefore, we can write

$$P(A|B) \propto P(B|A)P(A) \tag{3.83}$$

We decide $\hat{H} = H_1$ if

$$P(H_1 \mid o) \geq P(H_0 \mid o) \tag{3.84}$$

Now using Equations 3.82 and 3.84

$$P(o \mid H_1)P(H_1) \geq P(o \mid H_0)P(H_0) \tag{3.85}$$

Therefore, we can write

$$\frac{P(o \mid H_1)}{P(o \mid H_0)} \geq \frac{P(H_0)}{P(H_1)} = \frac{1-p}{p} \tag{3.86}$$

For IID, observations and using the probability mass function of Binomial random variable

$$P(o \mid H_1) = {}^{NM}C_o p_1^o (1-p_1)^{(NM-o)} \tag{3.87}$$

Similarly,

$$P(o \mid H_0) = {}^{NM}C_o p_0^o (1-p_0)^{(NM-o)} \tag{3.88}$$

Using Equations 3.86, 3.87, and 3.88

$$\frac{{}^{NM}C_o p_1^o (1-p_1)^{(NM-o)}}{{}^{NM}C_o p_0^o (1-p_0)^{(NM-o)}} \geq \frac{1-p}{p} \tag{3.89}$$

After simplification,

$$\left(\frac{p_1(1-p_0)}{p_0(1-p_1)}\right)^o \left(\frac{1-p_1}{1-p_0}\right)^{NM} \geq \frac{1-p}{p} \tag{3.90}$$

Taking log on both sides

$$o \ln \frac{p_1(1-p_0)}{p_0(1-p_1)} + NM \ln \left(\frac{1-p_1}{1-p_0}\right) \geq \ln \frac{1-p}{p} \tag{3.91}$$

Finally,

$$o \geq \frac{\ln\left(\frac{1-p}{p}\right) + NM \ln\left(\frac{1-p_0}{1-p_1}\right)}{\ln\left(\frac{p_1(1-p_0)}{p_0(1-p_1)}\right)} \tag{3.92}$$

$$= \lambda_c$$

$$= \text{Decision threshold for the centralized scheme}$$

We use celling function $\lceil \lambda_c \rceil$ for getting the next higher integer and $o \geq \lambda_c$.

Probabilities of Detection, False-Alarm: The probability of detection is

$$P_d = p(o \geq \lambda_c \mid H_1) = \sum_{o=\lceil \lambda_c \rceil}^{NM} {}^{NM}C_o p_1^o (1-p_1)^{(NM-o)} \tag{3.93}$$

The probability of false alarm is

$$P_f = p(o \geq \lambda_c \mid H_0) = \sum_{o=\lceil \lambda_c \rceil}^{NM} {}^{NM}C_o p_0^o (1-p_0)^{(NM-o)} \tag{3.94}$$

The overall probability of error is given by

$$P_e = (1 - P_d)p + P_f(1-p) \tag{3.95}$$

where p and $(1-p)$ are the prior probabilities for hypotheses H_1, and H_0, respectively. P_f is the probability of false alarm. $(1 - P_d)$ is the probability of missed detection.

3.6.4 Distributed Detection Scheme

We consider an identical local decision rule for each sensor node in a distributed detection scheme. This may not lead to optimality, however, the computational complexity is low. The scheme is then suitable for an IoT network. A sensor node does not have information about other sensor nodes. The local decision for each sensor node depend on $\{M, p, p_0, p_1\}$. The number of sensor nodes N is used for making the global decision. The local decision herein is like the centralized scheme. The identical threshold for all sensor nodes is given by

$$\lambda_d = \frac{\ln\left(\frac{1-p}{p}\right) + M\ln\left(\frac{1-p_0}{1-p_1}\right)}{\ln\left(\frac{p_1(1-p_0)}{p_0(1-p_1)}\right)} \tag{3.96}$$

We change the factor from NM to M. Thus, the local decision rule is

$$\widehat{H_i} = \begin{cases} H_1, & \text{if } o_i \geq \lambda_d \\ H_0, & \text{if } o_i < \lambda_d \end{cases} \tag{3.97}$$

Derivation of Threshold for Distributed Scheme: On the similar lines, the probability of detection is given by

$$P_D = p(o_i \geq \lambda_d \mid H_1) = \sum_{o_i = \lceil \lambda_d \rceil}^{M} {}^{M}C_{o_i} p_1^{o_i}(1-p_1)^{(M-o_i)} \tag{3.98}$$

and the probability of false alarm is given by

$$P_F = p(o_i \geq \lambda_d \mid H_0) = \sum_{o_i = \lceil \lambda_d \rceil}^{M} {}^{M}C_{o_i} p_0^{o_i}(1-p_0)^{(M-o_i)} \tag{3.99}$$

The final decision is made based on N one-bit local decisions $\{l_1, l_2, \ldots, l_N\}$. The statistics is the number of 1s out of the N local decisions, that is, $l = \sum_{i=1}^{N} l_i$. Similar to the centralized scheme, we can write

$$P(H_1 \mid l) \geq P(H_0 \mid l) \tag{3.100}$$

This is expressed if the final decision is to choose $\widehat{H} = H_1$. From Bayes' rule,

$$P(l \mid H_1)P(H_1) \geq P(l \mid H_0)P(H_0) \tag{3.101}$$

We can rewrite as

$$\frac{P(l \mid H_1)}{P(l \mid H_0)} \geq \frac{P(H_0)}{P(H_1)} = \frac{1-p}{p} \tag{3.102}$$

Using Equations 3.98, and 3.99

$$P(l \mid H_1) = P\left(\sum_{i=1}^{N} l_i = l \mid H_1\right) = {}^{N}C_l P_D^l (1-P_D)^{N-l} \tag{3.103}$$

Similarly,

$$P(l \mid H_0) = P\left(\sum_{i=1}^{N} l_i = l \mid H_0\right) = {}^{N}C_l P_F^l (1 - P_F)^{N-l} \tag{3.104}$$

Using Equations 3.102, 3.103, and 3.104

$$\frac{{}^{N}C_l P_D^l (1 - P_D)^{N-l}}{{}^{N}C_l P_F^l (1 - P_F)^{N-l}} = \frac{1-p}{p} \tag{3.105}$$

The threshold for distributed scheme is finally given as

$$l = \frac{\ln\left(\frac{1-p}{p}\right) + N \ln\left(\frac{1-P_F}{1-P_D}\right)}{\ln\left(\frac{P_D(1-P_F)}{P_F(1-P_D)}\right)}$$

$$= \lambda_D$$

$$= \text{ Global threshold for distributed scheme} \tag{3.106}$$

Hence, the final decision rule is

$$\widehat{H} = \begin{cases} H_1, & \text{if } l \geq \lambda_D \\ H_0, & \text{if } l < \lambda_D \end{cases} \tag{3.107}$$

Probabilities of Detection, False-Alarm: The probability of detection is

$$P_d = p(l \geq \lambda_D \mid H_1) = \sum_{l=\lceil \lambda_D \rceil}^{N} {}^{N}C_l P_D^l (1 - P_D)^{(N-l)} \tag{3.108}$$

The probability of false alarm is

$$P_f = p(l \geq \lambda_D \mid H_0) = \sum_{l=\lceil \lambda_D \rceil}^{N} {}^{N}C_l P_F^l (1 - P_F)^{(N-l)} \tag{3.109}$$

Finally, the probability of error is

$$P_e = (1 - P_d)p + P_f(1 - p) \tag{3.110}$$

Example 1: Determine P_f, P_d, and P_e for $M = 5$ and $N = 3$ for both centralized and distributed schemes. Given $p = P(H = H_1) = 0.60$, $p_0 = P(z_i^j = 1 \mid H_0) = 0.30$ and $p_1 = P(z_i^j = 1 \mid H_1) = 0.65$.

Solution: Let us first compute for the centralized scheme. Here, $p = 0.60$, $P(H = H_0) = 1 - p = 0.40$. The threshold is computed as follows using Equation 3.92

$$\lambda_c = \frac{\ln\left(\frac{1-p}{p}\right) + NM \ln\left(\frac{1-p_0}{1-p_1}\right)}{\ln\left(\frac{p_1(1-p_0)}{p_0(1-p_1)}\right)}$$

$$= \frac{\ln\left(\frac{1-0.6}{0.6}\right) + 3M \ln\left(\frac{1-0.30}{1-0.65}\right)}{\ln\left(\frac{0.65(1-0.30)}{0.3(1-0.65)}\right)} \tag{3.111}$$

$$= \frac{\ln 0.667 + 3M \ln 2}{\ln 4.333}$$

For $M = 5$, $\lambda_c = 6.81$ and hence, $\lceil \lambda_c \rceil = 7$. Now, $NM = 3 \times 5 = 15$. Using Equation 3.94, we can compute

$$P_f = \sum_{o=7}^{15} {}^{15}C_o(0.3)^o(0.7)^{15-o}$$
$$= 0.0811 + 0.03477 + 0.01159 + 2.98 \times 10^{-3} + 5.8 \times 10^{-4} + 8.29 \times 10^{-5}$$
$$+ 8.2 \times 10^{-6} + 5.02 \times 10^{-7} + 1.44 \times 10^{-8}$$
$$= 0.13.$$

$$(3.112)$$

Similarly, P_d is computed using Equation 3.93

$$P_d = \sum_{o=7}^{15} {}^{15}C_o(0.65)^o(1 - 0.65)^{15-o}$$
$$= 0.9578$$

$$(3.113)$$

Similarly, P_e is computed using Equation 3.95

$$P_e = (1 - 0.9578) \times 0.60 + 0.13 \times (1 - 0.6)$$
$$= 0.08$$

$$(3.114)$$

Now consider a distributed scheme. Using Equation 3.96, we can compute the local threshold for distributed scheme

$$\lambda_d = \frac{\ln\left(\frac{1-0.6}{0.6}\right) + 5\ln\left(\frac{1-0.30}{1-0.65}\right)}{\ln\left(\frac{0.65(1-0.30)}{0.30(1-0.65)}\right)}$$
$$= 2.0874$$

$$(3.115)$$

and hence, $\lceil \lambda_d \rceil = 3$. Using Equation 3.98, we can compute

$$P_D = \sum_{o_i=3}^{5} {}^{5}C_{o_i}(0.65)^{o_i}(1 - 0.65)^{5-o_i}$$
$$= 0.7648$$

$$(3.116)$$

we can compute the following using Equation 3.99

$$P_F = \sum_{o_i=3}^{5} {}^{5}C_{o_i}(0.30)^{o_i}(1 - 0.30)^{5-o_i}$$
$$= 0.1631.$$

$$(3.117)$$

Using Equation 3.106, we can compute the global threshold

$$\lambda_D = \frac{\ln\left(\frac{1-0.6}{0.6}\right) + 3\ln\left(\frac{1-0.1631}{1-0.7648}\right)}{\ln\left(\frac{0.7648(1-0.1631)}{0.1631(1-0.7648)}\right)}$$
$$= 1.2089$$

$$(3.118)$$

and hence, $\lceil \lambda_D \rceil = 2$. Using Equation 3.108 for overall probability of false alarm

$$P_f = \sum_{l=2}^{3} {}^3C_l(0.1631)^l(1 - 0.1631)^{3-l}$$

$$= 0.071$$

(3.119)

Using Equation 3.109 for overall probability of detection

$$P_d = \sum_{l=2}^{3} {}^3C_l(0.7648)^l(1 - 0.7648)^{3-l}$$

$$= 0.860.$$

(3.120)

Finally, using Equation 3.110 for overall probability of error

$$P_e = (1 - 0.860) \times 0.6 + 0.071 \times (1 - 0.6)$$

$$= 0.1124$$

(3.121)

Example 2: Compute P_f, P_d, and P_e for $M = 5$ to 10 for both centralized and distributed schemes and comment on it.

Solution: Let us consider first centralized scheme in Table 3.11. We can do similar computations like the previous example for different Ms. On the similar lines, the computations for distributed scheme is in Table 3.12. We can quantify these probabilities in percentage too. Ideally, P_d should be unity, and P_f and P_e be zeros. The performance of the distributed scheme is comparable. Hence, it is suited for energy-efficient IoT networks.

TABLE 3.11: P_f, P_d, and P_e for different Ms of a centralized scheme

M	λ_c	$\lceil \lambda_c \rceil$	P_f	P_d	P_e
5	6.81	7	0.13	0.96	0.08
6	8.23	9	0.06	0.94	0.06
7	9.65	10	0.07	0.97	0.05
8	11.07	12	0.03	0.96	0.04
9	12.48	13	0.04	0.98	0.03
10	13.90	14	0.04	0.99	0.02

3.7 Summary

Clustering and sensor data fusion techniques are presented in this chapter. The clustering is needed for partitioning the network. This is because the communication ranges of IoT devices are limited. Hence, two far-apart IoT

TABLE 3.12: P_f, P_d, and P_e for different M of a distributed scheme

M	λ_d	$\lceil \lambda_d \rceil$	P_D	P_F	λ_D	$\lceil \lambda_D \rceil$	P_f	P_d	P_e
5	2.09	3	0.77	0.16	1.21	2	0.07	0.86	0.11
6	2.56	3	0.88	0.26	1.66	2	0.16	0.96	0.09
7	3.03	4	0.80	0.13	1.21	2	0.04	0.90	0.08
8	3.51	4	0.89	0.19	1.60	2	0.10	0.97	0.06
9	3.98	4	0.95	0.27	1.92	2	0.18	0.99	0.08
10	4.45	5	0.91	0.15	1.55	2	0.06	0.98	0.04

devices cannot communicate directly. They can communicate via the cluster head of their cluster. Further, data fusion techniques, namely, Bayesian theory, Dempster-Shafer theory, and decision fusion are discussed. The multiple sensors provide complementary information. Hence, a better decision can be made using the fusion technique in an IoT network. This is helpful even if some of the sensors' data are missed due to node failure, communication blockage, and insufficient storage amongst others.

3.8 Exercises

1. (a) The distributed detection scheme is computationally efficient than a centralized detection scheme. That is why we prefer a distributed scheme for resource-constrained IoT networks. Is the statement correct?

   (b) If $P(\text{data}|\text{sensor}) = 0.9$, $P(\text{data}) = 0.3$ and $P(\text{sensor}) = 0.3$, what is the probability of $P(\text{sensor}|\text{data})$?

2. (a) $P(x = T_1|Y_0^1) = 0.5$, $P(x = T_1|Y_0^2) = 0.6$, $P(x = T_1|Y_0^1 Y_0^2) = 0.6$, $P(x = T_1|Y_1^1) = 0.7$, $P(x = T_1|Y_1^2) = 0.8$. What is unnormalized $P(x = T_1|Y_1^1 Y_1^2)$?

   (b) $P(x = T_1|Y_0^1) = 0.3$, $P(x = T_1|Y_0^2) = 0.2$, $P(x = T_1|Y_0^1 Y_0^2) = 0.3$, $P(x = T_1|Y_1^1) = 0.3$, $P(x = T_1|Y_1^2) = 0.1$. What is unnormalized $P(x = T_1|Y_1^1 Y_1^2)$?

3. How do you elect cluster head in clustering?

4. Consider one-dimensional measurements at 0, 1, 2, and 3 and initial cluster heads (CHs) are at 1.25 and 1.75. Determine the final cluster heads using the vector quantization technique.

5. Consider the Problem 4 again with initial cluster heads (CHs) are at 1.5 and 2. Determine the final cluster heads using the vector quantization technique.

6. If the transmit power increases exponentially as $\alpha_{LP} \exp(\beta_{LP} d)$ where α_{LP} and β_{LP} are the constants of the power model. Also, d denotes the distance between transmitter and receiver. What is the expected energy consumption by transmitter circuitry?

7. Consider two sensors for fusing data as shown in Table 3.13. The beliefs are initialized in terms of mass. Compute the fused belief using Dempster-Shafer's theory.

TABLE 3.13: Belief initialization

States in the power set	Sensor 1 (b^1)	Sensor 2 (b^2)
(T_1)	0.40	0.45
(T_2)	0.60	0.55
Total belief	1.00	1.00

8. In previous Problem 7, compute support, plausibility, and uncertainty interval.

9. Consider the example centralized scheme of decision fusion again with $M = 7$. Compute probabilities of false alarm, detection, and error. Make your observations from the computed results.

10. Consider the example distributed scheme of decision fusion again with $M = 7$. Compute probabilities of false alarm, detection, and error. Make your observations from the computed results.

11. **Do It Yourself**: Carry out human activity recognition of elderly people in a smart home system using Dempster-Shafer fusion of sensor data.

12. **Do It Yourself**: Find the expression of the threshold for faulty sensor data.

13. **Do It Yourself**: Explore Fuzzy logic and Kalman filter for decision fusion.

Chapter 4

Smart Device Localization

4.1 Introduction

Localization algorithm estimates the position, coordinates, or location of a smart device. A simple solution for localization and tracking is to use Global Positioning System (GPS). However, the cost and energy consumption of GPS is high. Additionally, GPS works well in line-of-sight scenarios like open space, not in underground or complex apartments. The applications of localization methods include sensing, monitoring, surveillance, and tracking. In a large agriculture field especially in hilly terrain, it is not possible to monitor farmers and animals manually. The location and time stamp are tagged with the sensed data. In another application, a camera can be used to locate elderly people in a smart home, however, it breaches privacy. Thus, the location of the person within a house is computed using opportunistic signals like Wi-Fi, geomagnetic, and visible light. If the user is located in the washroom frequently, then something is wrong with the person's health. In a large hospital equipped with several laboratories and departments, the patients, labs, or departments need to be tracked.

Further, the location of the intruder is important in order to locate or track and combat them. There is a need to keep track of our personnel and vehicles. This is required during stealth operation and surgical strikes for coordination among own personnel and resources. The location of the robot in a large indoor environment is also needed. The location information helps the robot in navigation in a constricted space. This also assumes importance in a multi-robot system so that two robots should not collide. Next, the environmental sensed data such as humidity, temperature, and pollution-causing particles levels in addition to the location and time stamp are essential. Lastly, pedestrian tracking and vehicle-to-vehicle communication also received significant attention recently. The chapter presents various distance-based and distance-free localization techniques along with their performance evaluation.

DOI: 10.1201/9781003225584-4

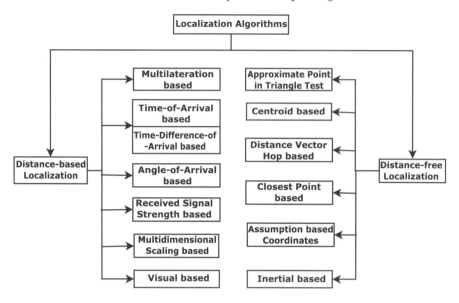

FIGURE 4.1: Classification of Localization Algorithms

4.2   Taxonomy of Localization Algorithms

In general, localization methods utilize the knowledge of the locations of a small subset of nodes. The node that is aware of its location is known as an anchor, beacon, source, or landmark. Localization is a one-time process for a static smart device, whereas tracking is the continuous localization of the mobile smart device over time. Localization methods can be classified as distance-free and distance-based methods in the literature as shown in Figure 4.1. Distance-based localization methods utilize the distance between the anchor and unknown node. On the other hand, distance-free methods utilize only connectivity information. Distance-based methods are fine-grained localization methods, whereas, distance-free methods are coarse-grained. A localization method can be chosen based on whether we need coarse-grained resolution, say, ($\pm$ 5 m) or fine-grained resolution, say, ($\pm$ 10 cm). The smart device refers to an unknown node. We are interested in estimating the location of unknown nodes given the measurements from anchors or other smart devices.

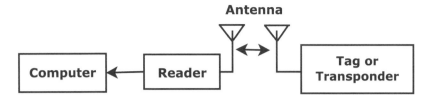

FIGURE 4.2: RFID based system for localization

4.3 Distance-based Localization Methods

Distance-based methods are based on multilateration, Time-of-Arrival (TOA), Time-Difference-of-Arrival (TDOA), Angle-of-Arrival (AOA)/Direction-of-Arrival (DOA), Received Signal Strength (RSS), Multidimensional Scaling (MDS), and visual information as shown in Figure 4.1. Localization algorithms using TOA and TDOA require precise synchronization. AOA and DOA-based algorithms need special hardware to estimate the angle at which the signal arrives at the antenna array. The time of arrival (TOA) method performs localization using the information about the time of arrival of the signal from different anchors. However, TOA requires a reference timestamp to synchronize the local clock of the nodes. To overcome this issue of reference offset, a time difference of arrival (TDOA) method is used. TDOA is based on the principle of the time difference of arrival of the anchor signals at a pair of nodes. In this method, one of the anchors is generally taken as a reference node. The TDOA method does not require synchronization between anchors and the unknown node. However, synchronization among different anchors is still needed. The visual-based localization algorithm is generally based on the distance between pixels in a spatio-temporal video. Notably, the algorithm requires a camera and breaches the privacy of the users.

Smart device localization using RSS provides a cost-effective solution. The RSS-based approach is also leveraged in Radio Frequency Identification (RFID) based positioning, which is suitable for IoT networks. The RFID based technique uses tag or transponder and reader or interrogator to locate the objects as shown in Figure 4.2. The RFID reader acts as a transceiver that detects and receives the RF wave originating from the RFID tag. The energy of RF signals decreases exponentially with the distance. The RFID reader is then connected to computing devices. The computing devices estimate the location of the objects using RSS signals. The RSS-based algorithm is marginally inaccurate, however, RSS measurements are easily accessible and low-cost. Hence, an RSS-based localization algorithm is suitable for IoT networks.

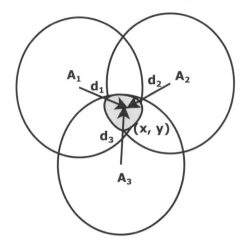

FIGURE 4.3: Illustration of a simple localization method

4.3.1   Multilateration Based Localization

Let the locations of the anchors be $A_1 = (x_1, y_1)$, $A_2 = (x_2, y_2)$, and $A_3 = (x_3, y_3)$ as shown in Figure 4.3. The location of the unknown node is denoted by (x, y). The Euclidean distance between A_ith anchor and unknown node:

$$(x_1 - x)^2 + (y_1 - y)^2 = d_1^2 \tag{4.1}$$

This can be further rewritten as

$$-2x_1 x - 2y_1 y + (x^2 + y^2) = d_1^2 - x_1^2 - y_1^2 \tag{4.2}$$

Similarly, we can write for A_2 and A_3 anchors as

$$\begin{aligned} -2x_2 x - 2y_2 y + (x^2 + y^2) = d_2^2 - x_2^2 - y_2^2 \\ -2x_3 x - 2y_3 y + (x^2 + y^2) = d_3^2 - x_3^2 - y_3^2 \end{aligned} \tag{4.3}$$

We can write Equations 4.2 and 4.3 in matrix form as

$$\underbrace{\begin{bmatrix} -2x_1 & -2y_1 & 1 \\ -2x_2 & -2y_2 & 1 \\ -2x_3 & -2y_3 & 1 \end{bmatrix}}_{=\mathbf{A}} \underbrace{\begin{bmatrix} x \\ y \\ x^2 + y^2 \end{bmatrix}}_{=\mathbf{X}} = \underbrace{\begin{bmatrix} d_1^2 - x_1^2 - y_1^2 \\ d_2^2 - x_2^2 - y_2^2 \\ d_3^2 - x_3^2 - y_3^2 \end{bmatrix}}_{=\mathbf{B}} \tag{4.4}$$

This can be succinctly written as

$$\mathbf{AX} = \mathbf{B} \tag{4.5}$$

The solution of this system of equations is the location of the unknown node. This is obtained by

$$\mathbf{X} = \mathbf{A}^{-1}\mathbf{B} \tag{4.6}$$

Now, assume the number of anchors is greater than three, that is, $N > 3$. In this case, matrices $\mathbf{A}$ and $\mathbf{B}$ are rectangular of sizes $N \times 3$ and $N \times 1$, respectively. In this case, the solution is obtained using the concept of pseudo-inverse for a rectangular matrix. The location of the unknown node for rectangular matrices is given by

$$\mathbf{X} = (\mathbf{A}^T \mathbf{A})^{-1} \mathbf{A}^T \mathbf{B} \tag{4.7}$$

This can easily be extended for a three-dimensional coordinates system.

4.3.2 Time-of-Arrival Based Localization

In Time-of-Arrival (TOA) based localization, consider the same variables from previous section on multilateration based localization. We know that speed multiplied with time elapsed gives the distance between transmitter and receiver. The difference between theoretical and observed distances is given by

$$g_i(\mathbf{X}) = v(t_i - \tau) - \sqrt{(x_i - x)^2 + (y_i - y)^2}, \quad i \in \mathcal{N} \tag{4.8}$$

where $\mathbf{X} = \begin{bmatrix} x & y & \tau \end{bmatrix}^T$ is the unknown parameter vector. v and $\mathcal{N}$ denote the speed of signal and and the set of unknown nodes. The first term on right hand side is the observed distance between the anchor and the smart device based on measurements. On the other hand, theoretical distance is shown using Euclidean distance in second term of right hand side. The error, g, is the difference between theoretical and measured distances. The cost function can be written as the sum of squared error. The cost function is given by

$$G(\mathbf{X}) = \sum_{i \in \mathcal{N}} w_i g_i^2(\mathbf{X}) \tag{4.9}$$

where w is the confidence parameter between 0 and 1. The expression is the function of the unknown node location. The w_i is the weight of the ith anchor and the smart device. The smaller the distance, the higher the weight or confidence parameter. This makes sense because nearby distance information is more reliable than larger distance.

Hence, the cost function is weighted sum of squared error. The location of unknown node can be estimated as

$$\tilde{\mathbf{X}} = \underset{\mathbf{X}}{\mathrm{argmin}} \; G(\mathbf{X}) \tag{4.10}$$

The TOA-based method requires synchronization between the unknown node and the anchor. This is because of the utilization of distance information between unknown nodes and anchors.

Example of ToA based Localization: The locations of the all the anchors are $\begin{bmatrix} x_1 & y_1 \end{bmatrix}^T = \begin{bmatrix} 0 & 0 \end{bmatrix}^T$, $\begin{bmatrix} x_2 & y_2 \end{bmatrix}^T = \begin{bmatrix} 0 & 1 \end{bmatrix}^T$, $\begin{bmatrix} x_3 & y_3 \end{bmatrix}^T = \begin{bmatrix} 1 & 0 \end{bmatrix}^T$, and $\begin{bmatrix} x_4 & y_4 \end{bmatrix}^T = \begin{bmatrix} 1 & 1 \end{bmatrix}^T$. The actual location of the unknown sensor node is assumed to be $\begin{bmatrix} x & y \end{bmatrix}^T = \begin{bmatrix} 0.5 & 0.5 \end{bmatrix}^T$.

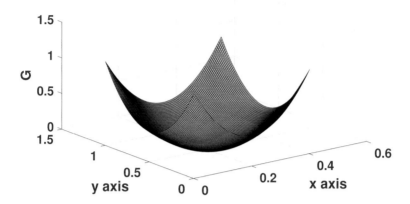

FIGURE 4.4: Sum of squared error versus network dimensions in TOA based localization method; The locations of the anchors are at the corners of the network.

Solution: Assume that all the sensor nodes have a radio communication range of 1.2 so that the unknown node can hear all the neighboring anchors. The Gaussian noise in distance measurement is considered to be $\mathcal{N}(0, 10^{-3})$. It can be seen that sum of square error is minimum at $\begin{bmatrix} 0.5 & 0.5 \end{bmatrix}$. The corresponding minimum value of the cost function is 3.1302×10^{-8}. That is, the estimated and actual node locations are the same which shows the efficacy of the TOA-based localization method. This is illustrated in Figure 4.4. Note that the confidence parameter is given by

$$w_i = \frac{1}{1 + \text{distance}} \tag{4.11}$$

is chosen to be inversely proportional to the distance between the anchor and the unknown node. If the distance is zero, w_i is one. On the other hand, if the distance is infinity then k_i is zero. We choose higher w_i closer to unity for a smaller distance. If the unknown node falls in the convex hull formed by the neighboring anchors, localization error is minimal. In that case, the region of the ambiguity is smaller. Refer to the problem of exercise.

4.3.3 Time-Difference-of-Arrival Based Localization

We explain Time-difference-of-arrival (TDOA) based localization now. The received signals at ith unknown node is given by

$$y_i(t) = \alpha_i^f(t)x(t - \tau_i) + \eta_i(t) \text{ for } i = \{1, 2\} \tag{4.12}$$

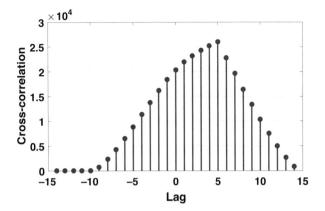

FIGURE 4.5: Correlation versus lag

where α_i^f represents the attenuation factor for the anchor and ith node. η_i is zero-mean Gaussian noise. τ_i denotes the time delay associated with the ith node. The estimated cross-correlation is expressed as

$$\tilde{R}_{y_1 y_2}(\tau) = \frac{1}{T} \int_0^T y_1(t) y_2(t - \tau) \, dt \qquad (4.13)$$

where T is the observation period. The TDOA can be estimated by maximizing the correlation function as

$$\text{TDOA} = \underset{\tau}{\text{argmax}} \ \tilde{R}_{y_1 y_2}(\tau) \qquad (4.14)$$

The TDOA information is used to further to locate the smart device.

Example of TDoA based localization: Two signals $y_1(t)$ and $y_2(t)$ are utilized for computing the cross-correlation. We consider 10 samples and 15 samples, respectively, in $y_1(t)$ and $y_2(t)$. The maximum correlation occurs when the lag is 5 as shown in Figure 4.5. This is expected since the difference between the number of samples in those two signals is 5.

The difference between TOAs of pair of nodes, that is, TDOA is utilized herein for obtaining the location of unknown sensor node. It requires precise synchronization among anchors. However, it does not require synchronization between the unknown node and anchors. It may be noted that TDOA is an efficient estimator as compared to the TOA-based method.

4.3.4 Angle-of-Arrival Based Localization

We first use trigonometry and geometry in Angle-of-Arrival (AOA) based localization. The angle and location relationship between the unknown node and anchor can be expressed as

$$(x_i - x) = (y_i - y) \tan \psi_i, \quad i \in \mathcal{N} \qquad (4.15)$$

where $\mathbf{X} = \begin{bmatrix} x & y \end{bmatrix}^T$ is an unknown node, and $\mathbf{X_i} = \begin{bmatrix} x_i & y_i \end{bmatrix}^T$ is ith anchor. The angle of arrival for ith anchor is denoted by ψ_i. The location of an unknown node using least-square method can be estimated as

$$\tilde{\mathbf{X}} = (A^T A)^{-1} A^T B \qquad (4.16)$$

where

$$\mathbf{A} = \begin{bmatrix} 1 & -\tan \psi_1 \\ 1 & -\tan \psi_2 \\ \vdots & \vdots \\ 1 & -\tan \psi_N \end{bmatrix} \text{ and } \mathbf{B} = \begin{bmatrix} x_1 - y_1 \tan \psi_1 \\ x_2 - y_2 \tan \psi_2 \\ \vdots \\ x_N - y_N \tan \psi_N \end{bmatrix}$$

Similar to multilateration based localization, the concept of pseudo-inverse is used herein for rectangular $\mathbf{A}$ and $\mathbf{B}$ matrices. It may be noted that the AOA-based method uses angle information. This increases cost and complexity because of the use of an antenna array.

Example of AoA based localization: Consider the locations of the all the anchors as $\begin{bmatrix} x_1 & y_1 \end{bmatrix}^T = \begin{bmatrix} 0 & 0 \end{bmatrix}^T$, $\begin{bmatrix} x_2 & y_2 \end{bmatrix}^T = \begin{bmatrix} 0 & 1 \end{bmatrix}^T$, $\begin{bmatrix} x_3 & y_3 \end{bmatrix}^T = \begin{bmatrix} 1 & 0 \end{bmatrix}^T$, and $\begin{bmatrix} x_4 & y_4 \end{bmatrix}^T = \begin{bmatrix} 1 & 1 \end{bmatrix}^T$. The actual location of the unknown sensor node is assumed to be $\begin{bmatrix} x & y \end{bmatrix}^T = \begin{bmatrix} 0.5 & 0.5 \end{bmatrix}^T$. The Gaussian noise in angle measurement is considered to be $\mathcal{N}(0, 10^{-3})$.

Solution: We get $\psi_1 = 180° + 45°$, $\psi_2 = 180° - 45°$, $\psi_3 = 360° - 45°$, and $\psi_4 = 45°$. Now, the matrices can be written as

$$\mathbf{A} = \begin{bmatrix} 1 & -1.0000 \\ 1 & 0.99930 \\ 1 & 0.99970 \\ 1 & -1.0016 \end{bmatrix} \text{ and } \mathbf{B} = \begin{bmatrix} 0.0000 \\ 0.99930 \\ 1 \\ -0.0016 \end{bmatrix} \qquad (4.17)$$

The estimated location of the unknown node is

$$\begin{bmatrix} 0.4998 \\ 0.5002 \end{bmatrix} \qquad (4.18)$$

The estimated location is closer to the actual location. Notably, if the unknown node lies in the convex hull formed by the neighboring anchors, the location estimate becomes accurate as expected.

4.3.5 Received Signal Strength Based Localization

We discuss next Received Signal Strength (RSS) based localization. The RSS measurements at the unknown node due to an anchor can be expressed as

$$P_r(d) = P_0(d_0) - 10\alpha^f \log\left(\frac{d}{d_0}\right) + \eta \qquad (4.19)$$

where d_0 denotes the reference distance from the transmitter and α^f represents the path loss exponent. η is Gaussian noise with zero mean and variance σ^2.

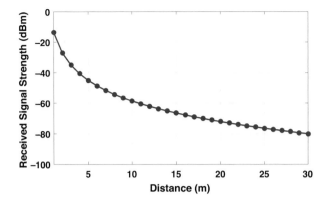

FIGURE 4.6: Received signal power with distance

P_0 is the power at reference distance d_0. Unbiased estimate of true distance using maximum likelihood estimate is given by

$$\tilde{d}_{ij} = d_0 \left(\frac{P_{ij}}{P_0(d_0)} \right)^{\frac{-1}{\eta}} \exp \left(\frac{-\log(10)\sigma^2}{20\eta^2} \right) \qquad (4.20)$$

RSS is a low-cost measurement and it depends upon the wireless channel. It may yield large errors because of the requirement of an accurate propagation model. We can also use the least-square method to estimate distance. Refer to the problem of exercise.

Example of RSS based localization: The path loss exponent η varies between 2 for free space to 6 for cluttered environment. This can be also estimated given the measurements. We consider $\eta = 4.5$, $d_0 = 1$ m. The received power is the function of transmitted power, distance, antenna parameter, and the state of the channel.

Given the received signal power, we estimate the distance and vice-versa. The received signal power decreases with the distance between the anchor and the unknown node as shown in Figure 4.6. Received signal strength below some threshold like -80 dBm or -90 dBm is generally considered to be the noise floor. This varies depending upon the specifications of the hardware and environmental conditions.

4.3.6 Multidimensional Scaling (MDS) Based Localization

The algorithm based on the MDS computes the location of the unknown node, given the set of distances between each pair of nodes. The squared distance matrix is given by

$$
\mathbf{D} = \begin{bmatrix} 0 & d_{12}^2 & \cdots & d_{1|\mathcal{N}|}^2 \\ d_{21}^2 & 0 & \cdots & d_{2|\mathcal{N}|}^2 \\ \vdots & \vdots & \vdots & \vdots \\ d_{|\mathcal{N}|1}^2 & d_{|\mathcal{N}|2}^2 & \cdots & 0 \end{bmatrix} \tag{4.21}
$$

Apply double centering matrix to D

$$
D_{\text{dc}} = JDJ \tag{4.22}
$$

where

$$
J = \mathbf{I}_{|\mathcal{N}| \times |\mathcal{N}|} - \frac{1}{|\mathcal{N}|} \mathbf{1}\mathbf{1}^T \tag{4.23}
$$

with $\mathbf{1}$ is the vector of all ones.

Apply Singular Value Decomposition (SVD) on D_{dc}

$$
D_{\text{dc}} = QAQ^T \tag{4.24}
$$

where A is the diagonal matrix having each element as eigenvalue and Q a matrix corresponding to the eigenvector. Choosing the first two eigenvalues and the corresponding eigenvectors for two-dimensional coordinates system

$$
D_{\text{new}} = Q_{\text{new}} A_{\text{new}} Q_{\text{new}}^T \tag{4.25}
$$

Transform the relative coordinates system

$$
\tilde{X} = Q_{\text{new}} A_{\text{new}}^{\frac{1}{2}} \tag{4.26}
$$

to absolute coordinates system using anchor nodes.

Example of MDS based Localization: The locations of the all the sensor nodes are $\begin{bmatrix} x_1 & y_1 \end{bmatrix}^T = \begin{bmatrix} 0 & 0 \end{bmatrix}$, $\begin{bmatrix} x_2 & y_2 \end{bmatrix}^T = \begin{bmatrix} 1 & 0 \end{bmatrix}$, $\begin{bmatrix} x_3 & y_3 \end{bmatrix}^T = \begin{bmatrix} 0 & 1 \end{bmatrix}$, $\begin{bmatrix} x_4 & y_4 \end{bmatrix}^T = \begin{bmatrix} 1 & 1 \end{bmatrix}$, and $\begin{bmatrix} x_5 & y_5 \end{bmatrix}^T = \begin{bmatrix} 0.5 & 0.5 \end{bmatrix}$.

Solution: The squared distance matrix

$$
\mathbf{D} = \begin{bmatrix} 0 & 1 & 1 & 2 & 0.5 \\ 1 & 0 & 2 & 1 & 0.5 \\ 1 & 2 & 0 & 1 & 0.5 \\ 2 & 1 & 1 & 0 & 0.5 \\ 0.5 & 0.5 & 0.5 & 0.5 & 0 \end{bmatrix} \tag{4.27}
$$

The double centering matrix

$$
\mathbf{J} = \begin{bmatrix} 0.8 & -0.2 & -0.2 & -0.2 & -0.2 \\ -0.2 & 0.8 & -0.2 & -0.2 & -0.2 \\ -0.2 & -0.2 & 0.8 & -0.2 & -0.2 \\ -0.2 & -0.2 & -0.2 & 0.8 & -0.2 \\ -0.2 & -0.2 & -0.2 & -0.2 & 0.8 \end{bmatrix} \tag{4.28}
$$

and

$$
D_{dc} = \begin{bmatrix} -1 & 0 & 0 & 1 & 0 \\ 0 & -1 & 1 & 0 & 0 \\ 0 & 1 & -1 & 0 & 0 \\ 1 & 0 & 0 & -1 & 0 \\ 0 & 0 & 0 & 0 & 0 \end{bmatrix} \tag{4.29}
$$

Therefore, using singular value decomposition,

$$
Q = \begin{bmatrix} 0 & -0.7071 & 0 & 0.7071 & 0 \\ 0.7071 & 0 & -0.7071 & 0 & 0 \\ -0.7071 & 0 & -0.7071 & 0 & 0 \\ 0 & 0.7071 & 0 & 0.7071 & 0 \\ 0 & 0 & 0 & 0 & 1 \end{bmatrix} \tag{4.30}
$$

and

$$
A = \begin{bmatrix} 2 & 0 & 0 & 0 & 0 \\ 0 & 2 & 0 & 0 & 0 \\ 0 & 0 & 0 & 0 & 0 \\ 0 & 0 & 0 & 0 & 0 \\ 0 & 0 & 0 & 0 & 0 \end{bmatrix} \tag{4.31}
$$

Hence, for two dimensional coordinate systems, considering fist two columns of Q and squared root of two dominant eigenvectors, we get

$$
\tilde{X} = \begin{bmatrix} 0 & -\frac{1}{\sqrt{2}} \\ \frac{1}{\sqrt{2}} & 0 \\ -\frac{1}{\sqrt{2}} & 0 \\ 0 & \frac{1}{\sqrt{2}} \\ 0 & 0 \end{bmatrix} \begin{bmatrix} \sqrt{2} & 0 \\ 0 & \sqrt{2} \end{bmatrix} = \begin{bmatrix} 0 & -1 \\ 1 & 0 \\ -1 & 0 \\ 0 & 1 \\ 0 & 0 \end{bmatrix} \tag{4.32}
$$

which is a translated, rotated, and scaled version of original location of the nodes. The MDS-based localization method only requires initial pairwise distance information. It also provides good initial coordinates for other localization methods. This method requires the set of anchors as reference nodes for converting the relative coordinate system to absolute coordinate system.

4.4 Distance-free Localization Methods

The distance-free based localization has low complexity than the distance-based method. Distance-free methods use connectivity information and yield coarser location estimates. Distance-free localization methods like Approximate Point in Triangle Test (APIT), Distance Vector-HOP, Centroid algorithm, Closest point-based method, and Assumption based coordinates method have been extensively dealt with in literature. The inertial based localization algorithm uses accelerometer and gyroscope for estimating the step counts and acceleration, respectively. Distance-free localization methods are based on distance-hop or geometric configuration of sensor nodes. These localization methods are good for coarse location in a large IoT network.

4.4.1   Centroid-based Localization

The centroid based localization is the most basic localization technique. This is very simple and effective for coarse location. The centroid-based localization method for sufficiently large number of anchor nodes is given by

$$
\begin{bmatrix} \hat{x} \\ \hat{y} \end{bmatrix} = \begin{bmatrix} \dfrac{\sum_{i=1}^{|\mathcal{S}|} \alpha_i^f x_i}{\sum_{i=1}^{|\mathcal{S}|} \alpha_i^f} \\[2em] \dfrac{\sum_{i=1}^{|\mathcal{S}|} \alpha_i^f y_i}{\sum_{i=1}^{|\mathcal{S}|} \alpha_i^f} \end{bmatrix} \tag{4.33}
$$

where $\begin{bmatrix} \hat{x} & \hat{y} \end{bmatrix}^T$ is the estimated location of unknown node. $\begin{bmatrix} x_i & y_i \end{bmatrix}^T$ denotes the ith anchor and α_i^f represents the confidence of ith anchor communication.

Example of Centroid Localization: Let the locations of all the anchors be $\begin{bmatrix} x_1 & y_1 \end{bmatrix}^T = \begin{bmatrix} 0 & 0 \end{bmatrix}$, $\begin{bmatrix} x_2 & y_2 \end{bmatrix}^T = \begin{bmatrix} 0 & 1 \end{bmatrix}$, $\begin{bmatrix} x_3 & y_3 \end{bmatrix}^T = \begin{bmatrix} 1 & 0 \end{bmatrix}$, and $\begin{bmatrix} x_4 & y_4 \end{bmatrix}^T = \begin{bmatrix} 1 & 1 \end{bmatrix}$. The location of the unknown sensor node is assumed to be $\begin{bmatrix} 0.2 & 0.2 \end{bmatrix}$.

The distances of the unknown node from the anchors are $d_1 = 0.2828$, $d_2 = 0.8246$, $d_3 = 0.8246$, and $d_4 = 1.1314$. The radio communication range of the anchor is denoted by R. Assume, the value of R is set to 0.9 without the loss of generality. The smart devices have limited communication range and hence it cannot hear all the anchors deployed in the network. Thus, the node can hear anchors located at $\begin{bmatrix} x_1 & y_1 \end{bmatrix}^T$, $\begin{bmatrix} x_2 & y_2 \end{bmatrix}^T$, and $\begin{bmatrix} x_3 & y_3 \end{bmatrix}^T$. Therefore, the centroid locations of the these three anchors is

$$
\begin{bmatrix} 0.33 \\ 0.33 \end{bmatrix} \tag{4.34}
$$

This is the estimated location of the unknown node. Notably, in order to increase the localization accuracy further, the confidence parameter α_i^f is also taken into account. The confidence parameter is expressed as $\alpha_i^f = \frac{1}{1+\text{distance}}$. The anchor which is located closer to the unknown node has larger weight. The estimated location is $\begin{bmatrix} 0.3 & 0.3 \end{bmatrix}^T$ for $\alpha_i^f = \frac{1}{\text{distance}}$. This is called weighted centroid based localization.

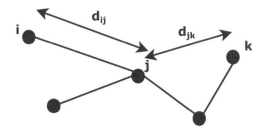

FIGURE 4.7: Illustration of the DV-HOP localization

4.4.2 Distance Vector Hop Based Localization

The Distance Vector (DV)-HOP localization method is based on the average hop distance between two sensor nodes as shown in Figure 4.7. The method does not utilize the absolute distance between two neighboring sensor node. Therefore, it gives coarse location of node than distance-based methods. The DV-HOP based localization method is given by

$$\text{Hop}_{\text{average}} = \frac{\sum_{i,j} \sqrt{(x_i - x_j)^2 + (y_i - y_j)^2}}{\sum_{i,j} h_{i,j}} \tag{4.35}$$

where (x_i, y_i) is the coordinates of the ith anchor, and $h_{i,j}$ is the hop count from ith node to jth node.

Example of DV Hop Based Localization: Let $d_{ij} = 0.5$ and $d_{jk} = 0.3$. The average hop distance using Equation 4.35 is given by

$$\frac{0.5 + 0.3}{1 + 2} = 0.29 \tag{4.36}$$

There are three hops between nodes i and k. Hence, the distance between i and k nodes are $3 \times 0.29 = 0.8$. This is a low-cost localization method for a small sensor network in line-of-sight scenario. However, it may be noted that computing the accurate distance between two sensor nodes is highly erroneous especially in an indoor scenario or a large IoT network. This is because of the loss due to obstruction such as wall and furniture. This creates non-line-of-sight conditions.

4.4.3 Closest Point Based Localization

The closest point localization method is employed for obtaining the cardinal location information. The coarse location of the unknown sensor node may be decided based on the following conditions:

- Which anchor is the closest to node receiving maximum power?

- Whether the node is in the communication range of ith anchor?

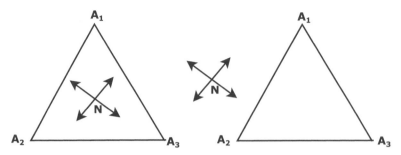

FIGURE 4.8: An illustration of point inside and outside of a triangle in APIT

- Direction at which nth node receives maximum energy?

- Near-far information between pair of nodes.

Example of Closest Point Based Localization: Consider the same set locations of all the anchors as follows: $\begin{bmatrix} x_1 & y_1 \end{bmatrix}^T = \begin{bmatrix} 0 & 0 \end{bmatrix}$, $\begin{bmatrix} x_2 & y_2 \end{bmatrix}^T = \begin{bmatrix} 0 & 1 \end{bmatrix}$, $\begin{bmatrix} x_3 & y_3 \end{bmatrix}^T = \begin{bmatrix} 1 & 0 \end{bmatrix}$, and $\begin{bmatrix} x_4 & y_4 \end{bmatrix}^T = \begin{bmatrix} 1 & 1 \end{bmatrix}$. The location of the unknown sensor node is assumed to be $\begin{bmatrix} 0.2 & 0.2 \end{bmatrix}$.

The distances of the unknown node from the anchors 1, 2, 3, and 4 are, respectively, $d_1 = 0.2828$, $d_2 = 0.8246$, $d_3 = 0.8246$, and $d_4 = 1.1314$. The radio communication range of the anchor is denoted by R. Assume, the value of R is set to 0.9 without the loss of generality. According to closest point based localization technique, the unknown node is in the vicinity of anchor 1. Hence, the coarse location of the unknown node is

$$\begin{bmatrix} x_1 \\ y_1 \end{bmatrix} = \begin{bmatrix} 0 \\ 0 \end{bmatrix} \tag{4.37}$$

Note that the closest point localization provides a low-cost solution, easily implementable, low energy consumption, and low resolution of the location estimate.

4.4.4 Approximate Point in Triangle Test (APIT)

We know that a few nodes that are equipped with high-powered transmitters are called anchors. The unknown node can obtain its location based on the information from the anchors. If there exists a direction of movement such that N is closer or further away to A_1, A_2, and A_3 simultaneously, then N is outside of $\Delta\ A_1 A_2 A_3$ as shown in Figure 4.8. Otherwise, N is inside Δ $A_1 A_2 A_3$.

Example of APIT: First, a grid array is formed and all the grids are initially assigned a zero value as shown in Figure 4.9. It is then scanned using a grid scan algorithm. If the node lies inside the triangle, it is incremented by

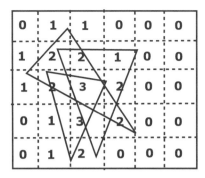

FIGURE 4.9: Illustration of the intersection of overlapping region in APIT

one. The grid array is used to choose the grid where the node is most likely to reside. In this example, the size of the grid is 0.2 times the radio communication range of the sensor. It is worth mentioning that the number of grids can be increased by decreasing the size for better accuracy. The number of the possible triangle for our scenario is three for illustration. However, in practice, all the possible combinations of the triangle are taken into account. APIT is a cost-effective approach and it has good localization accuracy, even in the presence of irregular radio patterns, and with the random node deployment.

4.4.5 Assumption Based Coordinates (ABC) Localization

Assumption Based Coordinates (ABC) is a distributed localization method. Initially, it is difficult to get the range measurements from more than three anchors for a 2D coordinate system. Therefore, a map based on the neighboring ranges is generated at the beginning of the network operation.

The Assumption Based Coordinates (ABC) localization method is shown in Figure 4.10. Here, we consider only positive value after square root operation. If the line joining origin and $(x_2, y_2, 0)$ subtends an angle ξ with x axis, then we can write using law of cosine as

$$\cos(\xi) = \frac{d_{01}^2 + d_{02}^2 - d_{12}^2}{2d_{01}d_{02}} \tag{4.38}$$

We can write x coordinate using $\cos(\xi) = \frac{x_2}{d_{02}}$ and Equation 4.38 as

$$x_2 = \frac{d_{01}^2 + d_{02}^2 - d_{12}^2}{2d_{01}} \tag{4.39}$$

Here, $d_{02} = \sqrt{(x_2 - 0)^2 + (y_2 - 0)^2 + (0 - 0)^2} = \sqrt{x_2^2 + y_2^2}$, we can write y coordinate as

$$y_2 = \sqrt{d_{02}^2 - x_2^2} \tag{4.40}$$

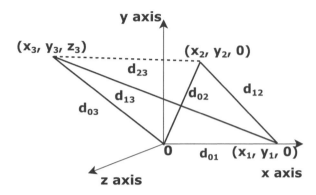

FIGURE 4.10: An illustration of node placement in ABC algorithm

Similarly, the following geometry based expressions for node location is given by

$$x_3 = \frac{d_{01}^2 + d_{03}^2 - d_{13}^2}{2d_{01}} \qquad (4.41)$$

$$y_3 = \frac{d_{02}^2 + d_{03}^2 - d_{23}^2 - 2x_2x_3}{2y_2} \qquad (4.42)$$

$$z_3 = \sqrt{d_{03}^2 - x_3^2 - y_3^2} \qquad (4.43)$$

The expressions for x_3 and z_3 are evident. Refer to the problem of exercise for determination of y_3 coordinate.

Example of ABC Localization: Let the actual locations of the sensors be $(x_1, y_1) = (1, 0)$, $(x_2, y_2) = (0.5, 1)$ and $(x_3, y_3, z_3) = (1, 1, 1)$. Subsequently, distances among nodes are $d_{01} = 1$, $d_{02} = 1.1180$, $d_{12} = 1.1180$, $d_{03} = 1.7321$, $d_{13} = 1.414$, and $d_{23} = 1.1180$. We add the noise $\mathcal{N}(0, 10^{-3})$ in the actual distance to get the estimated distances. We get the coordinates as follows:

$$x_2 = \frac{1.007^2 + 1.1180^2 - 1.1187^2}{2(1.007)} \qquad (4.44)$$

$$y_2 = \sqrt{1.1180^2 - 0.4995^2} \qquad (4.45)$$

$$x_3 = \frac{1.007^2 + 1.7318^2 - 1.4141^2}{2(1.0007)} \qquad (4.46)$$

$$y_3 = \frac{1.7318^2 - 1.1195^2 + 0.4995^2 + 1.002^2 - 2(0.4995)(0.9998)}{2(1.002)} \qquad (4.47)$$

$$z_3 = \sqrt{1.7318^2 - 0.9998^2 - 0.9983^2} \qquad (4.48)$$

The estimated locations of the sensors are $(\hat{x}_2, \hat{y}_2) = (0.4995, 1.002)$ and $(\hat{x}_3, \hat{y}_3, \hat{z}_3) = (0.9998, 0.9983, 1.0015)$ which is close to the actual locations of the sensors.

4.5 Performance Metrics

The performance of the localization algorithm is assessed by different metrics, namely, average localization error, the variance of localization error, the minimum variance of localization error by Cramer-Rao Lower Bound (CRLB), box and whisker analysis, and cumulative distribution function (CDF).

4.5.1 Average Localization Error

The motivation for using normalized localization error instead of absolute localization error is as follows: getting 0.2 m in 1 m × 1 m network is poorer than 0.2 m in 10 m × 10 m. The normalized errors are 20 % and 2 % for the former and latter scenarios, respectively. The normalized localization error is defined as the average of sum of Euclidean distance between the estimated and actual target locations per target and per network dimension. It is given by

$$\text{Normalized Localization Error} = \frac{1}{\mathcal{D}\mathcal{T}} \sum_{t=1}^{\mathcal{T}} ||\hat{\mathbf{x}}_t - \mathbf{x}_t|| \tag{4.49}$$

where $\mathcal{D}$ and $\mathcal{T}$ denote the network dimension and the number of targets, respectively. $\mathbf{x}_t$ and $\hat{\mathbf{x}}_t$ are the actual and the estimated target locations, respectively.

4.5.2 Cramer-Rao Lower Bound

In this section, Cramer-Rao Lower Bound (CRLB) analysis for the parameter of node location is presented. CRLB gives the lower bound on the variance of any unbiased estimator. It is used as a standard benchmark with respect to which variance of the estimator is compared. The parameters of node location is $\varphi = \begin{bmatrix} x & y \end{bmatrix}^T$, whose CRLB is to be estimated.

Consider $p = \alpha^f + \beta_f \log d_a$ as an RSS-distance model, where α^f and β_f are the parameters of Friss transmission formula. This depends on antenna gain, transmitted power, and wavelength of the carrier signal. For Gaussian RSP observations, that is, $\mathbf{p} \sim \mathcal{N}(\mu(\varphi), \mathbf{C}(\varphi))$, Fisher information matrix (FIM) is written using the expression of Kay et al. (1993) as

$$\text{FIM}(\varphi) = \left[\frac{\partial \mu(\varphi)}{\partial \varphi}\right]^T \mathbf{C}^{-1}(\varphi) \left[\frac{\partial \mu(\varphi)}{\partial \varphi}\right] + \frac{1}{2}\text{tr}\left[\left(\mathbf{C}^{-1}(\varphi)\frac{\partial \mathbf{C}(\varphi)}{\partial \varphi}\right)^2\right] \tag{4.50}$$

where tr(.) denotes trace of a matrix, which is sum of its diagonal elements. $\mathbf{C}$ is the covariance matrix which does not depend on φ. It can be shown that

$$\left[\frac{\partial \mu(\varphi)}{\partial \varphi}\right] = \begin{bmatrix} \beta_f \frac{(x-x_a)}{d_1^2} & \beta_f \frac{(y-y_a)}{d_1^2} \\ \beta_f \frac{(x-x_a)}{d_2^2} & \beta_f \frac{(y-y_a)}{d_2^2} \\ \vdots & \vdots \\ \beta_f \frac{(x-x_a)}{d_{\bar{A}}^2} & \beta_f \frac{(y-y_a)}{d_{\bar{A}}^2} \end{bmatrix} \quad (4.51)$$

Substitute Equation 4.51 into Equation 4.50 to get the following expression for FIM.

$\text{FIM}(\varphi) =$

$$\begin{bmatrix} \beta_f \frac{x-x_1}{d_1^2} & \beta_f \frac{x-x_2}{d_2^2} & \cdots & \beta_f \frac{x-x_A}{d_{\bar{A}}^2} \\ \beta_f \frac{y-y_1}{d_1^2} & \beta_f \frac{y-y_2}{d_2^2} & \cdots & \beta_f \frac{y-y_A}{d_{\bar{A}}^2} \end{bmatrix} \begin{bmatrix} \frac{1}{\sigma_1^2} & 0 & \cdots & 0 \\ 0 & \frac{1}{\sigma_2^2} & \cdots & 0 \\ \vdots & \vdots & \vdots & \vdots \\ 0 & 0 & \cdots & \frac{1}{\sigma_A^2} \end{bmatrix} \begin{bmatrix} \beta_f \frac{x-x_1}{d_1^2} & \beta_f \frac{y-y_1}{d_1^2} \\ \beta_f \frac{x-x_2}{d_2^2} & \beta_f \frac{y-y_2}{d_2^2} \\ \vdots & \vdots \\ \beta_f \frac{x-x_A}{d_{\bar{A}}^2} & \beta_f \frac{y-y_A}{d_{\bar{A}}^2} \end{bmatrix}$$

$$(4.52)$$

where σ_a^2 represents variance corresponding to each of the ath anchor, $\forall\, a \in \bar{A}$. The FIM for parameters of the node location is finally given as

$$\text{FIM}(\varphi) = \begin{bmatrix} \beta_f^2 \sum_{a=1}^{\bar{A}} \frac{(x-x_a)^2}{\sigma_a^2 d_a^4} & \beta_f^2 \sum_{a=1}^{\bar{A}} \frac{(x-x_a)(y-y_a)}{\sigma_a^2 d_a^4} \\ \beta_f^2 \sum_{a=1}^{\bar{A}} \frac{(x-x_a)(y-y_a)}{\sigma_a^2 d_a^4} & \beta_f^2 \sum_{a=1}^{\bar{A}} \frac{(y-y_a)^2}{\sigma_a^2 d_a^4} \end{bmatrix} \quad (4.53)$$

Since CRLB is the sum of diagonal elements of inverse of FIM

$$\text{CRLB}(\varphi) = [\mathbf{I}^{-1}]_{1,1} + [\mathbf{I}^{-1}]_{2,2} \quad (4.54)$$

If the variance of the location estimator is close to the CRLB, the estimator is said to be efficient as shown in Figure 4.11.

4.5.3   Box and Whisker Plot

Generally, observations are affected because of noise and multipath fading. Some of the observations follow a certain pattern and treated as normal, while some of them may not follow that distribution and are deemed as outliers. In order to detect the outliers, a box-and-whisker analysis plot is used. The plot is used for two purposes. First, to evaluate the effectiveness of the location estimator based on localization error. The location estimator is said to be efficient if the number of outliers is minimal. Second, it can be utilized for cleansing the raw signal strength data first and subsequently feeding it to the location estimator.

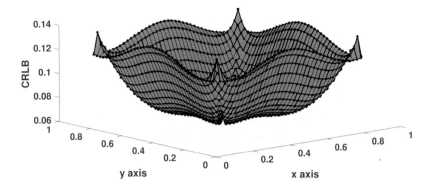

FIGURE 4.11: Cramer-Rao lower bound of the position estimator

Median error is shown by horizontal segment at the center of the box in Figure 4.12. Note that 25% and 75% percentile are first and third quartiles, respectively. These are denoted using lower and upper hinges of the box plot respectively. Minimum and maximum location errors are represented by lower and upper fences. The observation which is greater than one and half times the height of the box from the median is treated as an outlier. Hence, location error above the outer fence is considered to be an outlier as shown by cross symbols. Although, the number of extreme localization errors is more for method 1, however, the median localization error is small for method 1. Hence, it can be concluded that method 1 is good in average sense and method 2 in the outlier sense.

4.5.4 Cumulative Distribution Function

The cumulative distribution function (CDF) plot is utilized to investigate the distribution of localization error. For illustration purposes, we show the CDF plot for two methods in Figure 4.13. We mark the localization error and probability of error on x and y axes, respectively. The CDF curve should attain a unity probability rapidly. Ideally, it should resemble a unit step function. In this scenario, the probability of a large localization error is small. It can be seen from the figure that the performance of method 1 is better as compared to method 2.

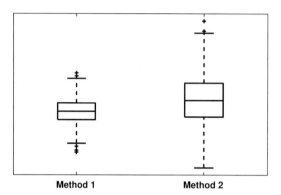

FIGURE 4.12: Box-plot

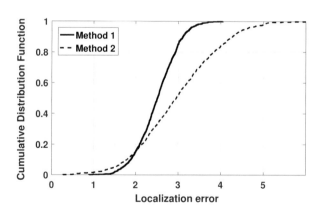

FIGURE 4.13: Cumulative distribution function plot

4.6 Summary

The localization accuracy of the distance-based methods depends upon the reliability of the radio propagation model. Fingerprinting localization yields good accuracy at the expense of extensive offline training. The primary aspects in choosing the method are accuracy, computational complexity, scalability, cost, and energy consumption. There is a trade-off between accuracy and available computational resources. For a one-shot process, one may choose the algorithm which has high accuracy. On the other hand, for real-time applications, the accuracy is tolerated up to some extent for low complexity algorithms. We can also utilize the available opportunistic signals in the environment such as light signal, acoustic signal, radio signal, geomagnetic disturbances, and crowd-sourcing for localization tasks.

4.7 Exercises

1. What is the average localization error using GPS in an indoor scenario?

2. Consider multilateration based localization using pseudo-inverse. There are three elements in unknown matrix $\mathbf{A}$. However, only two unknown variables x and y in the two-dimensional coordinates system are of interest. Explain.

3. Consider the location of the anchors $\begin{bmatrix} x_1 & y_1 \end{bmatrix}^T = \begin{bmatrix} 0.2 & 0.2 \end{bmatrix}$, $\begin{bmatrix} x_2 & y_2 \end{bmatrix}^T = \begin{bmatrix} 0.2 & 0.84 \end{bmatrix}$, $\begin{bmatrix} x_3 & y_3 \end{bmatrix}^T = \begin{bmatrix} 0.25 & 0 \end{bmatrix}$, and $\begin{bmatrix} x_4 & y_4 \end{bmatrix}^T = \begin{bmatrix} 0.82 & 0.82 \end{bmatrix}$ and unknown node $\begin{bmatrix} x & y \end{bmatrix}^T = \begin{bmatrix} 0.12 & 0.14 \end{bmatrix}$ are randomly deployed. Determine the location of the unknown node using ToA based technique.

4. What is the physical significance of lag in TDoA based localization?

5. If we use sound signal having speed 331 m/s in timing-based localization, how much would be an error in the distance for clock synchronization error of 1 s? Draw some inference.

6. How do we measure the angle in AoA/DoA based localization method?

7. When does the centroid-based localization give very poor accuracy?

8. If we consider a two-dimensional network $[0\ 1] \times [0\ 1]$. There are four anchors at the four corners of the network. If the node hears all four anchors, what is the estimated location using centroid-based localization?

9. Why do we take average hop size not absolute hop size in DV-Hop-based localization?

10. Determine the expression for y_3 coordinate of Assumption Based Coordinates (ABC) localization technique as mentioned in the theory section.

11. Let us assume that the average RSS at distance of 0.1 m, 2 m, and 3 m from the access point are, respectively, -30 dBm, -45 dBm, and -55 dBm. Estimate the distances between access points and smart devices.

12. Let the coordinates of three access points be $(x_1, y_1) = (0, 0)$, $(x_2, y_2) = (2, 1)$ and $(x_3, y_3) = (6, 6)$. Refer to Problem 11, perform multilateration based localization using the estimated distances.

13. How do we convert to the absolute coordinate system after using MDS-based localization?

14. Find CRLB for following FIMs: $\begin{bmatrix} 1 & 0 \\ 0 & 1 \end{bmatrix}$ and $\begin{bmatrix} 1 & 2 \\ -1 & 0 \end{bmatrix}$.

15. In performance evaluation, we calculate the localization error as the Euclidean distance between actual and estimate node locations. Mention other metrics that can be used.

16. **Do It Yourself**: Explore accelerometer and gyroscope and make a project on pedestrian tracking using measurements from these devices.

Chapter 5

Energy Harvesting and Control Optimization

5.1 Introduction

The energy is generally harvested from thermal, wind, and water current to name a few for resource-constrained IoT devices. This can be carried out using relay protocols, namely, time switching based relay (TSR) and power-splitting based relay (PSR). In the TSR protocol, the total time is divided into energy harvesting at the relay node, information processing at the relay node, which is transmitted from the source, and information transmission from the relay node to the destination. The fraction of time for each component is chosen judiciously to achieve maximum Signal-to-Noise Ratio (SNR) at the output. Similarly, in the PSR protocol, total power and time are divided. For instance, the power is divided into information processing at the relay node which is transmitted from the source, and energy harvesting at the relay node for the half-time duration. In the remaining half duration, information transmission from the relay node to the destination is carried out. Subsequently, model predictive control (MPC) for control action computation to get the desired output is presented. The control optimization is carried out using quadratic programming for both unconstrained and constrained MPC.

5.2 Energy Harvesting

Things in IoT networks are resource-constrained devices. Energy conservation is used for extending the battery life of things. We also do energy replenishment by recharging the battery. For recharge purposes, energy can be harvested from thermal energy, mechanical energy, wind energy, water current, or electromagnetic waves amongst others.

We can harvest energy from electromagnetic waves of access points, transmitter, or base station. This is also called Radio Frequency (RF) energy harvesting or RF energy transfer. The receiver converts the received signal power

DOI: 10.1201/9781003225584-5   143

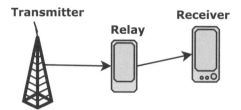

FIGURE 5.1: Illustration of a simple relay

to a DC voltage and the capacitor of the thing can store the harvested energy. Relay extracts energy and information from one device and transmits to other devices as shown in Figure 5.1. There are two types of basic relay protocols: Time-Switching based Relay (TSR) and Power-Splitting based Relay (PSR). This is discussed next.

5.2.1 Time-Switching Based Relay Protocol

In Time-Switching based Relay (TSR) protocol, $0 \leq a_E \leq 1$ is the fraction amount of time for energy harvesting by the relay node. T is the amount of time needed for information transmission from the source to the destination via a relay node. The total time T is divided into three segments in TSR protocol as shown in Figure 5.2. Therefore, T is given by

$$T = a_E T + (1 - a_E)\frac{T}{2} + (1 - a_E)\frac{T}{2} \tag{5.1}$$

Signal Model: The source or transmitter (S) transmits signals s^E with power P_s to the relay node (R). The received signal at the relay node, y_{SR}, is given by

$$y_{\mathrm{SR}} = \underbrace{\frac{\sqrt{P_s}h^E s^E}{\sqrt{d_{S,R}^\alpha}}}_{\text{desired signal}} + \underbrace{\sum_{i=1}^{I} \frac{\sqrt{P_i}g_i^E s_i^E}{\sqrt{d_{S_i R}^\alpha}}}_{\text{interference}} + \underbrace{\eta_R}_{\text{noise}} \tag{5.2}$$

where h^E is the channel gain and follows complex Gaussian distribution $\mathcal{CN}(0, \sigma_h^2)$. Now, ith interfering source transmits signal s_i^E with transmit power P_i. The channel gain follows $\mathcal{CN}(0, \sigma_g^2)$ between interfering source and relay node. The number of interfering sources is assumed to be I. The additive white Gaussian noise at the relay node is denoted by $\eta_R \sim \mathcal{N}(0, \sigma_R^2)$. The distance between the desired source (S) and relay is $d_{S,R}$, whereas the distance between interfering source (S_i) and relay is $d_{S_i R}$. Finally, α is the path loss exponent which varies between 2 (line-of-sight communication) and 6 (non-line-of-sight cluttered environment).

Signal-to-Interference-plus-Noise Ratio at Relay: The Signal-to-Interference-plus-Noise Ratio (SINR) at relay is

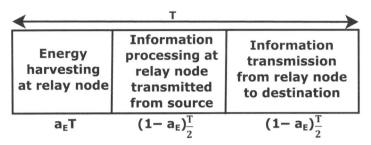

FIGURE 5.2: Time duration in TSR protocol

$$\text{SINR}_R = \frac{\text{Signal Power}}{\text{Interference Power} + \text{Noise Power}}$$

$$= \frac{\frac{P_s|h^E|^2}{d_{S,R}^\alpha}}{\sum_{i=1}^{I}\frac{P_i|g_i^E|^2}{d_{S_iR}^\alpha} + \sigma_R^2}$$

$$= \frac{\frac{P_s|h^E|^2}{\sigma_R^2 d_{S,R}^\alpha}}{\sum_{i=1}^{I}\frac{P_i|g_i^E|^2}{\sigma_R^2 d_{S_iR}^\alpha} + 1} \tag{5.3}$$

$$= \frac{\gamma_{\text{TSR}}}{I_{\text{TSR}} + 1}$$

where $\gamma_{\text{TSR}} = \frac{P_s|h^E|^2}{\sigma_R^2 d_{S,R}^\alpha}$ and $I_{\text{TSR}} = \sum_{i=1}^{I}\frac{P_i|g_i^E|^2}{\sigma_R^2 d_{S_iR}^\alpha}$. Here, transmit signal is assumed to have unity power, that is, $\mathbb{E}[(s^E)^2] = 1$. Notably, the power is calculated by taking expectation operator, $\mathbb{E}$. If SINR_R is greater than threshold, the received data is correctly decoded.

Harvested Energy and Transmission Power: The assumptions are as follows: all the energy harvested by the relay is used for transmitting the information to the destination. Consequently, the processing power of circuitry at the relay is very small. The relay harvests energy from the received signal and the interfering signals for $a_E T$ fraction of time.

$$\text{EH}_R = \kappa\left(\frac{P_s|h^E|^2}{d_{S,R}^\alpha} + \sum_{i=1}^{I}\frac{P_i|g_i^E|^2}{d_{S_iR}^\alpha}\right)a_E T \tag{5.4}$$

where $0 \leq \kappa \leq 1$ is the energy conversion efficiency. Therefore, the transmission power of relay is

$$P_R = \frac{\text{EH}_R}{(1 - a_E)\frac{T}{2}}$$

$$= 2\frac{\kappa\left(\frac{P_s|h^E|^2}{d_{S,R}^\alpha} + \sum_{i=1}^I \frac{P_i|g_i^E|^2}{d_{S_iR}^\alpha}\right)a_E T}{(1 - a_E)T}$$

$$= \frac{2a_E\kappa\left(\frac{P_s|h^E|^2}{d_{S,R}^\alpha} + \sum_{i=1}^I \frac{P_i|g_i^E|^2}{d_{S_iR}^\alpha}\right)}{(1 - a_E)}$$

$$= \frac{2a_E\kappa\sigma_R^2}{(1 - a_E)}(\gamma_{\text{TSR}} + I_{\text{TSR}}) \tag{5.5}$$

Signal-to-Noise Ratio at Destination: The received signal at destination is

$$y_{\text{RD}} = \frac{\sqrt{P_R}es_R^E}{\sqrt{d_{R,D}^\alpha}} + \eta_D \tag{5.6}$$

where s_R^E is the transmitted signal by the relay and having a unity power. e is the channel gain between the relay and the destination. This follows complex Gaussian noise $\text{CN}(0, \sigma_{h_1}^2)$ with zero mean and variance $\sigma_{h_1}^2$. Also, $\eta_D \sim \mathcal{N}(0, \sigma_D^2)$ is an additive white Gaussian noise with mean zero and variance σ_D^2.

Therefore, the Signal-to-Noise Ratio (SNR) at destination node is

$$\text{SNR}_D = \frac{P_R|e|^2}{d_{R,D}^\alpha\sigma_D^2}$$

$$= \frac{2a_E\kappa|e|^2\left(\frac{P_s|h^E|^2}{d_{S,R}^\alpha} + \sum_{i=1}^I \frac{P_i|g_i^E|^2}{d_{S_iR}^\alpha}\right)}{(1 - a_E)d_{R,D}^\alpha\sigma_D^2}$$

$$= \frac{2a_E\kappa}{(1 - a_E)d_{R,D}^\alpha}\frac{\sigma_R^2}{\sigma_D^2}|e|^2(\gamma_{\text{TSR}} + I_{\text{TSR}}) \tag{5.7}$$

Special Case of SNR at Destination: If we assume that there is no interfering signal, then the power due to interfering signal is zero. In this case, the SNR at destination node is

$$\text{SNR}_D = \frac{P_R|e|^2}{d_{R,D}^\alpha\sigma_D^2}$$

$$= \frac{2a_E\kappa|e|^2\left(\frac{P_s|h^E|^2}{d_{S,R}^\alpha}\right)}{(1 - a_E)d_{R,D}^\alpha\sigma_D^2}$$

$$= \frac{2a_E\kappa}{(1 - a_E)d_{R,D}^\alpha}\frac{\sigma_R^2}{\sigma_D^2}|e|^2\gamma_{\text{TSR}} \tag{5.8}$$

A high SNR is desirable.

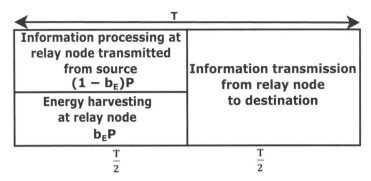

FIGURE 5.3: Time duration of PSR protocol

Remarks on TSR Protocol: If a_E increases and other parameters remain constant, the SNR at destination also increases. In fact, the factor $\frac{a_E}{(1-a_E)}$ increases with a_E. If a_E is equal to 0, the factor becomes $\frac{0}{1-0} = 0$. On the other hand, if a_E is equal to 0.5, the factor becomes $\frac{0.5}{1-0.5} = 1$. Finally, if a_E is equal to 1, the factor becomes ∞. This is because the fraction of time for harvesting the energy becomes full $1 \times T = T$ for $a_E \to 1$.

If the distance between the source and the relay or the relay and the destination increases, the SNR at the destination decreases. If the noise power (σ_D^2) increases, the SNR at the destination reduces as expected. This is evident from the derived expression too.

5.2.2 Power-Splitting Based Relaying Protocol

Consider $0 \leq b_E \leq 1$ in Figure 5.3 of a Power-Splitting based Relaying (PSR) protocol. $b_E p$ is the fraction of power that relay harvests from received signal (desired signal and interference) for the first $\frac{T}{2}$ duration. The remaining power $(1 - b_E)p$ is used for information processing at relay node which is transmitted from the transmitter or source node for the first $\frac{T}{2}$ duration.

Signal Model: We assume that the power splitting only reduces the signal power, not the noise power. We do this to analyze the worst-case performance of a relay node. The received signal at the relay node for information detection after power splitting is given by

$$y_{SR} = \frac{\sqrt{(1-b_E)P_s}}{\sqrt{d_{S,R}^\alpha}} h^E s^E + \sum_{i=1}^{I} \frac{\sqrt{(1-b_E)P_i}}{\sqrt{d_{S_i R}^\alpha}} g_i^E s_i^E + \eta_R \qquad (5.9)$$

where the symbols have their usual meaning as in TSR protocol. The SINR at relay node is expressed as

$$\text{SINR}_R = \frac{\text{Signal Power}}{\text{Interference Power} + \text{Noise Power}} \qquad (5.10)$$

SINR at Relay Node: On the similar lines of a TSR protocol, the SINR at relay node can be rewritten as

$$\text{SINR}_R = \frac{\frac{(1-b_E)P_s}{d_{S,R}^\alpha}|h^E|^2}{\sum_{i=1}^I \frac{(1-b_E)P_i}{d_{S_iR}^\alpha}|g_i^E|^2 + \sigma_R^2}$$

$$= \frac{\frac{(1-b_E)P_s}{d_{S,R}^\alpha \sigma_R^2}|h^E|^2}{\sum_{i=1}^I \frac{(1-b_E)P_i}{d_{S_iR}^\alpha \sigma_R^2}|g_i^E|^2 + 1} \tag{5.11}$$

$$= \frac{\gamma_{\text{PSR}}}{I_{\text{PSR}} + 1}$$

where $\gamma_{\text{PSR}} = \frac{(1-b_E)P_s}{d_{S,R}^\alpha \sigma_R^2}|h^E|^2$ and $I_{\text{PSR}} = \sum_{i=1}^I \frac{(1-b_E)P_i}{d_{S_iR}^\alpha \sigma_R^2}|g_i^E|^2$. Here, these expressions are different from a TSR protocol. However, the form of expression for SINR_R is the same.

Harvested Energy and Transmission Power: The assumption is as follows: all the energy harvested at the relay node is used for the transmission of information to the destination. In the duration of $\frac{T}{2}$, the relay harvests energy from the received signal (desired signal and interfering signal). The harvested energy at relay is given by

$$\text{EH}_R = \kappa b_E \left(\frac{P_s|h^E|^2}{d_{S,R}^\alpha} + \sum_{i=1}^I \frac{P_i|g_i^E|^2}{d_{S_iR}^\alpha} \right) \frac{T}{2} \tag{5.12}$$

The transmission power of relay node is

$$P_R = \frac{\text{EH}_R}{\frac{T}{2}}$$

$$= \frac{2}{T}\kappa b_E \left(\frac{P_s|h^E|^2}{d_{S,R}^\alpha} + \sum_{i=1}^I \frac{P_i|g_i^E|^2}{d_{S_iR}^\alpha} \right) \frac{T}{2} \tag{5.13}$$

$$= \kappa b_E \frac{\sigma_R^2}{(1-b_E)} \left(\frac{(1-b_E)P_s|h^E|^2}{d_{S,R}^\alpha \sigma_R^2} + \sum_{i=1}^I \frac{(1-b_E)P_i|g_i^E|^2}{d_{S_iR}^\alpha \sigma_R^2} \right)$$

SNR at Destination: The transmission power of a relay node can be rewritten as

$$P_R = \frac{\kappa b_E \sigma_R^2}{(1-b_E)}(\gamma_{\text{PSR}} + I_{\text{PSR}}) \tag{5.14}$$

Finally, the SNR at destination similar to a TSR protocol is given by

$$\text{SNR}_D = \frac{P_R|e|^2}{d_{R,D}^\alpha \sigma_D^2}$$

$$= \frac{\kappa b_E}{(1-b_E)d_{R,D}^\alpha} \frac{\sigma_R^2}{\sigma_D^2}|e|^2(\gamma_{\text{PSR}} + I_{\text{PSR}}) \tag{5.15}$$

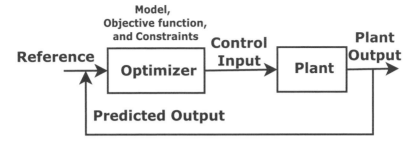

FIGURE 5.4: Model predictive control

Remarks on PSR Protocol: Similar to TSR protocol, after simplification of the expression for SNR at the destination, SNR_D varies with b_E assuming other parameters are constant. It may be noted that $1 - b_E$ from denominator and numerator are canceled out. Therefore, SNR_D increases with b_E. This makes sense since all the power $b_E P = P$ for $b_E \to 1$ is used for energy harvesting. Also, the SNR at destination decreases with the distance between the source and the relay or the relay and the destination. The SNR at the destination decreases with the noise variance (σ_D^2). The aforementioned conclusion is also intuitive.

5.3 Model Predictive Control

Model Predictive Control (MPC) is also called moving or receding horizon control. For a prediction horizon, the control action is computed and subsequently the output is predicted. A generic block diagram of the feedback MPC is shown in Figure 5.4. The plant output is fed back to the input of the optimizer. At each sampling instant, the model of the plant, current state, input and output are used to predict the future control action in a prediction horizon. This is shown in Figure 5.5. We consider a linear MPC using control and optimization techniques for building the foundations of the MPC technique.

5.3.1 Notations and State Space Model

Let N_p be the prediction horizon, $u(t)$ and $y(t)$ be the control input and the plant output at time t. $\theta_p(t+1|t)$ is the predicted θ_p at $t+1$ given θ_p at t, where $\theta_p = \{u, y\}$. Let the state at time t_0 be $\mathbf{x}(t_0)$ initially. The state-space model is given by

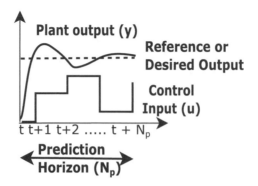

FIGURE 5.5: Control input and plant output in MPC

$$\dot{\mathbf{x}}(t) = \mathbf{A_c}\mathbf{x}(t) + \mathbf{B_c}\mathbf{u}(t)$$
$$\mathbf{y}(t) = \mathbf{C_c}\mathbf{x}(t) + \mathbf{D_c}\mathbf{u}(t) \tag{5.16}$$

Sample and hold circuit transforms a continuous time signal to discrete time signal as $\theta_p(kh)$, $kh \leq t \leq (k+1)h$. Therefore, the discretized input to the plant is given by $u(t) = u(kh)$, $kh \leq t \leq (k+1)h$. For brevity, we can write $u(k) = u(kh)$.

5.3.2 Solution of State Space Model

Consider a scalar case of the above state-space model

$$\dot{x}(t) - A_c x(t) = B_c u(t) \tag{5.17}$$

Multiplying both sides with $\exp(-A_c t)$ gives

$$\exp(-A_c t)\dot{x}(t) - \exp(-A_c t)A_c x(t) = \exp(-A_c t)B_c u(t) \tag{5.18}$$

We can rewrite the expression as follows

$$\frac{d}{dt}(\exp(-A_c t)x(t)) = \exp(-A_c t)B_c u(t) \tag{5.19}$$

Now, integrating the expression from t_0 to t gives

$$\int_{t_0}^{t} \frac{d}{d\tau}(\exp(-A_c \tau)x(\tau))\, d\tau = \int_{t_0}^{t} \exp(-A_c \tau)B_c u(\tau)\, d\tau \tag{5.20}$$

The left hand side of Equation 5.20 is

$$\exp(-A_c t)x(t)|_{t_0}^{t} = \exp(-A_c t)x(t) - \exp(-A_c t_0)x(t_0) \tag{5.21}$$

Multiply both sides with $\exp(A_c t)$ in Equations 5.20 and 5.21

$$x(t) = \exp(A_c(t - t_0))x(t_0) + \int_{t_0}^{t} \exp(A_c(t - \tau))B_c u(\tau)\, d\tau \tag{5.22}$$

Finally, for matrix case, we can write the solution as

$$\mathbf{x}(t) = \exp(\mathbf{A_c}(t - t_0))\mathbf{x}(t_0) + \int_{t_0}^{t} \exp(\mathbf{A_c}(t - \tau))\mathbf{B_c}\mathbf{u}(\tau)\, d\tau \quad (5.23)$$

5.3.3 Continuous to Discrete State Space Model

Denote $t_0 = kh$ and $t = (k + 1)h$, then $t - t_0 = (k + 1)h - kh = h$

$$\mathbf{x}(k + 1) = \exp(\mathbf{A_c}h)\mathbf{x}(k) + \int_{kh}^{(k+1)h} \exp(\mathbf{A_c}((k + 1)h - \tau))\mathbf{B_c}\mathbf{u}(k)\, d\tau \quad (5.24)$$

This can be rewritten as

$$\mathbf{x}(k + 1) = \exp(\mathbf{A_c}h)\mathbf{x}(k) + \int_{kh}^{(k+1)h} \exp(\mathbf{A_c}((k + 1)h - \tau))\mathbf{B_c}\, d\tau\, \mathbf{u}(k) \quad (5.25)$$

Denote $\alpha = (k + 1)h - \tau$. If $\tau = kh$, $\alpha = kh + h - kh = h$. If $\tau = (k + 1)h$, $\alpha = kh + h - (k + 1)h = 0$ and $d\alpha = -d\tau$. Therefore, we can write

$$\mathbf{x}(k + 1) = \exp(\mathbf{A_c}h)\mathbf{x}(k) + \int_{0}^{h} \exp(\mathbf{A_c}\alpha)\mathbf{B_c}\, d\alpha\, \mathbf{u}(k) \quad (5.26)$$

If $\mathbf{A_d} = \exp(\mathbf{A_c}h)$ and $\mathbf{B_d} = \int_{0}^{h} \exp(\mathbf{A_c}\alpha)\mathbf{B_c}\, d\alpha$, the state-space model can be written as

$$\begin{aligned} \mathbf{x}(k + 1) &= \mathbf{A_d}\mathbf{x}(k) + \mathbf{B_d}\mathbf{u}(k) \\ \mathbf{y}(k) &= \mathbf{C}\mathbf{x}(k) + \mathbf{D}\mathbf{u}(k) \end{aligned} \quad (5.27)$$

Example: Convert from continuous state space model to discrete state space model for $\mathbf{A}_c = \begin{bmatrix} 0 & 1 \\ 0 & 0 \end{bmatrix}$, $\mathbf{B}_c = \begin{bmatrix} 0 \\ 1 \end{bmatrix}$, $\mathbf{C} = \begin{bmatrix} 1 & 0 \end{bmatrix}$ and $\mathbf{D}$ is a zero matrix.

First Approach of Solution: This is based on Taylor series approximation for $\mathbf{A_d}$.

$$\mathbf{A}_d = \exp(\mathbf{A_c}h) = \mathbf{I} + \mathbf{A_c}h + \frac{\mathbf{A_c}^2 h^2}{2!} + \text{higher order terms} \quad (5.28)$$

where $\mathbf{I}$ denotes the identity matrix of appropriate dimension and ! is the factorial operation. If $h = 0.1$, then

$$\mathbf{A_d} = \begin{bmatrix} 1 & 0.1 \\ 0 & 1 \end{bmatrix} \quad (5.29)$$

using first order term. The answer is same even with second order term. Therefore, we can stop here. We can go to higher order depending upon $\mathbf{A_c}$.

Second Approach of Solution: This is based on inverse Laplace transform for

$$\mathbf{A_d} = \exp(\mathbf{A_c}t) = \text{ILT}[(s\mathbf{I} - \mathbf{A_c})^{-1}] \quad (5.30)$$

where

$$(s\mathbf{I} - \mathbf{A_c}) = \begin{bmatrix} s & -1 \\ 0 & s \end{bmatrix} \tag{5.31}$$

and

$$(s\mathbf{I} - \mathbf{A_c})^{-1} = \begin{bmatrix} \frac{1}{s} & \frac{1}{s^2} \\ 0 & \frac{1}{s} \end{bmatrix} \tag{5.32}$$

Subsequently,

$$\exp(\mathbf{A_c}t) = \begin{bmatrix} 1 & t \\ 0 & 1 \end{bmatrix} u(t) \tag{5.33}$$

where s is a complex frequency parameter and $u(t)$ is a unit step function. Hence,

$$\mathbf{A}_d = \exp(\mathbf{A_c}h) = \begin{bmatrix} 1 & h \\ 0 & 1 \end{bmatrix} u(h) = \begin{bmatrix} 1 & 0.1 \\ 0 & 1 \end{bmatrix} \tag{5.34}$$

Now for $\mathbf{B_d}$:

$$\mathbf{B_d} = \int_0^h \exp(\mathbf{A_c}\beta) \, d\beta \, \mathbf{B_c} \tag{5.35}$$

$$\mathbf{B_d} = \int_0^h \begin{bmatrix} 1 & \beta \\ 0 & 1 \end{bmatrix} d\beta \begin{bmatrix} 0 \\ 1 \end{bmatrix} \tag{5.36}$$

$$\mathbf{B_d} = \begin{bmatrix} h & \frac{h^2}{2} \\ 0 & h \end{bmatrix} \begin{bmatrix} 0 \\ 1 \end{bmatrix} = \begin{bmatrix} \frac{h^2}{2} \\ h \end{bmatrix} = \begin{bmatrix} 0.005 \\ 0.1 \end{bmatrix} \tag{5.37}$$

For $\mathbf{C}$ and $\mathbf{D}$, these matrices are the same in both continuous-time and discrete-time. Note that these matrices can be obtained using c2dm MATLAB® command.

5.3.4 Discrete Time MPC

We know that

$$\mathbf{x}(k+1) = \mathbf{A_d}\mathbf{x}(k) + \mathbf{B}_d\mathbf{u}(k) \tag{5.38}$$

Using a backward difference operator

$$\begin{aligned} \Delta \mathbf{x}(k+1) &= \mathbf{x}(k+1) - \mathbf{x}(k) \\ &= \mathbf{A_d}\mathbf{x}(k) + \mathbf{B}_d\mathbf{u}(k) - \mathbf{A_d}\mathbf{x}(k-1) - \mathbf{B}_d\mathbf{u}(k-1) \\ &= \mathbf{A_d}\Delta\mathbf{x}(k) + \mathbf{B}_d\Delta\mathbf{u}(k) \end{aligned} \tag{5.39}$$

Note that $\Delta\mathbf{x}(k) = \mathbf{x}(k) - \mathbf{x}(k-1)$ and $\Delta\mathbf{u}(k) = \mathbf{u}(k) - \mathbf{u}(k-1)$. Assuming $\mathbf{D}$ is a zero matrix, we can write the change in output as

$$\begin{aligned} \Delta\mathbf{y}(k+1) &= \mathbf{y}(k+1) - \mathbf{y}(k) \\ &= \mathbf{C}\mathbf{x}(k+1) - \mathbf{C}\mathbf{x}(k) \\ &= \mathbf{C}\Delta\mathbf{x}(k+1) \end{aligned} \tag{5.40}$$

Using Equations 5.39 and 5.40

$$\Delta\mathbf{y}(k+1) = \mathbf{C}(\mathbf{A_d}\Delta\mathbf{x}(k) + \mathbf{B_d}\Delta\mathbf{u}(k)) \tag{5.41}$$

Since $\Delta\mathbf{y}(k+1) = \mathbf{y}(k+1) - \mathbf{y}(k)$, we can rewrite above equation as

$$\mathbf{y}(k+1) = \mathbf{y}(k) + \mathbf{CA_d}\Delta\mathbf{x}(k) + \mathbf{CB_d}\Delta\mathbf{u}(k) \tag{5.42}$$

Using Equations 5.39 and 5.42

$$\underbrace{\begin{bmatrix} \Delta\mathbf{x}(k+1) \\ \mathbf{y}(k+1) \end{bmatrix}}_{=\mathbf{x}'(k+1)} = \underbrace{\begin{bmatrix} \mathbf{A_d} & \mathbf{0} \\ \mathbf{CA_d} & \mathbf{I} \end{bmatrix}}_{=\mathbf{A'_d}} \underbrace{\begin{bmatrix} \Delta\mathbf{x}(k) \\ \mathbf{y}(k) \end{bmatrix}}_{=\mathbf{x}'(k)} + \underbrace{\begin{bmatrix} \mathbf{B_d} \\ \mathbf{CB_d} \end{bmatrix}}_{=\mathbf{B'_d}} \begin{bmatrix} \Delta\mathbf{u}(k) \end{bmatrix} \tag{5.43}$$

where $\mathbf{0}$ and $\mathbf{I}$ are zero and identity matrices of appropriate dimensions. We can rewrite the output as

$$\mathbf{y}(k) = \underbrace{\begin{bmatrix} \mathbf{0} & \mathbf{I} \end{bmatrix}}_{=\mathbf{C}'} \underbrace{\begin{bmatrix} \Delta\mathbf{x}(k) \\ \mathbf{y}(k) \end{bmatrix}}_{=\mathbf{x}'(k)} \tag{5.44}$$

Finally, the state-space model is expressed as

$$\mathbf{x}'(k+1) = \mathbf{A'}_d\mathbf{x}'(k) + \mathbf{B'}_d\Delta\mathbf{u}(k) \tag{5.45}$$

$$\mathbf{y}(k) = \mathbf{C}'\mathbf{x}'(k) \tag{5.46}$$

Given the $\mathbf{x}'(k)$, we can find the change in the control sequence $\{\Delta\mathbf{u}(k), \Delta\mathbf{u}(k+1), \ldots, \Delta\mathbf{u}(k+N_p-1)\}$ for N_p prediction horizon. If no information is given, we can initialize $\mathbf{x}'(k)$ with sequence of zeros. Subsequently, the predicted state vector $\{\mathbf{x}'(k+1|k), \mathbf{x}'(k+2|k), \ldots, \mathbf{x}'(k+N_p|k)\}$ and predicted output of the plant $\{\mathbf{y}(k+1|k), \mathbf{y}(k+2|k), \ldots, \mathbf{y}(k+N_p|k)\}$ are computed as follows:

$$\mathbf{x}'(k+1|k) = \mathbf{A'}_d\mathbf{x}'(k) + \mathbf{B'}_d\Delta\mathbf{u}(k) \tag{5.47}$$

$$\begin{aligned} \mathbf{x}'(k+2|k) &= \mathbf{A'}_d\mathbf{x}'(k+1|k) + \mathbf{B'}_d\Delta\mathbf{u}(k+1) \\ &= \mathbf{A'}_d^2\mathbf{x}'(k) + \mathbf{A'}_d\mathbf{B'}_d\Delta\mathbf{u}(k) + \mathbf{B'}_d\Delta\mathbf{u}(k+1) \end{aligned} \tag{5.48}$$

Similarly,

$$\mathbf{x}'(k+N_p|k) = \mathbf{A'}_d^{N_p}\mathbf{x}'(k) + \mathbf{A'}_d^{N_p-1}\mathbf{B'}_d\Delta\mathbf{u}(k) + \ldots + \mathbf{B'}_d\Delta\mathbf{u}(k+N_p-1) \tag{5.49}$$

We can write the predicted state-vectors in matrix form using Equation 5.45 form as

$$
\begin{bmatrix} \mathbf{x}'(k+1|k) \\ \mathbf{x}'(k+2|k) \\ \vdots \\ \mathbf{x}'(k+N_p|k) \end{bmatrix} = \begin{bmatrix} \mathbf{A}'_d \\ \mathbf{A}'^2_d \\ \vdots \\ \mathbf{A}'^{N_p}_d \end{bmatrix} \mathbf{x}'(k) +
$$

$$
\begin{bmatrix} \mathbf{B}'_d & \mathbf{0} & \cdots & \mathbf{0} \\ \mathbf{A}'_d\mathbf{B}'_d & \mathbf{B}'_d & \cdots & \mathbf{0} \\ \vdots & \vdots & \vdots & \vdots \\ \mathbf{A}'^{N_p-1}_d\mathbf{B}'_d & \cdots & \cdots & \mathbf{B}'_d \end{bmatrix} \begin{bmatrix} \Delta\mathbf{u}(k) \\ \Delta\mathbf{u}(k+1) \\ \vdots \\ \Delta\mathbf{u}(k+N_p-1) \end{bmatrix} \tag{5.50}
$$

Now the predicted output can be written in matrix form using Equations 5.46 and 5.50 form as

$$
\begin{bmatrix} \mathbf{y}(k+1|k) \\ \mathbf{y}(k+2|k) \\ \vdots \\ \mathbf{y}(k+N_p|k) \end{bmatrix} = \begin{bmatrix} \mathbf{C}'\mathbf{x}'(k+1|k) \\ \mathbf{C}'\mathbf{x}'(k+2|k) \\ \vdots \\ \mathbf{C}'\mathbf{x}'(k+N_p|k) \end{bmatrix} \tag{5.51}
$$

This can be expanded using Equations 5.51 and 5.50 to

$$
\underbrace{\begin{bmatrix} \mathbf{y}(k+1|k) \\ \mathbf{y}(k+2|k) \\ \vdots \\ \mathbf{y}(k+N_p|k) \end{bmatrix}}_{=\mathbf{Y}} = \underbrace{\begin{bmatrix} \mathbf{C}'\mathbf{A}'_d \\ \mathbf{C}'\mathbf{A}'^2 \\ \vdots \\ \mathbf{C}'\mathbf{A}'^{N_p}_d \end{bmatrix}}_{=\mathbf{F}} \mathbf{x}'(k) +
$$

$$
\underbrace{\begin{bmatrix} \mathbf{C}'\mathbf{B}'_d & \mathbf{0} & \cdots & \mathbf{0} \\ \mathbf{C}'\mathbf{A}'_d\mathbf{B}'_d & \mathbf{C}'\mathbf{B}'_d & \cdots & \mathbf{0} \\ \vdots & \vdots & \vdots & \vdots \\ \mathbf{C}'\mathbf{A}'^{N_p-1}_d\mathbf{B}'_d & \cdots & \cdots & \mathbf{C}'\mathbf{B}'_d \end{bmatrix}}_{=\mathbf{H}} \underbrace{\begin{bmatrix} \Delta\mathbf{u}(k) \\ \Delta\mathbf{u}(k+1) \\ \vdots \\ \Delta\mathbf{u}(k+N_p-1) \end{bmatrix}}_{=\Delta\mathbf{U}} \tag{5.52}
$$

Finally, the above equation can be rewritten in condensed form as

$$
\mathbf{Y} = \mathbf{F}\mathbf{x}'(k) + \mathbf{H}\Delta\mathbf{U} \tag{5.53}
$$

5.3.5   Solution to Constrained MPC

If the desired (reference) signal is $\mathbf{s}$ for sampling instants $\{k+1, k+2, \ldots, k+N_p\}$, the optimization problem can be formulated as

$$
\begin{aligned}
&\min_{\Delta\mathbf{U}} \quad ||\mathbf{s} - \mathbf{Y}||^2 + ||\Delta\mathbf{U}||^2 \\
&\equiv \min_{\Delta\mathbf{U}} \quad ||\mathbf{s} - \mathbf{F}\mathbf{x}'(k) - \mathbf{H}\Delta\mathbf{U}||^2 + ||\Delta\mathbf{U}||^2
\end{aligned} \tag{5.54}
$$

The solution for this unconstrained problem can be given as follows. Taking the first-order derivative with respect to $\Delta \mathbf{U}$ and setting it equal to zero.

$$-2(\mathbf{s} - \mathbf{Fx}'(k) - \mathbf{H}\Delta \mathbf{U})^{\mathrm{T}}\mathbf{H} + 2\Delta \mathbf{U}^{\mathrm{T}} = \mathbf{0} \tag{5.55}$$

This can be rewritten as

$$\Delta \mathbf{U}^{\mathrm{T}} = \mathbf{s}^{\mathrm{T}}\mathbf{H} - \mathbf{x}'(k)^{\mathrm{T}}\mathbf{F}^{\mathrm{T}}\mathbf{H} - \Delta \mathbf{U}^{\mathrm{T}}\mathbf{H}^{\mathrm{T}}\mathbf{H} \tag{5.56}$$

We can recast it as

$$\Delta \mathbf{U}^{\mathrm{T}}(\mathbf{I} + \mathbf{H}^{\mathrm{T}}\mathbf{H}) = (\mathbf{s}^{\mathrm{T}} - \mathbf{x}'(k)^{\mathrm{T}}\mathbf{F}^{\mathrm{T}})\mathbf{H} \tag{5.57}$$

Taking transpose $(.)^{\mathrm{T}}$ both sides

$$(\mathbf{I} + \mathbf{H}^{\mathrm{T}}\mathbf{H})\Delta \mathbf{U} = \mathbf{H}^{\mathrm{T}}(\mathbf{s} - \mathbf{Fx}'(k)) \tag{5.58}$$

Finally, the solution to unconstrained problem is given by

$$\Delta \mathbf{U} = (\mathbf{I} + \mathbf{H}^{\mathrm{T}}\mathbf{H})^{-1}\mathbf{H}^{\mathrm{T}}(\mathbf{s} - \mathbf{Fx}'(k)) \tag{5.59}$$

Note that $(\mathbf{I} + \mathbf{H}^{\mathrm{T}}\mathbf{H})$ is invertible and is positive definite. The second-order derivative is equal to $(\mathbf{I} + \mathbf{H}^{\mathrm{T}}\mathbf{H}) > 0$. Hence, this ensures that the solution in Equation 5.59 indeed minimizes the objective function. Similarly, if the objective function is $(\mathbf{s} - \mathbf{Y})^{\mathrm{T}}\mathbf{W}_1(\mathbf{s} - \mathbf{Y}) + \Delta \mathbf{U}^{\mathrm{T}}\mathbf{W}_2\Delta \mathbf{U}$, the solution is given by

$$\Delta \mathbf{U} = (\mathbf{W}_2 + \mathbf{H}^{\mathrm{T}}\mathbf{W}_1\mathbf{H})^{-1}\mathbf{H}^{\mathrm{T}}\mathbf{W}_1(\mathbf{s} - \mathbf{Fx}'(k)) \tag{5.60}$$

where $\mathbf{W}_1$ and $\mathbf{W}_2$ are real symmetric positive definite matrices. We can get Equation 5.59 by assuming $\mathbf{W}_1 = \mathbf{W}_2 = \mathbf{I}$.

5.3.6 Example of Unconstrained MPC

Consider a discrete state-space model with $\mathbf{A}_d = \begin{bmatrix} 0.9752 & -0.2970 \\ 0.0990 & 0.9851 \end{bmatrix}$, $\mathbf{B}_d = \begin{bmatrix} 0.099 \\ 0.005 \end{bmatrix}$ and $\mathbf{C} = \begin{bmatrix} 0 & 10 \end{bmatrix}$. Apply unconstrained MPC for $N_p = 3$.

Solution:

$$\mathbf{A}'_d = \begin{bmatrix} \mathbf{A}_d & \mathbf{0} \\ \mathbf{CA_d} & \mathbf{I} \end{bmatrix} = \begin{bmatrix} 0.9752 & -0.2970 & 0 \\ 0.0990 & 0.9851 & 0 \\ 0.9900 & 9.8510 & 1 \end{bmatrix} \tag{5.61}$$

$$\mathbf{B}'_d = \begin{bmatrix} \mathbf{B}_d \\ \mathbf{CB}_d \end{bmatrix} = \begin{bmatrix} 0.099 \\ 0.005 \\ 0.050 \end{bmatrix} \tag{5.62}$$

and

$$\mathbf{C}' = \begin{bmatrix} \mathbf{0} & \mathbf{I} \end{bmatrix} = \begin{bmatrix} 0 & 0 & 1 \end{bmatrix} \tag{5.63}$$

$$F = \begin{bmatrix} C'A'_d \\ C'A'^2 \\ \vdots \\ C'A'^{N_p}_d \end{bmatrix} = \begin{bmatrix} 0.99 & 9.8510 & 1 \\ 2.9307 & 19.2610 & 1 \\ 5.7548 & 27.9545 & 1 \end{bmatrix} \tag{5.64}$$

$$H = \begin{bmatrix} C'B'_d & 0 & \cdots & 0 \\ C'A'_d B'_d & C'B'_d & \cdots & 0 \\ \vdots & \vdots & \vdots & \vdots \\ C'A'^{N_p-1}_d B'_d & \cdots & \cdots & C'B'_d \end{bmatrix} = \begin{bmatrix} 0.0497 & 0 & 0 \\ 0.1970 & 0.0497 & 0 \\ 0.4361 & 0.1970 & 0.0497 \end{bmatrix} \tag{5.65}$$

Assume $s = \begin{bmatrix} 1 \\ 1 \\ 1 \end{bmatrix}$ for first three sampling instants, that is, a unit step function. $W_1 = I_3$ and $W_2 = 0.01I_3$. There is no information about state vector and output. We can initialize with zero as $x'(k) = \begin{bmatrix} 0 \\ 0 \\ 0 \end{bmatrix}$. By substituting all the matrices, we get

$$\Delta U = (W_2 + H^T W_1 H)^{-1} H^T W_1 (s - Fx'(k))$$

$$\Delta U = \begin{bmatrix} \Delta u(k) \\ \Delta u(k+1) \\ \Delta u(k+2) \end{bmatrix} = \begin{bmatrix} 3.5872 \\ -1.7110 \\ -0.9060 \end{bmatrix} \tag{5.66}$$

Control output

$$u(k) = u(k-1) + \Delta u(k) = 0 + 3.5872 = 3.5872 \tag{5.67}$$

$$u(k+1) = u(k) + \Delta u(k+1) = 3.5872 - 1.7110 = 1.8763 \tag{5.68}$$

$$u(k+2) = u(k+1) + \Delta u(k+2) = 1.8763 - 0.9060 = 0.9702 \tag{5.69}$$

The output of plant

$$Y = Fx'(k) + H\Delta U = \begin{bmatrix} y(k+1|k) \\ y(k+2|k) \\ y(k+3|k) \end{bmatrix} = \begin{bmatrix} 0.1783 \\ 0.6216 \\ 1.1823 \end{bmatrix} \tag{5.70}$$

5.3.7 Constrained Rate of Change of Control Input

The rate of change of control input, $\Delta u(k)$, control input, $u(k)$, and output, Y, can be constrained based on prior knowledge for better performance. It may be noted that the change in time is equal to $(k+1) - k = 1$. For kth sampling instant, the rate of change of control input can be constrained between its minimum and maximum values $\Delta\mathbf{u}(k)^{\min} \leq \Delta\mathbf{u}(k) \leq \Delta\mathbf{u}(k)^{\max}$. This can be expressed in matrix form as

$$\begin{bmatrix} -\mathbf{I} \\ \mathbf{I} \end{bmatrix} \Delta\mathbf{u}(k) \leq \begin{bmatrix} -\Delta\mathbf{u}(k)^{\min} \\ \Delta\mathbf{u}(k)^{\max} \end{bmatrix} \tag{5.71}$$

For all sampling instants, we can write the above expression as

$$\begin{bmatrix} -\mathbf{I} & \mathbf{0} & \cdots & \mathbf{0} \\ \mathbf{I} & \mathbf{0} & \cdots & \mathbf{0} \\ \mathbf{0} & -\mathbf{I} & \cdots & \mathbf{0} \\ \mathbf{0} & \mathbf{I} & \cdots & \mathbf{0} \\ \vdots & \vdots & \vdots & \vdots \\ \mathbf{0} & \mathbf{0} & \cdots & -\mathbf{I} \\ \mathbf{0} & \mathbf{0} & \cdots & \mathbf{I} \end{bmatrix} \underbrace{\begin{bmatrix} \Delta\mathbf{u}(k) \\ \Delta\mathbf{u}(k+1) \\ \vdots \\ \Delta\mathbf{u}(k+N_p-1) \end{bmatrix}}_{=\Delta\mathbf{U}} \leq \begin{bmatrix} -\Delta\mathbf{u}^{\min} \\ \Delta\mathbf{u}^{\max} \\ -\Delta\mathbf{u}^{\min} \\ \Delta\mathbf{u}^{\max} \\ \vdots \\ -\Delta\mathbf{u}^{\min} \\ \Delta\mathbf{u}^{\max} \end{bmatrix} \tag{5.72}$$

5.3.8 Constrained Control Input

Similarly, the constraint on the control input is given as $\mathbf{u}(k)^{\min} \leq \mathbf{u}(k) \leq \mathbf{u}(k)^{\max}$. This can be expressed in matrix form as

$$\begin{bmatrix} -\mathbf{u}(k) \\ \mathbf{u}(k) \end{bmatrix} \leq \begin{bmatrix} -\mathbf{u}(k)^{\min} \\ \mathbf{u}(k)^{\max} \end{bmatrix} \tag{5.73}$$

We know that $\Delta\mathbf{u}(k) = \mathbf{u}(k) - \mathbf{u}(k-1)$, that is,

$$\mathbf{u}(k) = \Delta\mathbf{u}(k) + \mathbf{u}(k-1) \tag{5.74}$$

Using Equations 5.73 and 5.74,

$$\begin{bmatrix} -\Delta\mathbf{u}(k) - \mathbf{u}(k-1) \\ \Delta\mathbf{u}(k) + \mathbf{u}(k-1) \end{bmatrix} \leq \begin{bmatrix} -\mathbf{u}(k)^{\min} \\ \mathbf{u}(k)^{\max} \end{bmatrix} \tag{5.75}$$

Therefore, we can write the constraint finally as

$$\begin{bmatrix} -1 \\ 1 \end{bmatrix} \Delta\mathbf{u}(k) \leq \begin{bmatrix} -\mathbf{u}(k)^{\min} + \mathbf{u}(k-1) \\ \mathbf{u}(k)^{\max} - \mathbf{u}(k-1) \end{bmatrix} \tag{5.76}$$

Similarly, this can be carried out for $\{k+1, k+2, \ldots, k+N_p-1\}$ and concatenated in Equation 5.76.

5.3.9 Constrained on Output of Plant

We can impose constraint $\mathbf{Y}^{\min} \leq \mathbf{Y} \leq \mathbf{Y}^{\max}$. That is ,

$$\begin{bmatrix} -\mathbf{Y} \\ \mathbf{Y} \end{bmatrix} \leq \begin{bmatrix} -\mathbf{Y}^{\min} \\ \mathbf{Y}^{\max} \end{bmatrix} \tag{5.77}$$

We know that $\mathbf{Y} = \mathbf{F}\mathbf{x}'(k) + \mathbf{H}\Delta\mathbf{U}$. Therefore, we can rewrite

$$\begin{bmatrix} -\mathbf{H} \\ \mathbf{H} \end{bmatrix} \Delta\mathbf{U} \leq \begin{bmatrix} -\mathbf{Y}^{\min} + \mathbf{F}\mathbf{x}'(k) \\ \mathbf{Y}^{\max} - \mathbf{F}\mathbf{x}'(k) \end{bmatrix} \tag{5.78}$$

Example: Repeat the previous unconstrained problem with constraint imposed on the control input $-0.3 \leq u(k) \leq 0.5$.

Solution: We predict for $\{k+1, k+2, k+3\}$ with $N_p = 3$. Let the initial $\mathbf{x}'(k)$ be $\begin{bmatrix} 0 & 0 & 0 \end{bmatrix}^{\mathrm{T}}$

The output of plant

$$\mathbf{Y} = \mathbf{F}\mathbf{x}'(k) + \mathbf{H}\Delta\mathbf{U}$$

$$= \begin{bmatrix} 0.99 & 9.8509 & 1 \\ 2.9307 & 19.2610 & 1 \\ 5.7548 & 27.9545 & 1 \end{bmatrix} \begin{bmatrix} 0 \\ 0 \\ 0 \end{bmatrix} + \begin{bmatrix} 0.0497 & 0 & 0 \\ 0.1970 & 0.0497 & 0 \\ 0.4361 & 0.1970 & 0.0497 \end{bmatrix} \begin{bmatrix} \Delta u_1 \\ \Delta u_2 \\ \Delta u_3 \end{bmatrix} \tag{5.79}$$

$$= \begin{bmatrix} 0.0497\Delta u_1 \\ 0.197\Delta u_1 + 0.0497\Delta u_2 \\ 0.4361\Delta u_1 + 0.197\Delta u_2 + 0.0497\Delta u_3 \end{bmatrix}$$

Let $\mathbf{s}$ be $\begin{bmatrix} 1 & 1 & 1 \end{bmatrix}^{\mathrm{T}}$ for first three sampling instants, that is, a unit step function. $\mathbf{W}_1 = \mathbf{I}_3$ and $\mathbf{W}_2 = 0.01\mathbf{I}_3$. The objective function can be expressed as

$$0.5(\mathbf{s} - \mathbf{Y})^{\mathrm{T}}\mathbf{W}_1(\mathbf{s} - \mathbf{Y}) + 0.5\Delta\mathbf{U}^{\mathrm{T}}\mathbf{W}_2\Delta\mathbf{U} \tag{5.80}$$

This can be simplified to

$$0.5[(1 - 0.0497\Delta u_1)^2 + (1 - 0.197\Delta u_1 - 0.0497\Delta u_2)^2$$
$$+ (1 - 0.4361\Delta u_1 - 0.197\Delta u_2 - 0.0497\Delta u_3)^2] + 0.5 \times 0.01(\Delta u_1^2 + \Delta u_2^2 + \Delta u_3^2) \tag{5.81}$$

The factor 0.5 is used for simplifying the calculation without changing the minima. Also, the constants can be omitted in Equation 5.81 without changing the minima. This is a quadratic objective function which can be solved using, say, MATLAB® inbuilt function quadprog($\mathbf{P}, \mathbf{q}, \mathbf{C}_1, \mathbf{c}_2$). The quadratic optimization problem must be represented as

$$\min_{\Delta\mathbf{U}} \frac{1}{2}\Delta\mathbf{U}^{\mathrm{T}}\mathbf{P}\,\Delta\mathbf{U} + \mathbf{q}^{\mathrm{T}}\Delta\mathbf{U} \text{ such that } \mathbf{C}_1\Delta\mathbf{U} \leq \mathbf{c}_2 \tag{5.82}$$

Notably, the following matrix $\mathbf{P}$ will be same for all k.

$$\begin{bmatrix} \Delta u_1 & \Delta u_2 & \Delta u_3 \end{bmatrix} \underbrace{\begin{bmatrix} 0.2415 & 0.0957 & 0.0217 \\ 0.0957 & 0.0513 & 0.0098 \\ 0.0217 & 0.0098 & 0.0125 \end{bmatrix}}_{=\mathbf{P}} \begin{bmatrix} \Delta u_1 \\ \Delta u_2 \\ \Delta u_3 \end{bmatrix} \tag{5.83}$$

We use the following for writing the matrix $\mathbf{P}$:

- $0.5 \times (0.0497^2 + 0.197^2 + 0.4361^2 + 0.01)\Delta u_1^2 = 0.5 \times 0.2415\Delta u_1^2$

- $0.5 \times (0.0497^2 + 0.197^2 + 0.01)\Delta u_2^2 = 0.5 \times 0.0513\Delta u_2^2$

- $0.5 \times (0.0497^2 + 0.01)\Delta u_3^2 = 0.5 \times 0.0125\Delta u_3^2$

- $0.5 \times 2 \times (0.197 \times 0.0497 + 0.4361 \times 0.197)\Delta u_1\Delta u_2 = 0.5 \times 2 \times 0.0957\Delta u_1\Delta u_2$

- $0.5 \times 2 \times (0.197 \times 0.0497)\Delta u_2\Delta u_3 = 0.5 \times 2 \times 0.0098\Delta u_2\Delta u_3$

- $0.5 \times 2 \times (0.4361 \times 0.0497)\Delta u_1\Delta u_3 = 0.5 \times 2 \times 0.0217\Delta u_1\Delta u_3$

In each term related to $\Delta u_1\Delta u_2$, $\Delta u_2\Delta u_3$, and $\Delta u_1\Delta u_3$, there is a factor 2. That is why 0.0957, 0.0098, and 0.0217 appear twice in symmetric matrix $\mathbf{P}$. Now, the matrix $\mathbf{q}$ is written as

$$
0.5 \underbrace{\begin{bmatrix} -2 \times 0.0497 - 2 \times 0.197 - 2 \times 0.4361 \\ -2 \times 0.0497 - 2 \times 0.197 \\ -2 \times 0.0497 \end{bmatrix}}_{=\mathbf{q}}^{\mathrm{T}} \begin{bmatrix} \Delta u_1 \\ \Delta u_2 \\ \Delta u_3 \end{bmatrix} \Rightarrow \underbrace{\begin{bmatrix} -0.6828 \\ -0.2467 \\ -0.0497 \end{bmatrix}}_{=\mathbf{q}}^{\mathrm{T}} \tag{5.84}
$$

Note that $u(k-1) = 0$ in the following constraint

$$
\underbrace{\begin{bmatrix} -1 & 0 & 0 \\ -1 & -1 & 0 \\ -1 & -1 & -1 \\ 1 & 0 & 0 \\ 1 & 1 & 0 \\ 1 & 1 & 1 \end{bmatrix}}_{=\mathbf{C}_1} \begin{bmatrix} \Delta u(k) \\ \Delta u(k+1) \\ \Delta u(k+2) \end{bmatrix} \leq \underbrace{\begin{bmatrix} -(-0.3) + u(k-1) \\ -(-0.3) + u(k-1) \\ -(-0.3) + u(k-1) \\ 0.5 - u(k-1) \\ 0.5 - u(k-1) \\ 0.5 - u(k-1) \end{bmatrix}}_{=\mathbf{c}_2} \tag{5.85}
$$

The change in control input can be obtained as

$$
\Delta \mathbf{U} = \mathrm{quadprog}(\mathbf{P}, \mathbf{q}, \mathbf{C}_1, \mathbf{c}_2)
$$

$$
\begin{bmatrix} \Delta u(k) \\ \Delta u(k+1) \\ \Delta u(k+2) \end{bmatrix} = \begin{bmatrix} 0.5 \\ -3.56 \times 10^{-10} \approx 0 \\ -4.82 \times 10^{-7} \approx 0 \end{bmatrix} \tag{5.86}
$$

The control input can be computed as

$$
\begin{aligned}
u(k) &= u(k-1) + \Delta u(k) = 0 + 0.5 = 0.5 \\
u(k+1) &= u(k) + \Delta u(k+1) = 0.5 - 3.56 \times 10^{-10} = 0.5 \\
u(k+2) &= u(k+1) + \Delta u(k+2) = 0.5 - 4.82 \times 10^{-7} = 0.5
\end{aligned} \tag{5.87}
$$

The output of plant can be computed as

$$\mathbf{Y} = \mathbf{F}\mathbf{x}'(k) + \mathbf{H}\Delta\mathbf{U} = \begin{bmatrix} y(k+1|k) \\ y(k+2|k) \\ y(k+3|k) \end{bmatrix}$$

$$= \begin{bmatrix} 0.0497\Delta u_1 \\ 0.197\Delta u_1 + 0.0497\Delta u_2 \\ 0.4361\Delta u_1 + 0.197\Delta u_2 + 0.0497\Delta u_3 \end{bmatrix} = \begin{bmatrix} 0.0249 \\ 0.0985 \\ 0.2180 \end{bmatrix} \quad (5.88)$$

5.3.10 Remarks on MPC

- The output of the plant increases toward the desired output unity. It will attain unity after a few iterations. The fast convergence can be achieved with a proper choice of previous/current state vector and output in $\mathbf{x}'(k)$.

- We start with zero $\mathbf{x}'(k)$ if no prior information is available. In that scenario, it takes a larger number of iterations to attain the output of plant unity.

- Roughly, the control input $u(k)$ is maximum positive value 0.5 in $-0.3 \le u(k) \le 0.5$ for ramping up the plant output to unity.

- Similarly, $u(k)$ becomes negative if the output of the plant crosses unity and there is a need to decrease the output of the plant in order to follow the unit step.

- This is also related to the rate of change of control input, $\Delta u(k)$.

- Notably, we consider a linear constraints $(\mathbf{C}_1\Delta\mathbf{U} \le \mathbf{c}_2)$. A non-linear constraint can also be considered.

5.3.11 Optimization in MPC Using quadprog

quadprog function in MATLAB® uses the interior point algorithm. If $\mathbf{P}$ is positive definite matrix, the objective function of quadprog becomes a convex function. The positive definiteness is ensured by checking if all the eigenvalues of $\mathbf{P}$ are greater than zero. The quadratic optimization problem is given by

$$\min_{\mathbf{x}} \frac{1}{2}\mathbf{x}^{\mathrm{T}}\mathbf{P}\mathbf{x} + \mathbf{c}^{\mathrm{T}}\mathbf{x}$$
$$\text{such that } \mathbf{A}\mathbf{x} = \mathbf{b} \quad (5.89)$$
$$\mathbf{x} \ge 0$$

Note that, we can convert an equality $\mathbf{A_1x} = \mathbf{b_1}$ and an inequality constraints $\mathbf{A_2x} \leq \mathbf{b_2}$ into the above form $\mathbf{Ax} = \mathbf{b}$ as follows:

$$\underbrace{\begin{bmatrix} \mathbf{A}_1 & \mathbf{0} \\ \mathbf{A}_2 & \mathbf{I} \end{bmatrix}}_{\mathbf{A}} \begin{bmatrix} \mathbf{x} \\ \mathbf{sl} \end{bmatrix} = \underbrace{\begin{bmatrix} \mathbf{b}_1 \\ \mathbf{b}_2 \end{bmatrix}}_{\mathbf{b}} \tag{5.90}$$

where $\mathbf{sl}$ is a slack variable, $\mathbf{sl} \geq 0$. Similarly, the box constraint on $\mathbf{x}^{min} \leq \mathbf{x} \leq \mathbf{x}^{max}$ can be made positive like $\mathbf{x} \geq 0$ as follows:

$$\mathbf{x}^{max} - \mathbf{x} \geq 0$$
$$\mathbf{x} - \mathbf{x}^{min} \geq 0 \tag{5.91}$$

Logarithmic barrier function: In order to ensure that feasible set of non-negative variable $\mathbf{x}$ does not cross the boundary, we impose the penalty if $\mathbf{x}$ crosses the boundary $(\mathbf{x} < 0)$ because we know that if $\mathbf{x} \to 0$, $-\log(\mathbf{x}) \to \infty$. The objective function becomes a very large value at the boundary. Therefore, the barrier function introduces a barrier on crossing the boundary. The quadratic problem with barrier function for $\mathbf{x} \in \mathbb{R}^n$ is

$$\min_{\mathbf{x}} \frac{1}{2}\mathbf{x}^\mathsf{T}\mathbf{P}\mathbf{x} + \mathbf{c}^\mathsf{T}\mathbf{x} - \mu \sum_{i=1}^{n} \log x_i \tag{5.92}$$

such that $\mathbf{Ax} = \mathbf{b}$

The Lagrange function for the problem is

$$\mathcal{L}_\mu(\mathbf{x}, \boldsymbol{\lambda}) = \frac{1}{2}\mathbf{x}^\mathsf{T}\mathbf{P}\mathbf{x} + \mathbf{c}^\mathsf{T}\mathbf{x} - \boldsymbol{\lambda}^T(\mathbf{Ax} - \mathbf{b}) - \mu \sum_{i=1}^{n} \log x_i \tag{5.93}$$

Karush-Kuhn-Tucker (KKT) conditions for Lagrange function is given as

$$\frac{\partial \mathcal{L}_\mu}{\partial \mathbf{x}} = \mathbf{Px} + \mathbf{c} - \mathbf{A}^\mathsf{T}\boldsymbol{\lambda} - \mu \mathbf{X}^{-1}\mathbf{e} = 0$$
$$\frac{\partial \mathcal{L}_\mu}{\partial \boldsymbol{\lambda}} = \mathbf{Ax} - \mathbf{b} = 0 \tag{5.94}$$

where $\mathbf{X}^{-1} = \text{diag}\{x_1^{-1}, x_2^{-1}, \ldots, x_n^{-1}\}$ and $\mathbf{e}$ is the column of vector of all 1s. Denote $\mathbf{s} = \mu \mathbf{X}^{-1}\mathbf{e} \Rightarrow x_i s_i = \mu \ \forall \ i$. The KKT conditions can be rewritten as

$$\mathbf{A}^\mathsf{T}\boldsymbol{\lambda} + \mathbf{s} - \mathbf{Px} = \mathbf{c}$$
$$\mathbf{Ax} = \mathbf{b} \tag{5.95}$$
$$x_i s_i = \mu \ \forall \ i$$

For finding the Jacobian, compute the derivative of each KKT condition (row wise) with respect to $\mathbf{x}$, $\boldsymbol{\lambda}$, and $\mathbf{s}$, respectively (column wise). For fixed

μ, solve the above system of equations in Equation 5.95 $F_\mu(\mathbf{x}, \boldsymbol{\lambda}, \mathbf{s}) = 0$ using Newton's method of optimization. The steps are summarized below:

Step 1: Given an initial values of $(\mathbf{x}^0, \boldsymbol{\lambda}^0, \mathbf{s}^0)$, where $(\mathbf{x}^0, \mathbf{s}^0) > 0$

Step k: Solve the system of equations for kth iteration

$$\mathbf{J}_{F_\mu}(\mathbf{x}^k, \boldsymbol{\lambda}^k, \mathbf{s}^k)\Delta\mathbf{u} = -F_\mu(\mathbf{x}^k, \boldsymbol{\lambda}^k, \mathbf{s}^k) \qquad (5.96)$$

We can expand this as

$$\begin{bmatrix} -\mathbf{P} & \mathbf{A}^T & \mathbf{I} \\ \mathbf{A} & 0 & 0 \\ \mathbf{S} & 0 & \mathbf{X} \end{bmatrix} \begin{bmatrix} \Delta x^k \\ \Delta \lambda^k \\ \Delta s \end{bmatrix} = \begin{bmatrix} \mathbf{c} - \mathbf{A}^T\boldsymbol{\lambda} - \mathbf{s} + \mathbf{Px} \\ \mathbf{b} - \mathbf{Ax} \\ \mu\mathbf{e} - \mathbf{Xse} \end{bmatrix} \qquad (5.97)$$

where $\mathbf{J}_{F_\mu}$ is the Jacobian matrix. $\Delta\mathbf{u}$ is the search direction. For step-length α_k, we can compute as

$$x^{k+1} = x^k + \alpha^k \Delta x^k$$
$$\lambda^{k+1} = \lambda^k + \alpha^k \Delta \lambda^k \qquad (5.98)$$
$$s^{k+1} = s^k + \alpha^k \Delta s^k$$

We compute the values at $k + 1$ iteration using previous kth iteration, step-length and search direction.

5.4   Summary

Energy harvesting is needed for extracting energy from external sources for resource-constrained IoT devices. We discussed two relay protocols, in particular, TSR and PSR protocols. Further, a hybrid relay protocol that takes advantage of both TSR and PSR protocols can be explored. Subsequently, the model predictive control for coupling physical and cyber worlds is also presented. This is needed for control and optimization purposes. Finally, hand-solved numerical examples are discussed to test our understanding.

5.5   Exercises

1. What is the impact on received signal at the relay node if the path loss exponent increases?

2. Which one is a better metric between SNR and SINR?

3. What is the impact of fraction amount of time for energy harvesting by

the relay node (a_E) and distance between the source and relay (d_{SR}) on SNR at destination for TSR protocol.

4. What is the impact of the fraction of power that relay harvests from the received signal (b_E) and distance between the source and relay (d_{SR}) on SNR at destination for PSR protocol.

5. In TSR protocol, if $a_E = 0.7$, $\kappa = 0.5$, $P_s = 100$ Joules/sec, one interfering source with power $P_i = 50$ Joules/sec, $\sigma_R^2 = \sigma_D^2 = 1$, $\alpha = 3$, $d_{SR} = 2$ m, $d_{SD} = 3$ m, $d_{RD} = 2$ m, what is the average SNR at destination in dB for 10^6 trials?

6. In PSR protocol, if $b_E = 0.7$, $\kappa = 0.5$, $P_s = 100$ Joules/sec, one interfering source with power $P_i = 50$ Joules/sec, $\sigma_R^2 = \sigma_D^2 = 1$, $\alpha = 3$, $d_{SR} = 2$ m, $d_{SD} = 3$ m, $d_{RD} = 2$ m, what is the average SNR at destination in dB for 10^6 trials?

7. What is the state-space model? What is its role in MPC?

8. What is the role of a feedback system in MPC?

9. Which method is more accurate between Taylor series approximation and inverse Laplace transform for converting a continuous state-space model to discrete state-space model?

10. Convert to discrete state space model from continuous state space model if $\mathbf{A}_c = \begin{bmatrix} 0 & 1 \\ -2 & -3 \end{bmatrix}$, $\mathbf{B}_c = \begin{bmatrix} 0 \\ 1 \end{bmatrix}$ and $\mathbf{C} = \begin{bmatrix} 1 & 0 \end{bmatrix}$ and $h = 0.1$.

11. Using unconstrained MPC, predict control input for $\{k+3, k+4, k+5\}$ and output sequence for $\{k+4, k+5, k+6\}$. Given $\mathbf{A}_d = \begin{bmatrix} 0.9752 & -0.2970 \\ 0.0990 & 0.9851 \end{bmatrix}$, $\mathbf{B}_d = \begin{bmatrix} 0.099 \\ 0.005 \end{bmatrix}$, $\mathbf{C} = \begin{bmatrix} 0 & 10 \end{bmatrix}$, $\begin{bmatrix} \Delta u(k) \\ \Delta u(k+1) \\ \Delta u(k+2) \end{bmatrix} = \begin{bmatrix} 3.5872 \\ -1.7110 \\ -0.9060 \end{bmatrix}$, $\Delta \mathbf{x}(k) = \begin{bmatrix} 0 \\ 0 \end{bmatrix}$, $y(k+3) = 1.1823$ and $u(k+2) = 0.9702$.

12. Apply the constrained MPC for $\{k+4, k+5, k+6\}$ assuming the previous state vector and output of the plant with constrained imposed on the control input $-0.3 \le u(k) \le 0.5$. Note that $y(k+3|k) = 0.2180$, $u(k+2) = 0.5$ and $\begin{bmatrix} \Delta u(k) \\ \Delta u(k+1) \\ \Delta u(k+2) \end{bmatrix} = \begin{bmatrix} 0.5 \\ 0 \\ 0 \end{bmatrix}$.

13. **Do It Yourself**: Explore energy efficiency in relay protocols and understand how it is useful for IoT networks.

14. **Do It Yourself**: Study nonlinear model predictive control and list the motivation for the same.

Chapter 6

Things Data Analytics

6.1 Introduction

With the advent of the World Wide Web (WWW) in a year around 1990, and subsequently, cheap and fast processors in a year around 2000, the number of mobile devices started increasing exponentially on the Internet. Now adays, every person in the world has on average four to five smart devices as per the report. This leads to 20 to 30 billion IoT devices connected to the Internet. These smart things produce a large volume of data, which needs to be processed to get some insights. There is a need to analyze the data and extract some meaningful patterns or statistics for decision-making. This motivates us to study the things data analytics techniques.

Let us first define the term learning. Learning is attainment of new knowledge through practice or experience. We become familiar with insights into a task in the process of learning. According to American computer scientist, Tom M. Mitchell, learning is defined as a system that learns from the experience and improves the performance for a given task. We use machine learning for automation purposes. This helps in taking intellectual decisions by the system. A hard-coded algorithm for each application does not make it general or automated.

6.2 Understanding the Buzz Words

Artificial Intelligence (AI) helps in taking automated intellectual decisions like a human. We can use artificial intelligence algorithms in IoT networks for making decisions from a huge volume of data. Also, getting deep insight from the data is not possible for a human. Machine learning (ML) algorithms are used to learn from past experiences and data. Deep learning (DL) system involves learning using multi-layer perceptrons and takes more intelligent decisions. The role of computing in IoT networks is illustrated in Figure 6.1.

In traditional machine learning, features are extracted manually. Deep learning requires high-level abstract features which are extracted

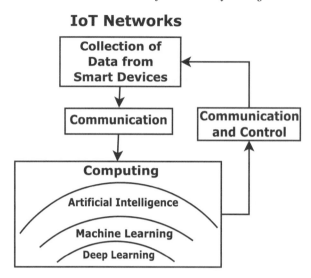

FIGURE 6.1: Artificial intelligence, machine learning, and deep learning

automatically using the data. The examples of features for face recognition in computer vision applications are the size of the nose, the distance between nose and lips, the number of ears, and the distance between them. The traditional machine learning techniques suffer from scalability problems, however, deep learning algorithms scale with the data. The applications of machine learning include analytics for smart environments (say, city, agriculture, health amongst others), social networks, natural language processing, e-commerce to name a few.

There are mainly four types of machine learning algorithms.

1. *Supervised Learning*: Training data includes labels or desired outputs. Example: classification and regression problems.

2. *Unsupervised Learning*: Training data does not include labels or desired outputs. Example: clustering problem.

3. *Semi-supervised Learning*: Training data includes a few labels or desired outputs. It is the combination of supervised and unsupervised learning.

4. *Reinforcement Learning*: Rewards from sequence of actions.

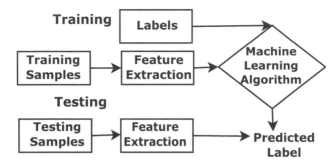

FIGURE 6.2: Supervised Learning

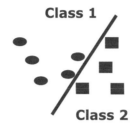

FIGURE 6.3: Classification in supervised learning

6.3 Supervised Learning

There are two types of data samples: Training and Testing. The training samples are used to extract features and train the machine learning algorithm. In fact, we optimize the weight parameters of the machine learning model in the training phase. Similarly, from the test samples, features are extracted and classified into a class using a trained machine learning algorithm. The machine learning model is used to predict the label for the given test data as shown in Figure 6.2. We use supervised learning for regression and classification tasks.

We categorize the test data among one of class in classification problem as shown in Figure 6.3. Predicting the dependent variable for the given test data is called a regression problem. In Figure 6.4, the dependent variable is Received Signal Strength Indicator (RSSI) and the independent variable is distance.

In supervised learning, the data (also called observations, measurements or samples) are labeled with classes. Given x samples for an output function $F(x)$, we use $(x, F(x))$ in supervised learning. We predict function $F(x)$ for new examples x, where discrete $F(x)$ is for classification problem and continuous $F(x)$ is for regression problem. The supervised learning has target labels. There are two types of supervised learning. First, the classification categorizes the samples into different classes. Figure 6.3 illustrates classification for two

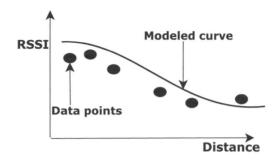

FIGURE 6.4: Regression in supervised learning

classes. Second, the regression predicts an expected dependent variable using interpolation and extrapolation as shown in Figure 6.4. The next section presents some widely used supervised learning techniques.

6.3.1 k-Nearest Neighbor

A supervised learning technique in which $k_n \in [1 \ n]$ is the number of nearest samples with respect to a test sample. Note that n is the total number of samples. Based on majority voting among k_n nearest neighbors, the sample is classified into the majority class. Let us understand it with an example.

Example: Perform kNN classification on the following raw dataset of a smart home as shown in Table 6.1. Determine the class for Temperature = 4 and Humidity = 8 with $k_n = 3$. Note that the dataset is just assumed for the sake of illustration.

TABLE 6.1: Raw dataset for kNN example

	Temperature	Humidity	Class
a	8	8	Warm
b	8	5	Warm
c	4	5	Cool
d	2	5	Cool
e	9	9	Warm

Solution: Denote the test sample with x and training samples with a, b, c and d. The Euclidean distance of the test sample with respect to the training sample is given as

$$\sqrt{\sum_{i=1}^{2}(\text{test sample} - \text{training sample})^2} \qquad (6.1)$$

The different distances are computed as follows:

$$D(x, a) = \sqrt{(4-8)^2 + (8-8)^2} = 4,$$
$$D(x, b) = \sqrt{(4-8)^2 + (8-5)^2} = 5,$$
$$D(x, c) = \sqrt{(4-4)^2 + (8-5)^2} = 3, \tag{6.2}$$
$$D(x, d) = \sqrt{(4-2)^2 + (8-5)^2} = 3.6 \text{ and}$$
$$D(x, e) = \sqrt{(4-9)^2 + (8-9)^2} = 5.1$$

Therefore, it can be observed that a, c, and d are $k_n = 3$ nearest neighbors of the test sample x. The majority of the neighbors fall in the cool class. Therefore, the given test sample belongs to the cool class.

6.3.2 Naive Bayes Classification

Let us discuss now Naive Bayes classification algorithm. We know from the probability theory that the probability of A when B is true

$$P(A|B) = \frac{P(A \cap B)}{P(B)} \tag{6.3}$$

The probability of B when A is true

$$P(B|A) = \frac{P(B \cap A)}{P(A)} \tag{6.4}$$

Therefore, we can write the following using Equations 6.3 and 6.4.

$$P(A|B) = \frac{P(B|A)P(A)}{P(B)} \tag{6.5}$$

We apply the Naive Bayes classification algorithm in the next example for illustration purposes.

Example: Consider the given raw dataset as shown in Table 6.2. Perform Naive Bayes classification algorithm and determine the posterior probability if the weather is windy. Note that the dataset is just assumed for the sake of illustration.

TABLE 6.2: Dataset of number of occurrence for Naive Bayes classification problem

Weather	No	Yes	Probability
Sunny	1	2	$\frac{3}{12}$
Rainy	0	4	$\frac{4}{12}$
Windy	2	3	$\frac{5}{12}$
Probability	$\frac{3}{12}$	$\frac{9}{12}$	

Solution: The probability is computed given the number of occurrences. This is shown in Table 6.2. From the Bayes' theorem,

$$P(\text{Yes}|\text{Windy}) = \frac{P(\text{Windy}|\text{Yes})P(\text{Yes})}{P(\text{Windy})}$$

$$= \frac{\frac{3}{9} \times \frac{9}{12}}{\frac{5}{12}} = 0.6 \tag{6.6}$$

6.3.3 Linear Regression

In regression, we predict the value of a continuous dependent variable given a new independent variable. In linear regression, the fitted or modeled curve is linear. Examples of regression include RSSI prediction at a given distance, heart-rate prediction, and productivity prediction amongst others. The regression takes a vector $x \in \mathbb{R}^n$ and predict scalar $y \in \mathbb{R}$. The predicted value is represented as $\hat{y} = w^\top x$, where w is a vector of weight parameters.

Regression problem: Apply linear regression, $y = a_l x + b_l$ for the following data of Table 6.3. Estimate the value of y when $x = 10$ using least square method. Here, x and y represent the day index and temperature of the corresponding day, respectively. Note that the dataset is just assumed for the sake of illustration.

TABLE 6.3: Raw dataset for regression problem

x = days	1	2	4	6	7
y = productivity	2	3	5	4	10

Solution: In this problem, we predict the value of y when $x = 8$ from the given dataset. Consider the following linear regression for n number of measurements:

$$y_i = a_l x_i + b_l \text{ for } i = 1 \text{ to } n \tag{6.7}$$

We first need the parameters a_l and b_l. In determining so, minimize the sum of square error and take the derivative with respect to b_l

$$\frac{\partial \text{ Error}}{\partial b} = \frac{\partial \sum_{i=1}^{n}(y_i - a_l x_i - b_l)^2}{\partial b} = 0 \tag{6.8}$$

This can be rewritten as

$$\sum_{i=1}^{n} y_i - a_l \sum_{i=1}^{n} x_i - nb_l = 0 \tag{6.9}$$

Therefore, the expression for b is expressed as

$$b_l = \frac{\sum_{i=1}^{n} y_i - a_l \sum_{i=1}^{n} x_i}{n} \tag{6.10}$$

Now, taking the derivative with respect to a

$$\frac{\partial \text{ Error}}{\partial a_l} = \frac{\partial \sum_{i=1}^{n}(y_i - a_l x_i - b_l)^2}{\partial a_l} = 0 \tag{6.11}$$

This can be rewritten as

$$\sum_{i=1}^{n} x_i y_i - a_l \sum_{i=1}^{n} x_i^2 - b_l \sum_{i=1}^{n} x_i = 0 \tag{6.12}$$

Substituting expression of b in the above expression, we get

$$\sum_{i=1}^{n} x_i y_i - a_l \sum_{i=1}^{n} x_i^2 - \frac{1}{n} \sum_{i=1}^{n} x_i \left(\sum_{i=1}^{n} y_i - a_l \sum_{i=1}^{n} x_i \right) \tag{6.13}$$

Finally the expression for a is

$$a_l = \frac{n \sum_{i=1}^{n} x_i y_i - \sum_{i=1}^{n} x_i \sum_{i=1}^{n} y_i}{n \sum_{i=1}^{n} x_i^2 - \left(\sum_{i=1}^{n} x_i \right)^2} \tag{6.14}$$

Now, we compute the parameters using Equations 6.14 and 6.10 for the given data

$$a_l = \frac{5 \times (2 + 6 + 20 + 24 + 70) - 20 \times 24}{5 \times 106 - (20)^2} = \frac{610 - 480}{130} = 1 \tag{6.15}$$

$$b_l = \frac{24 - 1 \times 20}{5} = 0.8 \tag{6.16}$$

where n is number of examples. Therefore, we can write

$$y = 1 \times x + 0.8 \tag{6.17}$$

using estimated parameters a and b. This gives $y = 8.8$ when $x = 8$.

Limitations of Linear Regression: A linear regression gives outcome any value that may be less than zero, greater than one, and between zero and one. On the other hand, the logistic regression gives output zero or one. If the output is greater than some threshold, say, 0.5, the logistic regression gives unity, otherwise zero.

6.3.4 Logistic Regression

Linear regression model represents the probability as

$$p(x) = w_1 x + w_0 \tag{6.18}$$

where w_1 and w_0 are the weights of a linear regression model. In logistic regression, the probability is represented as

$$p(x) = \frac{e^{w_1 x + w_0}}{1 + e^{w_1 x + w_0}} \tag{6.19}$$

TABLE 6.4: Raw values of glucose level for logistic regression problem. Here, 1 and 0 in result column, respectively, show disease and disease-free cases.

Glucose level	Result
18	0
16	0
32	1
27	1
40	1

such that we have a mapping of the probability of sigmoid between 0 and 1.

Notably, if the exponent tends to infinity, $p(x)$ tends to one as dividing numerator and denominator by infinity in limiting case gives $\frac{1}{0+1} = 1$. On the the other hand, if the exponent tends to zero, $p(x)$ tends to a half as $\frac{1}{1+1} = \frac{1}{2}$. Finally, if the exponent tends to minus infinity, $p(x)$ tends to zero as $\frac{0}{1+0} = 0$. Logistic regression is similar to linear regression, except that the output is mapped between zero to one by a sigmoid function. If we represents $\theta^\top x$ as $w_1 x + w_0$ in Equation 6.19, we can write the following by dividing the numerator and denominator by $e^{w_1 x + w_0}$.

$$p(y|x, \theta) = \sigma_f(\theta^\top x) = \frac{1}{1 + \exp(-\theta^\top x)} \tag{6.20}$$

where $(.)^\top$ and σ_f denote the transpose operation of matrix and sigmoid function, respectively. The sigmoid function has variants like tanh function instead of a logistic sigmoid. In that case, the range is $[-1, 1]$.

Example: The dataset of disease or disease-free for five patients is given in Table 6.4. Use logistic regression as the classifier. Assume the hypothesis for linear regression is $2 \times$ glucose level $- 56$. Note that the dataset is just assumed for the sake of illustration. Answer the following questions:

1. Determine the probability of having a disease who has glucose level 30.

2. At least how much glucose level ensures disease case with a probability of more than 98%?

Solution:

1. The hypothesis for logistic regression is

$$p = \frac{1}{1 + e^{-z}} \tag{6.21}$$

Now,

$$z = 2 \times \text{glucose level} - 64 \quad = 2 \times 30 - 56 = 4 \tag{6.22}$$

Hence,

$$P = \frac{1}{1 + e^{-4}} = 0.982 \tag{6.23}$$

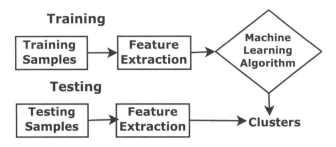

FIGURE 6.5: Unsupervised Learning

Therefore, a patient having glucose level 30 has 98.2% chance of having disease.

2. Given $P = 0.98$, we solve for z. Therefore, we have

$$0.98 = \frac{1}{1 + e^{-z}} \tag{6.24}$$

This gives $z = 3.89$. Putting the value of z in the given equation, we have

$$3.89 = 2 \times \text{glucose level} - 56 \tag{6.25}$$

This gives glucose level $= 29.95$. Therefore, a patient must have a glucose level of 29.95 for more than a 98% probability of having a disease.

6.4 Unsupervised Learning

We use unsupervised learning when labels of data are unknown. We know that the clustering is an example of unsupervised learning. Given data samples, we group the similar data or features. The flow-chart of unsupervised learning is shown in Figure 6.5. The number of clusters can be chosen based on heuristics like Elbow method or some criteria such as Akaike information criterion (AIC), Bayesian information criterion (BIC), or the Deviance information criterion (DIC). In unsupervised learning, the data samples or features are grouped into clusters as shown in Figure 6.6. Although we group the data into two clusters, however, multiple clusters can be formed depending on the datasets. Notably, there are no target labels to get classified. Clustering technique along with examples are presented in Clustering and Data Fusion chapter. Let us discuss widely used Principal Component Analysis.

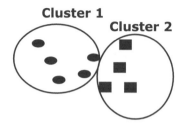

FIGURE 6.6: Clustering problem

TABLE 6.5: Smart agriculture data for PCA problem

x = **Soil Moisture**	2	1	0	−1
y = **Leaf Wetness**	4	3	1	0.5

6.4.1 Principal Component Analysis

Principal Component Analysis (PCA) is an unsupervised learning approach for dimensionality reduction technique of a large dataset. The original large dataset is transformed for dimensionality reduction and reduced dimensionality eliminates redundancy. This maximizes the variance along a few axes or dimensions. Before applying PCA, we make the data set having zero mean using the centering technique.

Problem: Find the first principal component of the following data of Table 6.5.

Solution: We determine the values as shown in Table 6.6 before we apply PCA . Therefore, we get

$$
\begin{aligned}
\text{Cov}(X, X) &= \frac{\sum_{i=1}^{n}(x_i - \hat{x})^2}{n - 1} \\
&= \frac{\sum A^2}{n - 1} \\
&= \frac{5}{3} = 1.67
\end{aligned} \tag{6.26}
$$

TABLE 6.6: Transformation of data for PCA problem

x	y	$A = (x_i - \hat{x})$	$B = (y_i - \hat{y})$	AB	A^2	B^2
2	4	1.5	1.875	2.8125	2.25	3.5156
1	3	0.5	0.875	0.4375	0.25	0.7656
0	1	−0.5	−1.125	0.5625	0.25	1.2656
−1	0.5	−1.5	−1.625	0.4925	2.25	2.6406

Similarly, we can write

$$\text{Cov}(Y,Y) = \frac{\sum_{i=1}^{n}(y_i - \hat{y})^2}{n-1}$$
$$= \frac{\sum B^2}{n-1} \tag{6.27}$$
$$= \frac{8.1875}{3} = 2.73$$

and finally

$$\text{Cov}(X,Y) = \text{Cov}(Y,X)$$
$$= \frac{\sum AB \text{ or } BA}{n-1} \tag{6.28}$$
$$= \frac{6.25}{3} = 2.08$$

Therefore, we can write the covariance matrix using computed values in Equations 6.26, 6.27, and 6.28 as

$$S = \begin{bmatrix} \text{Cov}(X,X) & \text{Cov}(X,Y) \\ \text{Cov}(Y,X) & \text{Cov}(Y,Y) \end{bmatrix} = \begin{bmatrix} 1.67 & 2.08 \\ 2.08 & 2.73 \end{bmatrix} \tag{6.29}$$

Now,

$$\left| S - \lambda_e I \right| = 0 \Rightarrow \left| \begin{bmatrix} 1.67 & 2.08 \\ 2.08 & 2.73 \end{bmatrix} - \lambda_e \begin{bmatrix} 1 & 0 \\ 0 & 1 \end{bmatrix} \right| = 0 \tag{6.30}$$

On solving, we get

$$\lambda_e^2 - 4.4\lambda_e + 0.23 = 0 \tag{6.31}$$

The eigenvalues, λ_e, are 4.35 and 0.051 by solving Equation 6.31. Considering the largest eigenvalue, we get the first principal component from the eigenvector direction. Therefore, we take $\lambda_e = 4.35$. We can write the following expression using Equation 6.30 for getting the eigenvector.

$$\begin{bmatrix} 1.67 - 4.35 & 2.08 \\ 2.08 & 2.73 - 4.35 \end{bmatrix} \begin{bmatrix} e_{11} \\ e_{21} \end{bmatrix} = 0 \tag{6.32}$$

From this, we get

$$-2.68e_{11} + 2.08e_{21} = 0 \tag{6.33}$$

that is,

$$\frac{e_{11}}{e_{21}} = \frac{2.08}{2.68} = 0.78 \tag{6.34}$$

and

$$2.08e_{11} - 1.62e_{21} = 0 \tag{6.35}$$

that is,

$$\frac{e_{11}}{e_{21}} = \frac{1.62}{2.08} = 0.78 \tag{6.36}$$

We get the eigenvector corresponding to eigenvalue 4.35 as

$$
\begin{bmatrix} e_{11} \\ e_{21} \end{bmatrix} = \begin{bmatrix} 0.61 \\ 0.79 \end{bmatrix} \tag{6.37}
$$

Note that $\frac{0.61}{0.79} = 0.77$, the ratio remains the same. In order to calculate these numbers we compute the normalized value as

$$
\frac{2.08}{\sqrt{2.08^2 + 2.68^2}} = \frac{1.62}{\sqrt{1.62^2 + 2.08^2}} = 0.61 \tag{6.38}
$$

and

$$
\frac{2.68}{\sqrt{2.08^2 + 2.68^2}} = \frac{2.08}{\sqrt{1.62^2 + 2.08^2}} = 0.79 \tag{6.39}
$$

Now, the 2D data is reduced to 1D in the direction of the principal component. Therefore, transforming the data into a new subspace as

$$
\begin{bmatrix} 0.61 & 0.79 \end{bmatrix} \begin{bmatrix} 1.5 & 0.5 & -0.5 & -1.5 \\ 1.875 & 0.875 & -1.125 & -1.625 \end{bmatrix}
$$
$$
= \begin{bmatrix} 2.4 & 1 & -1.2 & -2.2 \end{bmatrix} \tag{6.40}
$$

In this example, we reduce from the original two dimensions data to one dimension by PCA.

6.5   Bias and Variance Tradeoff

In under-fitting, the data is modeled by an order lower than the actual order of the model. This is referred to as the high bias condition. The error is high for the training and testing phases. On the other hand, in over-fitting, the data is modeled by an order higher than the actual order of the model. This is also called high variance condition. In this scenario, the model memorizes the training data. If we apply unseen test data to this over-fitted model, the error is high. This is because the learning of the model is not proper for unseen data. This is illustrated in Figure 6.7. Therefore, we need to choose the order of the model properly. This is called the optimal capacity. There is a trade-off between under-fitting and over-fitting.

Example of Underfitting and Overfitting: Let us consider the dataset as shown in Table 6.7. This is also plotted for visualization purposes in Figure 6.8. It is evident from the plot that the data follows a quadratic model.

The different order curves are modeled using cftool toolbox of MATLAB®. This can be also carried out using least square method as discussed in this chapter. The RMSE is 1.724, 0.3696, 0.3227 for first, second, and third order

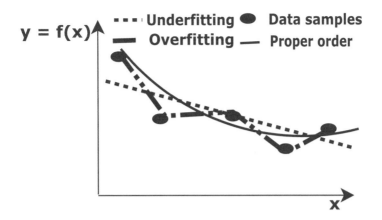

FIGURE 6.7: Data samples and different order curves

TABLE 6.7: Dataset for Underfitting and Overfitting

x	0	1	2	3	4
data	0	1	4.8	9.4	15.5

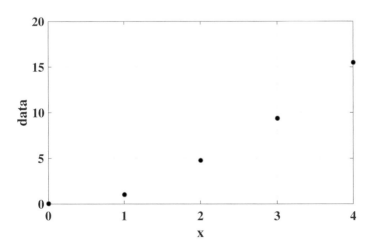

FIGURE 6.8: Scatter diagram of data

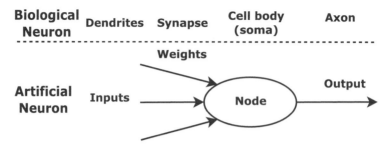

FIGURE 6.9: Terminologies in biological and artificial neurons

models, respectively. The first, second and third order models, respectively, are

$$\text{data} = 3.94x - 1.74 \tag{6.41}$$

$$\text{data} = 0.7857x^2 + 0.7971x - 0.1686 \tag{6.42}$$

and

$$\text{data} = -0.1083x^3 + 1.436x^2 - 0.1345x - 0.03857 \tag{6.43}$$

Note that the RMSE is minimum for the third order, however, the data follows the second-order model.

6.6   Artificial Neural Networks

A deep neural network is similar to the biological neural network. Dendrites, synapse, cell body (or soma), and axon of a biological neuron act like input, weight, node, and output of an artificial neuron, respectively, as shown in Figure 6.9. Dendrites are the thin fiber that carries information from other neurons. The information transmitted between the dendrites and axons is carried out by synapse. This information is then passed to the cell body for processing. Axon carries impulses from the cell body to other cells. Finally, we get the output if the sum of weighted information is greater than a threshold.

6.6.1   Perceptron Model

A single artificial neuron is called perceptron for computation purpose. Let x_i be the ith input with the corresponding weight w_i as shown in Figure 6.10. The output is unity if the weighted sum of the input is greater than zero. That is,

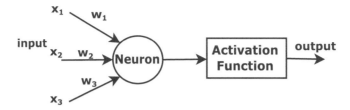

FIGURE 6.10: Perceptron model

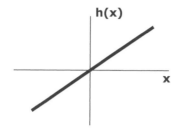

FIGURE 6.11: Linear activation function

$$y = 1 \text{ if } \sum_{i=1}^{n} w_i x_i > 0$$

$$= 0 \text{ otherwise} \tag{6.44}$$

Example: If $x_1 = 1$, $x_2 = 1$, $x_3 = 0$, $w_1 = 4$, $w_2 = 3$, and $w_3 = 5$, the weighted sum of inputs is 7 and hence the output is 1. On the other hand, if $x_1 = 1$, $x_2 = 0$, $x_3 = -1$, $w_1 = 4$, $w_2 = 3$, and $w_3 = 5$, the weighted sum of inputs is -1 and hence the output is 0.

6.6.2 Activation Function

Activation function decides whether a neuron should be activated or not. The function helps the network to utilize useful information and suppress irrelevant information. When the neurons are sufficiently activated, the output is one, otherwise zero. The activation function with a bounded range is called the squashing function. We usually consider a non-linear function for learning complex data and makes a multi-layer network powerful. Notably, the activation function is the last block of a perceptron model. There are different activation functions. Let us discuss it one by one.

Linear Activation or Identity Function: There is no change in the values as the derivative of the linear or identity function is constant. The linear activation is shown in Figure 6.11 for input x and function $h(x)$. There is a huge range in $(-\infty, \infty)$ for the function. This linear activation function is given by

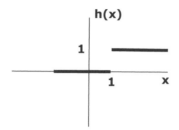

FIGURE 6.12: Binary step function

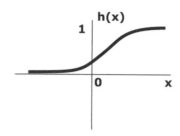

FIGURE 6.13: Sigmoid activation function

$$h(x) = x \qquad (6.45)$$

Binary Step Function: The function is also known as threshold or Heaviside function. The output is either of two values say zero or one as shown in Figure 6.12. It is used for a single-layer network. The function is given by

$$\begin{aligned} h(x) &= 1 \text{ if } x > 1 \\ &= 0 \text{ otherwise} \end{aligned} \qquad (6.46)$$

Sigmoid Activation Function: The range is from 0 to 1 and hence bounded as shown in Figure 6.13. This is strictly an increasing function and not symmetric around the origin. This is popular for backpropagation as it is a differentiable function. The function is expressed as

$$h(x) = \frac{1}{1 + \exp(-x)} \qquad (6.47)$$

Bipolar Sigmoid or Tanh Activation Function: This function is a scaled version of the sigmoid and symmetric around the origin and bounded. The values lie between -1 and 1 as shown in Figure 6.14. This is strictly an increasing function. The function is expressed as

$$h(x) = \tanh(x) = \frac{\exp(x) - \exp(-x)}{\exp(x) + \exp(-x)} \qquad (6.48)$$

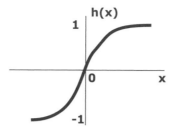

FIGURE 6.14: Tanh activation function

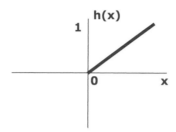

FIGURE 6.15: ReLu activation function

Rectified Linear unit (ReLu) Activation Function: The function is lower bounded by zero and not upper bounded. This is strictly an increasing function as shown in Figure 6.15. The function is given by

$$h(x) = \text{ReLu}(x) = \max(0, x) \tag{6.49}$$

6.6.3 Loss Functions

The objective functions in neural networks is to minimize the loss function. The different loss functions are discussed next.

Mean Absolute Error (MAE): This is the average of the absolute differences between actual (y) and predicted observation $(\hat{y})$. This is given by

$$\text{MAE} = \frac{1}{n}(|y - \hat{y}|) \tag{6.50}$$

Mean Squared Error (MSE): The quadratic loss function is widely used in linear regression as the performance measure because of differentiability and continuity properties. It is always non-negative, and values closer to zero are better.

$$\text{MSE} = \frac{1}{n}||(y - \hat{y})||^2 \tag{6.51}$$

Cross Entropy: This is used in the field of information theory. This has the unit of bits. The cross-entropy is between a true distribution p and an estimated distribution q. This can be re-written in terms of the entropy and

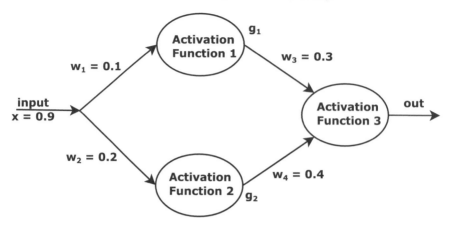

FIGURE 6.16: Back-propagation in feed-forward neural network

Kullback-Leibler divergence between the two distributions. The cross-entropy is given by

$$H(p, q) = -\sum_x p(x) \log q(x) = H(p) + D_{\text{KL}}(p||q) \qquad (6.52)$$

6.6.4   Back-propagation and Its Example

The backpropagation is used to train neural networks. This can update the weights very efficiently. We compute the gradient of a cost function with respect to all the weights in the network.

Example of Back-propagation: Let us consider an example shown in Figure 6.16. Here, $w_1 x = 0.9 \times 0.1 = 0.09$. We use sigmoid activation function for illustration purpose herein. g_1 is computed by applying activation function on weighted input.

$$g_1 = h(w_1 x)$$
$$= \frac{1}{1 + \exp(-w_1 x)} \qquad (6.53)$$
$$= \frac{1}{1 + 0.91} = 0.52$$

Now, we compute g_2 using $w_2 x = 0.2 \times 0.9 = 0.18$ as follows:

$$g_2 = h(w_2 x)$$
$$= \frac{1}{1 + \exp(-w_2 x)} \qquad (6.54)$$
$$= \frac{1}{1 + 0.84} = 0.55$$

In order to calculate the out, we need $w_3 g_1 + w_4 g_2 = 0.3 \times 0.52 + 0.4 \times 0.55$

$$= 0.38.$$

$$\text{out} = h(w_3 g_1 + w_4 g_2)$$

$$= \frac{1}{1 + \exp(-w_3 g_1 - w_4 g_2)} \quad (6.55)$$

$$= \frac{1}{1 + 0.68} = 0.59$$

Subsequently, the loss is computed using mean squared error as

$$\text{loss} = (\text{desired} - \text{out})^2$$

$$= (1 - 0.59)^2 = 0.17 \quad (6.56)$$

For backpropagating, the derivative of the loss function with respect to out is given as

$$\frac{\partial \text{loss}}{\partial \text{out}} = -2(\text{desired} - \text{out})$$

$$= -2(1 - 0.59) = -0.81 \quad (6.57)$$

If we denote $w_3 g_1 + w_4 g_2 = x_3$, then

$$\text{out} = h(x_3) = \frac{1}{1 + \exp(-x_3)} \quad (6.58)$$

We can write the derivative as follows

$$\frac{\partial \text{out}}{\partial x_3} = \frac{\exp(-x_3)}{(1 + \exp(-x_3))^2}$$

$$= \frac{\exp(-0.38)}{(1 + \exp(-0.38))^2} = 0.24 \quad (6.59)$$

Also, using $w_3 g_1 + w_4 g_2 = x_3$, we can write

$$\frac{\partial x_3}{\partial g_1} = w_3 = 0.3 \quad (6.60)$$

and

$$\frac{\partial x_3}{\partial g_2} = w_4 = 0.4 \quad (6.61)$$

Similarly, if we denote $a_1 = w_1 x$ and $a_2 = w_2 x$, then

$$g_1 = h(w_1 x)$$

$$= h(a_1)$$

$$= \frac{1}{1 + \exp(-a_1)} \quad (6.62)$$

and

$$g_2 = h(w_2 x)$$

$$= h(a_2)$$

$$= \frac{1}{1 + \exp(-a_2)} \quad (6.63)$$

Therefore, the derivatives can be written as

$$\frac{\partial g_1}{\partial a_1} = \frac{\exp(-a_1)}{(1 + \exp(-a_1))^2}$$
$$= \frac{\exp(-0.09)}{(1 + \exp(-0.09))^2} = 0.25 \tag{6.64}$$

and

$$\frac{\partial g_2}{\partial a_2} = \frac{\exp(-a_2)}{(1 + \exp(-a_2))^2}$$
$$= \frac{\exp(-0.18)}{(1 + \exp(-0.18))^2} = 0.25 \tag{6.65}$$

Finally, using $a_1 = w_1 x$ and $a_2 = w_2 x$, we can write the derivatives as

$$\frac{\partial a_1}{\partial w_1} = x = 0.9 \tag{6.66}$$

and

$$\frac{\partial a_2}{\partial w_2} = x = 0.9 \tag{6.67}$$

Assume the learning rate $\eta = 0.05$. Using the chain rule of derivatives, we can write the derivative of loss with respect to w_1 as follows

$$\frac{\partial \text{loss}}{\partial w_1} = \frac{\partial \text{loss}}{\partial \text{out}} \times \frac{\partial \text{out}}{\partial x_3} \times \frac{\partial x_3}{\partial g_1} \times \frac{\partial g_1}{\partial a_1} \times \frac{\partial a_1}{\partial w_1} \tag{6.68}$$
$$= -0.81 \times 0.24 \times 0.3 \times 0.25 \times 0.9 = -0.013$$

Hence, the updated weight w_1 can be written as

$$w_1 = w_1 - \eta \frac{\partial \text{loss}}{\partial w_1} \tag{6.69}$$
$$= 0.1 - 0.05 \times -0.013 = 0.10065$$

On the same lines, carry out the same for other weights w_2, w_3, and w_4. Refer to the problems of exercise.

6.6.5 Optimization in Back Propagation

We present gradient descent, mini-batch gradient descent and stochastic gradient descent methods herein for optimization in back propagation.

Gradient Descent Method: The first derivative of a scalar function $E(w)$ with respect to a vector $w = [w_1, w_2]^\top$ is called the gradient of $E(w)$ or $\nabla E(w)$.

$$\nabla E(w) = \frac{d}{dw} E(w) = \begin{bmatrix} \frac{\partial E}{\partial w_1} \\ \frac{\partial E}{\partial w_2} \end{bmatrix} \tag{6.70}$$

The second derivative of a scalar function $E(w)$ with respect to a vector $w = [w_1, w_2]^\top$ is a matrix called the Hessian of $E(w)$ or $\nabla^2 E(w)$.

$$H = \nabla^2 E(w) = \frac{d^2}{dw^2} E(w) = \begin{bmatrix} \frac{\partial^2 E}{\partial w_1^2} & \frac{\partial^2 E}{\partial w_1 \partial w_2} \\ \frac{\partial^2 E}{\partial w_2 \partial w_1} & \frac{\partial^2 E}{\partial w_2^2} \end{bmatrix} \qquad (6.71)$$

This is also called batch gradient descent which computes the gradient of the cost function with respect to the parameters w for the entire training dataset. For a function $y = f(w)$, derivative (slope at point w) of it is $f'(w) = \frac{dy}{dw}$. A small change (ϵ) in the input can cause output to move to a value given by $f(w + \epsilon) \approx f(w) + \epsilon f'(w)$ which is the first order Taylor series. We need to take a jump so that y reduces assuming a minimization problem. Gradient descent proposes weight update as

$$w' = w - \eta_l \frac{1}{m} \sum_{i=1}^{m} \nabla_w f(x^{(i)}, y^{(i)}, w) \qquad (6.72)$$

where η_l is the learning rate and m is the batchsize.

Example: Let there be 100 samples in a dataset that are used for training a model. Here, number of batches $\times$ batch size = total number of samples = 100. For gradient descent, we have batch size (m) = 100 and number of batches = 1. Therefore, the updated weight w' is obtained by summing the gradients of all losses considering all samples, and then averaging them.

$$w' = w - \eta_l \frac{1}{100} \sum_{i=1}^{100} \nabla_w (\text{loss}_1 + \text{loss}_2 + \ldots + \text{loss}_{100}) \qquad (6.73)$$

where $\text{loss}_i = \text{desired}_i - \text{predicted}_i = y_i - w_i x_i$.

Let there be 6 examples in a dataset. Say, the target values corresponding to examples $x_1, x_2, x_3, x_4, x_5,$ and x_6 be $y_1, y_2, y_3, y_4, y_5,$ and y_6 respectively. The weights associated with these examples are $w_1 = 0.6$, $w_2 = 0.4$, $w_3 = 0.3$, $w_4 = 0.4$, $w_5 = 0.5$, and $w_6 = 0.5$. Let the derivative of loss $\nabla_{w_i}(y_i - w_i x_i)$ for $i \in [1, 6]$ be 0.5, 0.2, 0.7, 0.4, 0.7, and 0.6 respectively initially. Using gradient descent, we update weight w_1 as follows:

$$w_1 = w_1 - \eta_l \frac{1}{6}(0.5 + 0.2 + 0.7 + 0.4 + 0.7 + 0.6)$$
$$= 0.6 - 0.01 \times 0.52 = 0.5948 \qquad (6.74)$$

where we consider learning rate $\eta_l = 0.01$. Similarly, we update all the weights and iterate till convergence or maximum number of allowed iterations.

Minibatch Gradient Descent: We perform update for every mini-batch of n examples. In minibatch gradient descent, the weight is updated as

$$w' = w - \eta_l \frac{1}{n} \sum_{i=1}^{n} \nabla_w f(x^{(i)}, y^{(i)}, w) \qquad (6.75)$$

where η_l is the learning rate and $n \leq m$. Here, minibatch size is a hyperparameter.

Example: Let there be 100 samples in a dataset that are used for training a model. The number of mini-batches is 5 each containing 20 samples. Therefore, the size of each minibatch = 20. Note that number of batches × batch size = the total number of samples = 100. For minibatch gradient descent, we have batch size $(m) = 20$ and number of batches = 5. Therefore, the updated weight w' is obtained by summing the gradients of losses considering 20 samples and then averaging them.

$$w' = w - \eta_l \frac{1}{20} \sum_{i=1}^{20} \nabla_w (\text{loss}_1 + \text{loss}_2 + \ldots + \text{loss}_{20}) \tag{6.76}$$

where $\text{loss}_i = \text{target}_i - \text{predicted}_i = y_i - w_i x_i$. We update weight for each mini-batch till convergence or maximum number of allowed iterations.

Consider the same example of gradient descent except with 2 minibatches with batchsize of 3. Using minibatch gradient descent, we update weight w_1 as follows

$$
\begin{aligned}
w_1 &= w_1 - \eta_l \frac{1}{3}(0.5 + 0.2 + 0.7) \\
&= 0.6 - 0.01 \times 0.47 = 0.5953
\end{aligned}
\tag{6.77}
$$

where we consider learning rate $\eta_l = 0.01$. Similarly, we update all the weights and iterate till convergence or maximum number of iterations.

Stochastic Gradient Descent: In Stochastic Gradient Descent (SGD), a single parameter update takes place. This is much faster as avoid redundancy that exists in the batch gradient descent method. It performs frequent updates with a high variance that cause the objective function to fluctuate heavily.

Example: Let there be 100 samples in a dataset that are used for training a model. Note that number of batches × batch size = the total number of samples = 100. For SGD, we have batch size $(m) = 1$ and the number of batches = 100. Therefore, the updated weight w' is obtained by summing the gradients of loss of each sample at a time.

$$w'_i = w_i - \eta_l \nabla_{w_i} (L = \text{loss}_i) \tag{6.78}$$

where $\text{loss}_i = \text{desired}_i - \text{predicted}_i = y_i - w_i x_i$. The weight is updated for every single sample and so the oscillation is too much as compared to gradient descent before reaching global optima. Consider the same example of gradient descent method. Using SGD, we update weight w_1 as follows

$$w_1 = w_1 - \eta_l \times 0.5 = 0.6 - 0.01 \times 0.5 = 0.595 \tag{6.79}$$

where we consider learning rate η_l of 0.01. Similarly, we update all the weights and iterate till convergence or maximum number of allowed iterations. The SGD is much faster as compared to GD, however, weight update oscillates with SGD. GD guarantees convergence without much oscillations.

6.7 Evaluation Method

We partition the data in the cross-validation method. One part is used for training and the other for testing. Next, to assess the performance of the algorithm, performance metrics are used.

6.7.1 Cross-validation Method

We discuss herein holdout set, validation set, n-fold cross-validation, and leave-one-out cross validation.

Holdout Set: The available data set D is divided into two disjoint subsets. The training set is used for learning a model and the test set for testing the model. Note that the training set should not be used in testing and the test set should not be used in learning. The test set is also called the holdout set. The examples in the original data set D are all labeled with classes. This method is mainly used when the dataset D is large.

Validation Set: The available data is divided into three subsets: training set, validation set, and test set. A validation set is used frequently for estimating hyperparameters in learning algorithms. In such cases, the values that give the best accuracy on the validation set are used as the final parameter.

n-fold Cross-validation: The available data (all training and testing) is partitioned into n equal-size disjoint subsets. We use each subset as the test set and combine the rest $n-1$ subset as the training set to learn a classifier. The procedure is run n times, which gives n accuracies. The final estimated accuracy of learning is the average of the n accuracies. This method is used when the available data is not large.

Leave-one-out Cross-validation: This method is used when the data set is very small. Each fold of the cross-validation has only a single test example and all the rest of the data is used in training. If the original data has m examples, this is m-fold cross-validation.

6.7.2 Performance Metrics

The different measures to test the model performance are as follows:

- *Accuracy*: Ratio of number of correctly predicted results to total number of predicted results

- *Precision*: Number of correctly classified positive examples divided by the total number of examples that are classified as positive.

- *Recall*: Number of correctly classified positive examples divided by the total number of actual positive examples in the test set.

- *F1-score*: Combination precision and recall into one measure.

	Classified Positive	Classified Negative
Actual Positive	**True Positive (TP)**	**False Negative (FN)**
Actual Negative	**False Positive (FP)**	**True Negative (TN)**

FIGURE 6.17: Confusion matrix

Accuracy, precision, recall, and F1-score can be determined from a confusion matrix as shown in Figure 6.17. Ideally, FP and FN should be zero. The non-zero FP and FN reduce the precision and recall, respectively. Therefore, all performance metrics such as accuracy, precision, recall, and F1-score should be ideally unity.

We can represent the performance metrics as

$$\text{Accuracy} = \frac{(\text{TP} + \text{TN})}{(\text{TP} + \text{TN} + \text{FP} + \text{FN})} \tag{6.80}$$

$$\text{Precision} = \frac{\text{TP}}{(\text{TP} + \text{FP})} \tag{6.81}$$

$$\text{Recall or Sensitivity} = \frac{\text{TP}}{(\text{TP} + \text{FN})} \tag{6.82}$$

$$\text{F1 Score} = 2 \times \frac{(\text{Precison} \times \text{Recall})}{(\text{Precision} + \text{Recall})} \tag{6.83}$$

$$\text{F1 Score} = \frac{2\text{TP}}{2\text{TP} + \text{FP} + \text{FN}} \tag{6.84}$$

If FP and FN = 0, the F1 score = $\frac{2\text{TP}}{2\text{TP}} = 1$.

Example of Performance Metrics: If TP = 1, TN = 1000, FP = 0, and FN = 99, then from confusion matrix, we get: accuracy = 91 %, precision $p = 100$ %, recall $r = 1$ %.

Here we only classify one positive example correctly (TP = 1) and no negative examples wrongly (FP = 0). Note that the precision and recall only measure classification on the positive class (TP).

Here, F1 Score = $\frac{2(p \times r)}{(p+r)}$, therefore the F1-score tends to be closer to the smaller of the two-precision and recall because F1-score is a harmonic mean. We are generally interested in the worst performance. This is why we choose a Harmonic mean metric that gives a value closer to the smaller of those two not closer to the larger of those two.

6.8   Summary

We know that in an IoT network, the data are generated from plenty of devices. This needs to be processed using a machine learning algorithm for automated decision purposes. We classified the test point or predict the dependent variable for a new independent test variable. Some of the popular supervised and unsupervised techniques are presented. We also discussed the fundamentals of neural networks along with back-propagation hand-solved examples. The performance metrics are presented to evaluate the effectiveness of the machine learning algorithms.

6.9   Exercises

1. Suppose we have two levels of electrical voltages +5 Volt and 0 Volt. If these levels are sent through a communication channel, these values are corrupted by noise. How do you simply detect these levels using thresholding at the receiver? How many classes are there in this classification problem?

2. Suppose that data x and y is received as $x + n$ and $y + n$, where n is the noise. What is the impact of differential data applied to machine learning algorithms?

3. How to determine the number of clusters in k-means clustering?

4. What is the significance of maximum eigenvalue and the corresponding eigenvector in PCA?

5. Determine the maximum eigenvalue and the corresponding eigenvector for matrix $\mathbf{A} = \begin{bmatrix} 1 & 2 \\ 0 & 4 \end{bmatrix}$.

6. Is Rectified Linear unit (ReLu) activation function linear or non-linear? Is it continuous and differentiable?

7. Which one should we choose between GD and SGD?

8. How to decide the mini-batch size in mini-batch GD?

9. Is false-positive good in healthcare IoT network?

10. Given TP = 40, TN = 30, FP = 20 and, FN = 10, determine accuracy, precision, recall (sensitivity), and F1 score.

11. Does high accuracy means high precision for different trials of the result and vice versa?

12. Which one is better between underfitting and overfitting?

13. If we consider the index x as [0 1 2 3] and data as [0 0.9 2.2 3], what are the RMSEs if we model using cftool box of MATLAB®. What are those models.

14. Refer to Problem 13, predict the value of data when $x = 5$ using both regression models.

15. Repeat the backpropagation example of theory for weight w_2.

16. Repeat the back propagation example of theory for weights w_3 and w_4.

17. **Do It Yourself**: Study deep learning techniques and understand how it is useful for IoT networks.

18. **Do It Yourself**: Explore big data analytics for a huge volume of data of IoT networks.

Chapter 7

Fog Computing

7.1 Introduction

Cloud computing is a shared pool of dedicated computing resources provided to all users. The features of cloud computing are as follows:

- *Resource pooling*: Multiple users use same resources and services like storage, processing and bandwidth.

- *Scalability*: On-demand resources and services can be changed based on the user demand.

On the other hand, fog computing is a platform that provides distributed storage, computing, and networking services. The computing is implemented on IoT devices themselves or gateways at the edge of the networks. This brings the computations closer to the things, sensors, or devices where the data is generated. The fog and cloud levels are shown in Figure 7.1. Note that fog computing is not a replacement, rather an augmentation of cloud computing. The user can choose fog or cloud service depending on the application's specific requirements.

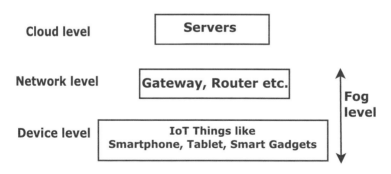

FIGURE 7.1: Fog and cloud levels

DOI: 10.1201/9781003225584-7   191

7.1.1 Motivation for Fog Computing

Billions of devices are connected to the Internet. Those devices generate a huge volume of data from different applications. According to Moore's law, the capacity of storage and compute technologies gets doubled every 18 months. On the other hand, Nielsen's law states that the bandwidth of network edge gets doubled every 24 months. That is the user's connection speed increases by 50 % every year. Moore's law allows computational and storage facilities at the network edge instead of sending all data to the cloud.

Multipath fading and interference affect the network conditions because of the user's mobility. This leads to loss of packets even in cloud computing architecture. As we move, there is a need for the physical movement of computing and storage facilities. We do virtual movement for getting the facilities from the network edge. Hence, fog augments the cloud by providing pervasiveness and reliability during mobility. In control and actuation, sensing and actuating devices are resource-constrained devices. Thus, all data cannot be processed by those devices themselves. Hence, there is a requirement to *offload* the storage and compute functions to fog nodes.

The applications of fog computing include real-time analytics, and distributed and hierarchical data management. For instance, in a smart environment application, noise sensors record a stream of noise levels continuously. Sending all data to the cloud proves to be inefficient. Fog computing does local processing and sends filtered data to the cloud as and when needed.

7.1.2 Cloud Computing versus Fog Computing

Both cloud and fog computing have storage, computing, and networking functionalities. These are some similarities. However, there some differences that are listed in Table 7.1. Cloud computing uses generally wired connectivity using Gigabit Ethernet with a speed of 10 Gbps to 100 Gbps. On the other hand, fog computing has low latency because the fog node is closer to the data source. This also supports heterogeneous devices and mobility in a distributed wireless environment. The distance to the data source is small, however, the number of nodes is large. Fog computing also uses location information of the users. In short, the characteristics of fog and cloud computing are opposite.

7.2 Technologies for Fog Computing

7.2.1 Virtualization Technology

The fog node processes the data near the source of data. This is carried out using lightweight virtualization technology. The technology combines or

TABLE 7.1: Comparison of cloud computing and fog computing

Characteristics	Cloud Computing	Fog Computing
Connectivity	Wired	Wireless
Delay	High	Low
Operation	Core	Edge
Resource type	Homogeneous	Heterogeneous
Architecture	Centralized	Distributed
Nodes density	Small	Large
Mobility	No	Yes
Distance to things	Large	Small
Localization	No	Yes
Analytics	Real-time	Batch processing

partitions the computing resources to provide multiple operating environments. This is performed using hardware and software aggregation or partition, hardware emulation, resource sharing, or time multiplexing. The advantages are as follows:

1. Consolidates both hardware and applications and therefore, reduces procuring and managing overhead of underutilized infrastructure.

2. Provides the application with isolated execution environments

3. Supports multiple operating systems over the same hardware infrastructure.

4. Easy movement of applications from one hardware or physical location to another

Virtualization at CPU Instruction Level: The emulator provides to an application the illusion of running on one processor architecture. However, the actual hardware belongs to a different architecture. The guest instruction set of an application is translated to the host instruction set of actual hardware.

Virtualization at Hardware Abstraction Level: The hardware abstraction layer uses a virtual machine manager or hypervisor, which is a software layer that sits above the physical hardware or bare metal. This provides a virtualized view of all its services. The hypervisor creates multiple Virtual Machines (VMs) and VMs run different operating systems. Applications run on the respective operating system. Further, the applications are unaware of the underlying virtualization.

Virtualization at Operating System Level: The operating system level relies on virtualization software that runs on top of or as a module within the operating system. This provides an abstraction of the kernel-space system calls to user-space applications. Also, it provides security and isolation capabilities to prevent one application from causing damage to another.

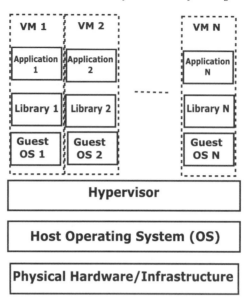

FIGURE 7.2: Virtual machine

7.2.2   Terminologies in Computing

Virtual Machine (VM): This is used at the hardware abstraction level in cloud computing as shown in Figure 7.2. VMs provide an abstraction of a compute platform's hardware and software resources. This is complete with all the drivers, full Operating System (OS), and libraries.

Containers: This is used at the operating system level in cloud computing as shown in Figure 7.3. This includes portions of the operating system and selected libraries. These are minimal components to run an application. Containers share the same operating system and common libraries.

Advantages of Containers over VM: The containers are lightweight in terms of memory and processing. A large number of containers can be supported for the given resources than VMs. Therefore, the container provides scalability for both cloud computing and fog computing. Compact memory footprint for containers gives them another advantage. Containers can be migrated faster from one host to another. LINUX operating system supports both VMs and containers.

Limitations of Containers: The containers cannot be used for applications that require different OS versions or environments. This is because it shares the OS unlike VM. There is a security issue since containers use the same OS, unlike VM.

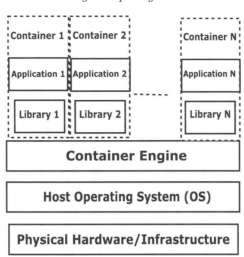

FIGURE 7.3: Container

7.3 Mobility in Fog Framework

There are two types of addresses of end devices for message delivery. These are defined below:

- Media Access Control (MAC) address: This is used for unique identification over the network. The address is burnt into the device called identity address.

- Internet Protocol (IP) address: This is the geographical location of the end device. It is also called the location address.

We use identity and location addresses, respectively, at the edge and core of the network for scalability. Mapping by the network is done by associating these two addresses. Let us consider an analogy of a post-office service for illustration purposes. If someone moves from one locality to another, one needs to update his/her name (identity address) from an old house (old location address) to a new house (new location address). This is illustrated in Figure 7.4.

7.3.1 Ethernet Virtual Private Network

Ethernet Virtual Private Network (EVPN) is standardized by Internet Engineering Task Force (IETF) in Request for Comments (RFC) 7432. Only network elements at the edge of the network are supported by EVPN because EVPN is an overlay technology. The literal meaning of overlay is to cover the

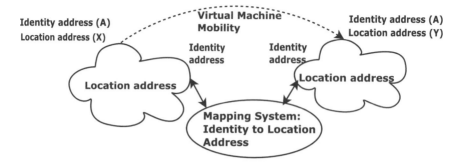

FIGURE 7.4: Identity and location addresses

surface of something. EVPN uses Border Gateway Protocol (BGP) to build the forwarding table. Mapping from identity address to location address is carried out by centralized or distributed protocols. EVPN and Locator/Identier Separation Protocol (LISP) are an example of these, which will be used by fog computing.

How does EVPN work? The Provider Edge (PE) learns the MAC address of host which is the Customer Edge (CE) from local interfaces or remote PE. PE sends MAC advertisement route messages to other network elements in case of learning a new MAC address. There are two route messages for the MAC address: an old (wrong) one and a new (correct) one. EVPN decides the correct MAC route based on the highest sequence number which is found in MAC mobility extended community field. In the case of a tie of sequence numbers, the lowest PE IP address is used. The sequence number starts at 0 and it is increased for every MAC address mobility event. The old PE withdraws the PE route and installs a new one directing to the new PE.

Example of EVPN: As shown in Figure 7.5, the following steps are involved.

- MAC advertisement route message is sent by PE 1.

- MAC address is moved to a new server from PE 1 to PE 3.

- Then, PE 3 learns a new local MAC address and sends a new advertisement route message.

- In case of different sequence numbers

    1. If PE 1 and PE 3 have MAC address with a sequence numbers 4 and 5 (incremented by 1), respectively, then PE 3 advertises the local MAC route because it has a higher sequence number.

    2. PE 1, PE 2, and PE 4 install the remote MAC advertisement route from PE 3 because PE 3 has a higher sequence number.

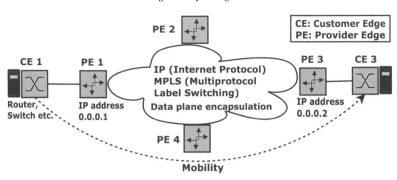

FIGURE 7.5: EVPN Mobility

- In case of the same sequence numbers

  1. If PE 1 and PE 3 have MAC address with same sequence numbers, then PE 1 will advertise the local MAC route because PE1 has the lower IP address (0.0.0.1).

  2. PE 2, PE 3, and PE 4 will install the remote MAC advertisement route from PE1 because PE1 has the lower IP address

7.3.2 Default IP Gateway

In the event of mobility, VM's configurations like RAM, disk image, and address of default IP gateway remain unchanged. A default IP gateway is needed for forwarding the traffic to the remote server. This must be in the vicinity of the host server which ensures optimal forwarding of traffic. EVPN declares PE which is at the edge of the network to act as a default IP gateway. In the event of Address Resolution Protocol (ARP) request for the default IP Gateway IP address from the host, PE reads the ARP message and sends its own MAC address.

Example of Default IP Gateway: As shown in Figure 7.6,

- The source VM on server 1 communicates to destination VM using optimal forwarding path via default IP gateway. This is shown using a dashed line.

- After mobility, the VM on server 2 communicates to destination VM using sub-optimal forwarding path via same default IP gateway. This is shown using a dotted line.

- Finally, the communications happen through PE. This is shown using a solid line.

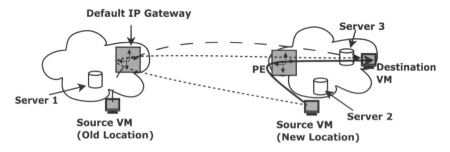

FIGURE 7.6: Illustration of default IP gateway

7.3.3 Locator/Identifier Separation Protocol

LISP is standardized in IETF RFC 6830. Endpoint Identifiers (EIDs) are the identity addresses of an end device. Routing Locators (RLOCs) are the location addresses of routers. LISP dynamically maps between EIDs and RLOCs. EIDs can be associated with different RLOCs based on the EID-RLOC mappings. RLOCs are fixed with the network topology and are contactable by routing. LISP decouples identity from the topology. EID is mobile without changing the routing that interconnects the locator IP space.

Architecture of LISP: Ingress Tunnel Routers (ITRs) receive and encapsulate traffic of end device for transporting over the LISP network. Egress Tunnel Routers (ETRs) decapsulate the tunneled traffic and forward to their destinations. Identification of ITRs and ETRs are based on their RLOCs. To forward traffic, ITR uses a map resolver to determine the RLOC of the ETR of the destination EID. The map server has all EID-ETR mapping. The map resolver forward to the map server for determining appropriate ETR. This destination ETR responds to source ETR the list of RLOCs associated with EID. The overall working of LISP is shown with dotted lines in Figure 7.7. The steps involved in LISP are summarized below:

- The traffic of VM is sent from a new location to a new nearby ETR. This is shown with A on the arrow.

- The MAP server is updated with new EID-ETR mapping. This is shown with B on the arrow.

- The de-registration of EID from old ETR takes place. This is shown with C on the arrow.

- If the ITR sends traffic to EID via old ETR, it is shown with D on the arrow.

- Then the old ETR responds with solicit-map-request to ITR to update map-cache. This is shown with E on the arrow.

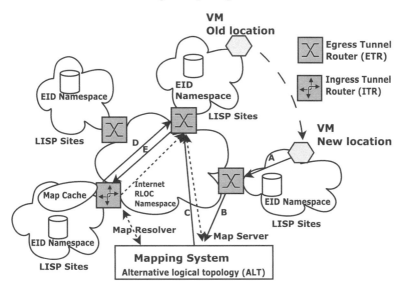

FIGURE 7.7: Illustration of LISP

7.4 Fog Orchestration

The literal meaning of orchestration is to plan or coordinate the elements of a scenario to produce the desired effect. Fog orchestration provisions and manages compute, storage and network facilities. The fog orchestration block is shown in Figure 7.8. The tasks of orchestration are deploying, debug, patch, and update of applications or operating systems, setting up network connectivity between application entities, reserving bandwidth, and allocating and expanding disk space. The orchestration also handles the heterogeneous systems which are distributed across multiple locations. In contrast to cloud orchestration, fog orchestration does topology management, things connectivity, and network performance guarantees.

7.5 Localization in Fog Computing Framework

Wi-Fi-based localization is widely used than inertial based methods such as accelerometer, gyroscope, and magnetometer. Further, fingerprinting based localization performs better than path loss model based in terms of localization accuracy. In fingerprinting-based localization, there are two steps: training and testing. In the training phase, we collect RSS and corresponding location

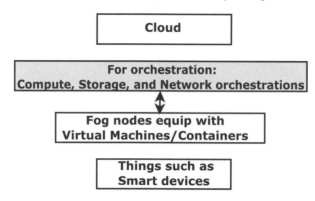

FIGURE 7.8: Fog orchestration

information at reference points. In the testing phase, given a new RSS at the smart device, we estimate the corresponding location. We can offload fingerprinting computations to fog nodes. In offloading, we move the computational load from the local device to the fog device. The fog node in the vicinity may be powerful than the local node. The fog computing framework is shown in Figure 7.9. In the fog computing framework, we move the cloud computing capabilities toward the edge of the network. This is also called edge computing. The benefits of task offloading are lower latency, lower energy consumption of the smart device, and sharing of computations among several devices.

7.5.1   Fingerprinting Based Localization

The user runs the fingerprinting-based localization algorithm. If the available computational power is less than a set threshold, then a nearby device is requested for computations. This is also called device-to-device communication using Wi-Fi direct. If the nearby device is not available for any reason, the local processing unit or cloud server is requested. Note that the fog computing framework saves energy and extends the lifetime of a resource-constrained smart device.

7.5.2   Getting Device Information

If the available computational power is less than the threshold, (ε_1), then look for nearby device for running localization algorithm. The smart device sends the status to the fog node. In second and third columns of Table 7.2, the value is [0 1]. Note that 1 denotes the high availability of battery and/or CPU. The only integer is allowed in the fourth column. It may be noted that 1, 2, and 3 are for Wi-Fi, Bluetooth, and LoRaWAN, respectively.

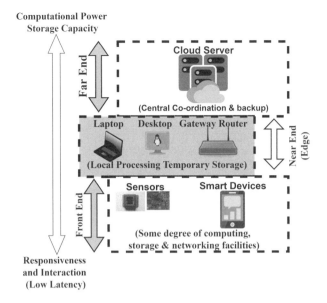

FIGURE 7.9: Fog Computing Framework

TABLE 7.2: Given data of three devices for offloading

Smart Device	Battery Level	Computation	Communication Interface, m_i
D_1	0.90	0.80	1
D_2	0.95	0.20	3
D_3	0.50	0.80	2

7.5.3 Computing Cost Function

The cost function is computed as

$$J = \sum_{n=1}^{N} m_n w_n \qquad (7.1)$$

where m_n and w_n denote metric and weight, respectively, for ith device. Also, $0 \leq w_i \leq 1$ and the sum of weights of all devices is equal to 1. We choose the device for offloading if J is greater than and equal to some new threshold, ε_2.

7.5.4 Example of Offloading

Suppose $N = 3$, $\mathbf{w} = \left[\frac{1}{3}, \frac{1}{3}, \frac{1}{3}\right]$, and $\varepsilon_2 = 0.6$. The data of Table 7.2 is used to fill up Table 7.3. Now, let us choose first two metrics only for easy

TABLE 7.3: Offloading scenario for three devices

Offloading Percentage		O_p	O_n	Offloading	
	J			Start	End
Device 1	$0.9 \times \frac{1}{3} + 0.8 \times \frac{1}{3} + 1 \times \frac{1}{3} = 0.9$	41%	10	1	10
Device 2	$0.95 \times \frac{1}{3} + 0.2 \times \frac{1}{3} + 3 \times \frac{1}{3} = 1.38$	28%	7	11	17
Device 3	$0.5 \times \frac{1}{3} + 0.8 \times \frac{1}{3} + 2 \times \frac{1}{3} = 1.1$	31%	8	18	25

illustration. For nth device

$$O_p = \frac{m_1^n w_1 + m_2^n w_2}{\sum_{n=1}^{N} m_1^n w_1 + m_2^n w_2} \times 100\% \qquad (7.2)$$

If we offload to the first fog device, the offloading percentage is

$$O_p = \frac{0.9 \times \frac{1}{3} + 0.8 \times \frac{1}{3}}{(0.9 \times \frac{1}{3} + 0.8 \times \frac{1}{3}) + (0.95 \times \frac{1}{3} + 0.2 \times \frac{1}{3}) + (0.5 \times \frac{1}{3} + 0.8 \times \frac{1}{3})} \qquad (7.3)$$

$$= \frac{0.9 + 0.8}{(0.9 + 0.8) + (0.95 + 0.2) + (0.5 + 0.8)} = \frac{1.7}{4.15} = 41\%$$

Similarly, if we offload to second and third fog devices, the offloading percentages are $\frac{0.95+0.2}{4.15} = 27.7\%$ and $\frac{0.5+0.8}{4.15} = 31.3\%$. Now, we distribute load based on O_p. Let the total number of locations be 25. The number of locations for each fog node is given by

$$O_n = [O_p \times 25] \qquad (7.4)$$

where [.] denotes the operator for the nearest integer. The offloading period is computed as follows:

$$O_1 = 0.41 \times 25 = 10.25 \approx 10$$
$$O_2 = 0.28 \times 25 = 7 \qquad (7.5)$$
$$O_3 = 0.31 \times 25 = 7.75 \approx 8$$

1. Device 1 does localization from 1st to 10th locations.

2. Device 2 does localization from 11th to 17th locations.

3. Device 3 does localization from 18th to 25th locations.

After computations, these three devices return their results to the initiating smart device.

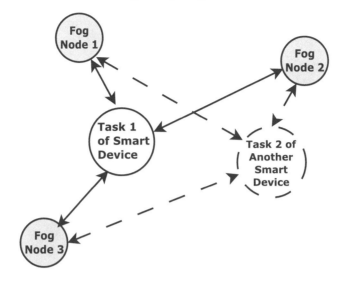

FIGURE 7.10: Three fog nodes and two tasks in a fog framework

7.6   Task Offloading

Let there be two tasks at two smart devices and three fog nodes as shown in Figure 7.10. The received signal power at the smart device due to fog node is P_r. The distance between smart device and fog node is d. According to Friss transmission formula, $P_r \propto \frac{1}{d^2}$. Given P_r, we can estimate d. Say, the distances of Task 1 with fog nodes are $\begin{bmatrix} 8 & 9 & 18 \end{bmatrix}$ m and the distances of Task 2 with fog nodes are $\begin{bmatrix} 15 & 6 & 12 \end{bmatrix}$ m. The coverage of fog nodes are assumed to be $\begin{bmatrix} 10 & 12 & 15 \end{bmatrix}$ m. The bandwidth between smart device and fog nodes is $\begin{bmatrix} 1.5 & 1.8 & 1.9 \end{bmatrix}$ Mbps. The computational power of fog nodes is $\begin{bmatrix} 20 & 30 & 25 \end{bmatrix}$ Mega flops. The energy expenditure per unit of data in transferring between smart device and fog nodes is $\begin{bmatrix} 0.2 & 0.4 & 0.5 \end{bmatrix}$ Joule/Mb. The cost for processing unit data at fog nodes is $\begin{bmatrix} 0.002 & 0.002 & 0.002 \end{bmatrix}$ per kb. The weights for execution time, energy consumption and cost are $\begin{bmatrix} \frac{1}{3} & \frac{1}{3} & \frac{1}{3} \end{bmatrix}$. The size of upload data to fog node for smart devices is $\begin{bmatrix} 50 & 60 \end{bmatrix}$ kb. The size of returned result from fog node to smart device is 1 kb.

7.6.1   Offloading Task 1 to Fog Nodes

The distance of Task 1 lies in the coverage of fog node 1 and fog node 2. Therefore, the selected fog nodes are shown with $\begin{bmatrix} 1 & 1 & 0 \end{bmatrix}$, where 1 and 0 show, respectively, the presence and absence of the fog node for Task 1. There are four types of execution times for fog node 1 and 2:

- Let t_i be the time required for data collection and taking a call for offloading decision. This is equal to $\begin{bmatrix} 0.001 & 0.001 \end{bmatrix}$ s.

- Let t_u be the time required for data upload to fog nodes from the smart device. This is equal to $\begin{bmatrix} \frac{50\text{kb}}{1.5\text{Mbps}} & \frac{50\text{kb}}{1.8\text{Mbps}} \end{bmatrix} = \begin{bmatrix} 0.033 & 0.028 \end{bmatrix}$ s.

- Let t_e be the time needed for task execution at fog nodes $= \begin{bmatrix} \frac{50\text{kb}}{20\text{Mega flops}} & \frac{50\text{kb}}{30\text{Mega flops}} \end{bmatrix} = \begin{bmatrix} 0.0025 & 0.00167 \end{bmatrix}$ s.

- Let t_d be the time for downloading the result at smart device from fog node. This is equal to $\begin{bmatrix} \frac{1\text{kb}}{1.5\text{Mbps}} & \frac{1\text{kb}}{1.8\text{Mbps}} \end{bmatrix} = \begin{bmatrix} 0.000667 & 0.00056 \end{bmatrix}$ s.

The total execution time (in second) for fog nodes 1 and 2 is

$$t_i + t_u + t_e + t_d = \begin{bmatrix} 0.001 + 0.033 + 0.0025 + 0.000667 \\ 0.001 + 0.028 + 0.00167 + 0.00056 \end{bmatrix}^T = \begin{bmatrix} 0.037 \\ 0.031 \end{bmatrix}^T \quad (7.6)$$

We make the decision to offload the data to fog nodes if

$$t_i + t_u + t_e + t_d < T_{\text{sd}} \quad (7.7)$$

where T_{sd} is the time required for executing the task at smart device itself.

The energy expenditure (in Joule) to upload the data from the smart device and download the result from fog node is

$$\begin{bmatrix} (50 + 1)\text{kb} \times 0.2\text{J/Mb} & (50 + 1)\text{kb} \times 0.4\text{J/Mb} \end{bmatrix} = \begin{bmatrix} 0.0102 & 0.0204 \end{bmatrix} \quad (7.8)$$

We make the decision to offload the data to fog nodes if

$$\text{Energy expenditure} < E_{\text{sd}} \quad (7.9)$$

where E_{sd} is the energy expenditure for executing the task at smart device itself. The normalized execution time is

$$\begin{bmatrix} \frac{0.037}{0.037+0.031} & \frac{0.031}{0.037+0.031} \end{bmatrix} = \begin{bmatrix} 0.544 & 0.456 \end{bmatrix} \quad (7.10)$$

Similarly, the normalized energy expenditure is

$$\begin{bmatrix} \frac{0.0102}{0.0102+0.0204} & \frac{0.0204}{0.0102+0.0204} \end{bmatrix} = \begin{bmatrix} 0.33 & 0.67 \end{bmatrix} \quad (7.11)$$

Finally, the cost function is

$$\begin{bmatrix} \frac{1}{3} \times 0.544 + \frac{1}{3} \times 0.33 + \frac{1}{3} \times 0.002 \times 50 \\ \frac{1}{3} \times 0.456 + \frac{1}{3} \times 0.67 + \frac{1}{3} \times 0.002 \times 50 \end{bmatrix}^T = \begin{bmatrix} 0.325 \\ 0.409 \end{bmatrix}^T \quad (7.12)$$

Since the cost function is minimum for Fog node 1, the Task 1 is offloaded to Fog node 1. Note that Fog node 1 has larger execution time than Fog node 2. However, the energy consumption is lower for Fog node 1 for Task 1.

7.6.2   Offloading Task 2 to Fog Nodes

We can proceed similar to Task 1. Task 2 is offloaded to Fog node 2. Refer to the problem of exercise.

7.7   Summary

In this chapter, we first introduced the cloud and fog computing frameworks. Fog computing is not a replacement rather augments cloud computing. The role of virtualization technology is also presented for combining or partitioning the resources in a fog network. Finally, two applications, namely, fingerprinting-based localization and task offloading to fog nodes are discussed. We considered different parameters like a real application for task offloading problems.

7.8   Exercises

1. What is data in motion paradigm in fog network?

2. Differentiate among cloud, fog, mist, and edge computing.

3. What is the role of data management technology and how is it useful for fog platforms?

4. In the example of the theory section, determine the fog node for offloading task 2.

5. In the solved example of task offloading, we observe that the cost function is minimum, however, execution time is larger and the energy consumption is lower than other fog nodes. Notably, this is not true in general and the result can be opposite/in between two fog nodes for the minimum cost function.

   Repeat the example of theory for Task 1 by considering one more fog node. The coverage of this fog node is 20 m and the distance with Task 1 and 2 are 10 m and 14 m, respectively. The bandwidth is 1.2 Mbps, computational power is 40 Mega flops, energy expenditure and cost per unit of data are 0.6 Joule/Mb and 0.002, respectively.

6. The number of tasks can be increased from now 1 to 2. It can be increased further too depending on the requirements.

Repeat the example of theory for Task 2 by considering one more fog node. The coverage of this fog node is 20 m and the distance with Task 1 and 2 are 10 m and 14 m, respectively. The bandwidth is 1.2 Mbps, computational power is 40 Mega flops, energy expenditure and cost per unit of data are 0.6 Joule/Mb and 0.002, respectively.

7. In the task offloading example of theory, analyze the gain and loss if we use offloading approach for both the tasks.

8. **Do It Yourself**: Explore task partitioning in fog framework.

Chapter 8

Privacy and Security of Things Data

8.1 Introduction

Several devices communicate among themselves in an IoT network. Consider an example: when your neighbors get access to all your personal details like eating habits, disease, date of birth, income amongst others. This may pose threat to your bank account, credit card, and health card. Nobody likes it if everyone knows our private data. Therefore, things data needs to be anonymized before storing that in a hospital, bank, or government organization. This ensures prevention from unauthorized manipulation even if illegitimate persons get hold of it. Consider another example: the user turns on or off a smart air conditioner, smart refrigerator, smart bulb, smart door remotely in a smart home application. Imagine a situation, when some intruders intercept the communication of devices and get access to it. Nobody likes it if they control and trespass through our building. These two examples motivate us to study the privacy and security of things data. There are several other examples of IoT applications like smart grid, smart manufacturing, smart transportation, and smart parking where there is a need to anonymize and secure the things data. In particular, the chapter discusses data privacy, elliptic curve cryptography (ECC), and blockchain technology.

8.2 Data Privacy

The organization often maintains a database of the employees or users like name, age, gender, area code, health conditions, and many more. Generally, the database has sensitive attributes like a disease of a patient in a hospital, income of a person in a government department, location of the user for a mobile network amongst others. We anonymize data for research or analysis purposes. The anonymized data must not disclose sensitive attributes like the name of disease and income of the user. Also, at the same time, we should have enough information. The data anonymization preserves the privacy of the user.

TABLE 8.1: Dataset for *k*-anonymity. Entries in normal and italic fonts of two blocks are for distinction purpose only.

Record No.	Non-Sensitive Age	Non-Sensitive Area Code	Non-Sensitive Country	Sensitive Disease
1	*27*	*800101*	*	*Stomach*
2	*32*	*800120*	*	*Flu*
3	65	800105	*	Heart
4	43	800283	*	Heart
5	*19*	*800140*	*	*Stomach*
6	52	800787	*	Heart

There are several techniques for data anonymization. Among them, three common techniques are *k-anonymity*, *l-diversity*, and *t-closeness*. In *k*-anonymity, each user is not distinguishable from at least $k - 1$ number of users in each block. In *l*-diversity, there are at least *l* different sensitive attributes in each block. A simple approach for anonymization is to suppress the name of the user. However, the malicious user can extract the user's sensitive attributes using non-sensitive attributes such as age, gender, or pin code of the user's area and prior knowledge. For example, in a linking attack, the malicious user can combine the published data like a medical database that has sensitive attributes, and external data like voter registration details. This is further used to determine the disease of a user. *k*-anonymity is not vulnerable against this attack. Note that the row of a table is called *record* or *tuple*, while the column is an *attribute*.

8.2.1 Privacy Using *k*-anonymity

We do *generalization* and *suppression* to anonymize the data. Consider a dataset as in Table 8.1 for anonymization purpose. For example, if there are three records in each group, the non-sensitive attributes are generalized using less than or greater than some value, say, 30. Further, some digits of non-sensitive area code are suppressed by asterisks. The name of the country is completely suppressed. In the 3-anonymized table, at least 2 records are not distinguishable with each record in each block. Notably, the name of the person is suppressed to provide a first level of anonymization. The 3-anonymized dataset is shown in Table 8.2.

Drawbacks of *k*-anonymity: In a homogeneity attack, the malicious user is a neighbor and friend of the legitimate user. Therefore, the malicious user knows the user's area code and age which is 30+ years. The malicious user is interested in his friend's disease as he or she often goes to the hospital. Now, the malicious user gets the published 2-anonymized table and shortlisted records number 4, 6, and 3 of block 2 with the help of age and area code. Hence, the malicious user comes to know that his friend is suffering

TABLE 8.2: 3-anonymized table

Record No.	Age	Area Code	Country	Disease
5	≤ 30	8001**	*	Stomach
1	≤ 30	8001**	*	Stomach
2	≤ 30	8001**	*	Flu
4	> 30	800***	*	Heart
6	> 30	800***	*	Heart
3	> 30	800***	*	Heart

from heart disease because the sensitive attribute of heart disease is common for all three records. Hence, we need a diversity of sensitive attributes in each group.

TABLE 8.3: Dataset for *l*-diversity. Entries in normal and italic fonts of two blocks are for distinction purpose only.

	Non-Sensitive	Non-Sensitive	Non-Sensitive	Sensitive
Record No.	Age	Area Code	Country	Disease
1	*27*	*800101*	*	*Stomach*
2	*32*	*800120*	*	*Flu*
3	65	800105	*	Heart
4	*43*	*800183*	*	*Heart*
5	50	800140	*	Stomach
6	52	800787	*	Flu

In attack with prior knowledge, let the malicious user knows his other best friend whose age is less than 30 years. Since he or she is a friend, so, the malicious user knows his or her area code as well. Now, assume that the malicious user has prior knowledge that he or she eats sufficient fiber-rich foods. This means that he or she may not be suffering from the flu and he or she may have a stomach-related disease.

8.2.2 Privacy Using *l*-diversity

If a block contains at-least *l* different sensitive attributes, then it is called *l*-diverse. If every block of the table is *l*-diverse, so is the table. Let us consider the dataset of Table 8.3. The 3-diverse anonymized table is in Table 8.4.

We carried out some minor changes in the original table of *k*-anonymity to fit for *l*-diversity problem as we don't have a large number of records. Note that, *k* and *l* need not be the same. In each block, there are 3 records and at least 3 different sensitive attributes, namely, stomach, heart, and flu. Notably, these two numbers can be different but they must have at least 3 different sensitive attributes. Now, the malicious user needs at least $l - 1 = 2$ pieces of prior knowledge to discard two records in each block. In k-anonymity, we need just 1 piece of prior knowledge to obtain the sensitive attribute of a person. Hence, l-diversity is a better anonymization technique than k-anonymity.

TABLE 8.4: 3-diverse anonymized table

Record No.	Age	Area Code	Country	Disease
1	≤ 45	8001**	*	Stomach
2	≤ 45	8001**	*	Flu
4	≤ 45	8001**	*	Heart
3	> 45	800***	*	Heart
5	> 45	800***	*	Stomach
6	> 45	800***	*	Flu

Drawbacks of l-diversity: At times, it is difficult to achieve anonymity for some problems. For example, there are only negative and positive test reports of disease. These are the sensitive attributes and negative attributes dominate, say, 95% of 1000 records. Most of the blocks contain both negative attributes using 2-diversity. There can be at-most $5\% \times 1000 = 50$ distinct 2-diverse blocks. In literature, an efficient anonymization technique such as t-closeness is proposed.

8.3 Elliptic Curve Cryptography

Earlier, we had a *symmetric key cryptography*, where only one key called *private key* is used. The sender and receiver exchange the private key. This can be vulnerable since it can eavesdrop on the communication medium. The solution is to use *asymmetric key* where two keys are used, namely, *private and public keys*. The private key is like a password and is kept secretly with each party. On the other hand, the public key is like an email id and is announced to the external world. *Public key cryptography* was developed by Diffie and Hellman in 1976. Public key cryptography is also called asymmetric key cryptography because it uses two keys: private and public. RSA and ECC are examples of public-key cryptography. RSA algorithm was developed by MIT researchers Ron **R**ivest, Adi **S**hamir, and Leonard **A**dleman in 1977. RSA algorithm addresses the issue of secrecy or private key cryptography, however, it has higher computational complexity.

Elliptic Curve Cryptography (ECC) was developed by Neal Koblitz and Victor Miller who had worked at IBM in 1985. If the RSA algorithm uses 3072 bits public key, then the ECC algorithm uses only 256 bits public key for a comparable level of security. ECC algorithm uses a smaller key size and hence suitable for IoT networks. Notably, the elliptic curve has nothing to

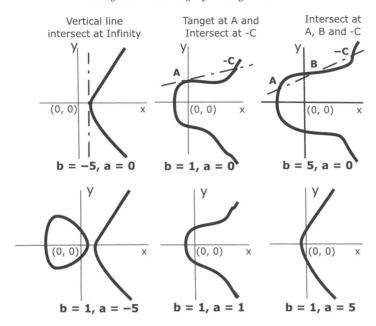

FIGURE 8.1: ECC curves

do with an ellipse. The elliptic curve is described using a quadratic curve. In ECC, addition does not mean the simple algebraic addition. Similarly, the doubling of points does not mean the simple multiplication of each coordinate by two. Nevertheless, we use the same terminologies.

8.3.1 ECC over Real Numbers

Elliptic curve over real number is described using

$$y^2 = x^3 + ax + b \tag{8.1}$$

where x, y, a, $b \in \mathbb{R}$, a set of real numbers and $4a^3 + 27b^2 \neq 0$. This cubic form is of degree 3.

ECC uses *trapdoor or one way function*. That is, given the public key, it is difficult to derive the private key. Public and private keys are generated using points of an elliptic curve. The curve is parametrized by $\{a, b, p_r, n_r, g\}$. Note that, a and b are the parameters of the elliptic curve. Figure 8.1 shows the elliptic curves for different values of the parameters. Here, p_r imposes the maximum limits along the x and y axes. p_r is a prime number and used in the elliptic curve over a finite field. n_r is a cyclic group and this many times operations are repeated to get a private key. g is the generator or base point on the elliptic curve. This is used to compute other points on the curve.

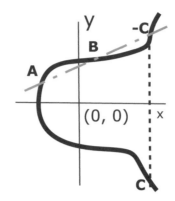

FIGURE 8.2: ECC addition

8.3.2 Dot Operations over Real Numbers

Some characteristics of an elliptic curve are as follows: First, the curve is symmetric about x axis. Second, if we draw a line, it touches the curve at a maximum of three points. Third, the curve extends to infinity on both ends. There are also the following properties:

- If a line intersects two points A and B on the curve, then it also intersects a third point, that is, $-C$ on the curve.

- If a line is a tangent to the curve at point A, then it also intersects another point $-C$ on the curve.

- The vertical line intersects the curve at infinity.

There are two operations called dot operations. These are called point addition and point doubling. Let us discuss that.

Point Addition: Let A and B be (x_A, y_A) and (x_B, y_B), respectively. A straight line between points A and B intersects at point $-C$. The reflection of point $-C$ about x axis gives the point C which is the addition of points A and B as shown in Figure 8.2. Let

$$\theta_a = \frac{y_B - y_A}{x_B - x_A} \tag{8.2}$$

be the slope of the straight line connecting A and B. Now, make it a general straight line by replacing (x_B, y_B) with (x, y). That is,

$$\theta_a(x - x_A) = (y - y_A) \tag{8.3}$$

We can rewrite it as follows:

$$y = \theta_a x + y_A - \theta_a x_A \tag{8.4}$$

In order to find the coordinates of point $-C \equiv (x_C, -y_C)$, solve equation of the curve $y^2 = x^3 + ax + b$ and Equation 8.4. That is,

$$x^3 + ax + b = (\theta_a x + y_A - \theta_a x_A)^2 \tag{8.5}$$

This can be further recast as

$$x^3 - \theta_a^2 x^2 + [a - 2\theta_a(y_A - \theta_a x_A)]x + b - (y_A - \theta_a x_A)^2 = 0 \tag{8.6}$$

This is a monic polynomial. It has the coefficient of highest power of x (that is, x^3) equal to 1. We can write the following using the property of monic polynomial:

$$x_A + x_B + x_C = -(-\theta_a^2) \tag{8.7}$$

That is,

$$x_C = \theta_a^2 - x_A - x_B \tag{8.8}$$

Replace (x, y) with $(x_C, -y_C)$ in Equation 8.3. That is,

$$- y_C = y_A + \theta_a(x_C - x_A) \tag{8.9}$$

Hence, y_C for point reflected point C is

$$y_C = -y_A + \theta_a(x_A - x_C) \tag{8.10}$$

Doubling Operation: The tangent line at point A intersects the elliptic curve at point $-C$. The reflected point of $-C$ about x axis gives the doubling point C of point P. Taking the derivative of the elliptic curve $y^2 = x^3 + ax + b$ with respect to x gives

$$2y\frac{dy}{dx} = 3x^2 + a \tag{8.11}$$

That is, replacing (x, y) with (x_A, y_A)

$$\theta_d = \frac{dy}{dx} = \frac{3x_A^2 + a}{2y_A} \tag{8.12}$$

at point A. We may consider $A = B$ for point doubling. From final expression of x_C of point addition, we can write

$$x_C = \theta_d^2 - 2x_A$$
$$y_C = -y_A + \theta_d(x_A - x_C) \tag{8.13}$$

8.3.3   Operations over Finite Field

The computation using real numbers is easy to understand. However, it requires high computational time for performing various operations. There is also inaccuracy due to rounding error. At times, the number becomes extremely large and floating-point cannot hold it. The solution is to use the cryptographic algorithm which needs accurate and fast computations. Hence, carry out the computation on a finite field $(0, 1, \ldots, p_r - 1)$ of integers modulo p_r, where p_r is a prime number. Here, x and $y \in \mathbb{Z}$, a set of integers. Using expressions of point addition and doubling operations, we can summarize the following for operations over a finite field:

Addition:

$$\theta_a = \left(\frac{y_B - y_A}{x_B - x_A}\right) \bmod p_r$$
$$x_C = (\theta_a^2 - x_A - x_B) \bmod p_r \qquad (8.14)$$
$$y_C = -y_A + \theta_a(x_A - x_C) \bmod p_r$$

Doubling:

$$\theta_d = \left(\frac{3x_A^2 + a}{2y_A}\right) \bmod p_r$$
$$x_C = (\theta_d^2 - 2x_A) \bmod p_r \qquad (8.15)$$
$$y_C = (-y_A + \theta_d(x_A - x_C)) \bmod p_r$$

Negation: If $A \equiv (x_A, y_A)$ is a point on the curve, then $-A$ is obtained by reflection about x-axis. That is,

$$-A \equiv (x_A, -y_A \bmod p_r) \qquad (8.16)$$

Identity element: The point at infinity O is an identity element under addition operation.

- If we add the points A with $-A$, then the straight line becomes vertical. It is assumed that the line intersects the curve at infinity. Hence, the finite length of the reflected line remains at infinity. That is to say, $A + (-A) = O$.

- Addition of a point A and infinity O gives the point itself. That is, $A + O = A$.

  In the last case, there was no other option other than going to infinity for the third intersection. However, in this case, we have the possibility of a third intersection on the actual curve. So, there is no need to go to infinity to find the third intersection with the curve.

8.3.4 Trapdoor Function

Let g and q be two points on the elliptic curve described in the following manner

$$q = n_r g, \qquad (8.17)$$

where $n_r < p_r$. According to the property of commutative group, q will be also the point of the elliptic group. Since it uses the trapdoor function, given n_r and g, it is easy to find q. However, given q and g, it is very difficult to find n_r for a large n_r. This is called the *discrete logarithm problem* for an elliptic

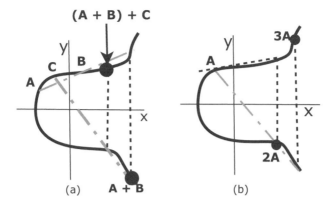

FIGURE 8.3: Jump in ECC

curve. Here, start point (g) and end point (q) on an elliptic curve act as the public keys. The number of jumps to go from g to q is a private key.

8.3.5 Beauty of ECC

We take a straight path and then jump to another side to get $A + B$ as shown in Figure 8.3(a). This is done in order to lose our enemy. However, the enemy may still follow us. Let us repeat the same trick. Start from $A + B$ and go to C. Then again jump to another side, that is, $(A + B) + C$. If the number of jumps (n_r) is large enough, then it becomes difficult for the enemy to track us.

We can consider the special case for illustration purposes in Figure 8.3(b). Let us move along the tangent for easy illustration when $A = B$. Using the previous trick, we can get $2A$, then $3A$, and so on till $n_r A$ to lose our enemy for a large n_r. We can go from A to $n_r A$ if we know the n_r. However, it is very difficult for the enemy to crack n_r, given A and $n_r A$. The elliptic curve parameters a and b, and generator or base point, g or A, are the public information. The sender and receiver are agreed to use these parameters. The final point $n_r g$ or $n_r A$ is a public key, however, n_r is the private key. The enemy can track us if n_r is small and we do the operation slowly.

The solution is to carry out the operation very fastly. Also, if we do some operations on points on the curve, the result still belongs to the group. Further, the add operation follows the associativity property. That is, $(A + B) + C = A + (B + C)$. The proof is difficult, however, it can be verified easily by taking points on the curve. Hence, the order does not matter.

Example: Let us consider a numerical example to understand the concepts that we have learned so far. Suppose that we want to get $13A$. There are two approaches for the same. First, we can add A in thirteen steps, we can get $13A$. Second, convert decimal to binary equivalent. Then, $(13)_{10}A = (1101)_2 A = 2^3 A + 2^2 A + 2^0 A = 8A + 4A + A$. (a) Add A and then double A, (b) Double

$2A$, (c) Add $4A$ and then double $4A$, and (d) Add $8A$. Therefore, we can do it in only 4 steps. Both the approaches produce the same result. Doubling is easier and order of addition does not matter. We can trick the enemy by doing doubling quickly on an elliptic curve rather than adding one by one. The second approach requires only 4 steps and hence faster than the first approach which requires 13 steps. Note that $n_r = 13$ is a very small number herein. We consider it for visualization purpose.

We can do the computation with order of $O(\log_2 n_r)$. Even if $n_r = 2^{200}$, we can do the computation in only 200 double and add very fast steps. If n_r is a very large number, then it becomes difficult for the enemy to determine the number of jumps. This is called *elliptic curve discrete logarithm*. For a secure message exchange between sender and receiver, they must agree upon the parameters of an elliptic curve, that is, a, b, and a large prime number p_r. They then pick a generator or base point g on the elliptic curve.

8.3.6   Key Generation and Exchange

In key generation, the private keys are chosen, which are the large prime numbers between 0 and $p_r - 1$. Let the private keys of sender and receiver be s_{priv} and r_{priv}, respectively. We compute the public keys for sender and receiver as

$$s_{\text{pub}} = s_{\text{priv}}g \text{ and}$$
$$r_{\text{pub}} = r_{\text{priv}}g, \tag{8.18}$$

respectively. After generation of public keys, they exchange these between each other. Now, in key exchange, the public key of receiver (or sender) is with sender (or receiver). We calculate the secret keys for the sender and the receiver, respectively, as

$$s_{\text{key}} = s_{\text{priv}}r_{\text{pub}} \text{ and}$$
$$r_{\text{key}} = r_{\text{priv}}s_{\text{pub}}. \tag{8.19}$$

Note that both are the same as

$$s_{\text{priv}}r_{\text{pub}} = s_{\text{priv}}r_{\text{priv}}g$$
$$= r_{\text{priv}}(s_{\text{priv}}g) \quad = r_{\text{priv}}s_{\text{pub}}. \tag{8.20}$$

Notably, we can get s_{pub} (or r_{pub}) by adding g, s_{priv} (or r_{priv}) times. Now, in key exchange, the sender (or receiver) adds $r_{\text{priv}}g$ (or $s_{\text{priv}}g$), s_{priv} (or r_{priv}) times. We can trick enemy by using double and add method and using a large s_{priv} and r_{priv}.

8.3.7   Encryption and Decryption

Let us consider a simple elliptic curve encryption and decryption for illustration purpose. In encryption, the original message is encoded by mapping

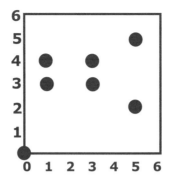

FIGURE 8.4: ECC finite field for $p_r = 7$

to a point on the curve. The data to be encoded is Message. The encrypted or ciphered message which is sent from the sender to the receiver is given by

$$C_M = \{s_{\text{priv}}g, \text{Message} + s_{\text{key}} \text{ or } r_{\text{key}}\} \text{ as } s_{\text{key}} = r_{\text{key}} \tag{8.21}$$

Hence,

$$C_M = \{s_{\text{priv}}g, \text{Message} + s_{\text{priv}}r_{\text{pub}}\} \tag{8.22}$$

which is again the x and y coordinates on the elliptic curve.

In decryption, the receiver subtracts the product of receiver's private key and first coordinate of C_M from the second coordinate of C_M. That is,

$$\text{Message} + s_{\text{priv}}r_{\text{pub}} - (r_{\text{priv}}s_{\text{priv}}g) = \text{Message} + s_{\text{priv}}r_{\text{priv}}g - (r_{\text{priv}}s_{\text{priv}}g) \tag{8.23}$$

where $r_{\text{pub}} = r_{\text{priv}}g$. Hence, we can simplify to

$$\text{Message} + s_{\text{priv}}r_{\text{priv}}g - s_{\text{priv}}r_{\text{priv}}g = \text{Message} \tag{8.24}$$

which is in fact the original message.

Example for Generation of Points: Generate the points for an elliptic curve $y^2 = (x^3 + ax + b) \bmod p_r$ for $a = 1$, $b = 0$, and $p_r = 7$.

Solution: The points of the elliptic curve over the finite field are $(0, 0)$, $(1, 3)$, $(1, 4)$, $(3, 3)$, $(3, 4)$, $(5, 2)$, and $(5, 5)$ as shown in Figure 8.4. We can easily verify these points below:

- *For (0, 0)*: $0^2 \bmod 7 = 0^3 + 1 \times 0 + 0 \bmod 7$. This gives $0 = 0$.

- *For (1, 3)*: $3^2 \bmod 7 = 1^3 + 1 \times 1 + 0 \bmod 7$. This gives $2 = 2$.

- *For (1, 4)*: $4^2 \bmod 7 = 1^3 + 1 \times 1 + 0 \bmod 7$. This gives $2 = 2$.

- *For (3, 3)*: $3^2 \bmod 7 = 3^3 + 1 \times 3 + 0 \bmod 7$. This gives $2 = 2$.

- *For (3, 4)*: $4^2 \bmod 7 = 3^3 + 1 \times 3 + 0 \bmod 7$. This gives $2 = 2$.

TABLE 8.5: Values of $3\theta_d \mod 7$

θ_d	1	2	3	4	5	6	7
$3\theta_d$	3	6	9	12	15	18	21
$3\theta_d \mod 7$	3	6	2	5	1	4	0

TABLE 8.6: Values of $2\theta_a \mod 7$

θ_a	1	2	3
$2\theta_a$	2	4	6
$2\theta_a \mod 7$	2	4	6

- *For (5, 2)*: $2^2 \mod 7 = 5^3 + 1 \times 5 + 0 \mod 7$. This gives $4 = 4$.

- *For (5, 5)*: $5^2 \mod 7 = 5^3 + 1 \times 5 + 0 \mod 7$. This gives $4 = 4$.

The following example utilizes all the concepts like point adding, doubling, and negation operations in detail.

Example of ECC Encryption and Decryption: Consider the elliptic curve of the last example with generator point $g \equiv (x_g, y_g) = (3, 3)$ and encoded message on the curve, Message $\equiv (x_M, y_M) = (3, 4)$. Assume the private key for sender and receiver are respectively 3 and 2. Carry out the ECC encryption and decryption.

Solution: Here, $s_{\mathrm{priv}} = 3$ and $r_{\mathrm{priv}} = 2$. Let us compute the public key of the sender. $s_{\mathrm{pub}} = s_{\mathrm{priv}} g = 3 \times (3, 3) = (3)_{10} g = (11)_2 g = (2^1 + 2^0)g = 2g + g$. Hence, (a) Add g and then double g (b) Add $2g$.

Now, we double g as $2g = (x_C, y_C)$ say. $\theta_d = \left(\frac{3x_g^2 + a}{2y_g}\right) \mod p_r = \left(\frac{3 \times 3^2 + 1}{2 \times 3}\right) \mod 7 = \left(\frac{14}{3}\right) \mod 7$. That is $3\theta_d = 14 \mod 7 = 0$. For $\theta_d = 7$, the condition is satisfied as shown in Table 8.5. Therefore, $x_C = (\theta_d^2 - 2x_g) \mod p_r = (7^2 - 2 \times 3) \mod 7 = 1$. Now, $y_C = (-y_g + \theta_d(x_g - x_C)) \mod p_r = (-3 + 7(3 - 1)) \mod 7 = 4$. Hence, $2g = (1, 4) = (x_C, y_C)$ (say).

Now, we add g and $2g \equiv (x_D, y_D)$. Here, $\theta_a = \left(\frac{y_g - y_C}{x_g - x_C}\right) \mod p_r = \left(\frac{3-4}{3-1}\right) \mod 7 = \left(\frac{-1}{2}\right) \mod 7$. This is $2\theta_a = -1 + 7 \mod 7 = 6$. Therefore, $\theta_a = 3$ as shown in Table 8.6. Let us add. $x_D = (\theta_a^2 - x_g - x_C) \mod p_r = (3^2 - 3 - 1) \mod 7 = 5$ and $y_D = -y_g + \theta_a(x_g - x_D) \mod p_r = -3 + 3(3 - 5) \mod 7 = -9 \mod 7 = -9 + 7 \times 2 \mod 7 = 5$. Hence, $g + 2g = (5, 5) \equiv (x_D, y_D)$.

We determine the public key of receiver as: $r_{\mathrm{pub}} = r_{\mathrm{priv}} g = 2 \times (3, 3) = (1, 4) \equiv (x_E, y_E)$ as computed previously. This is the first part of s_{pub}. The secret key after key exchange for the sender is computed as follows: $s_{\mathrm{key}} = s_{\mathrm{priv}} r_{\mathrm{pub}} = 3 \times (1, 4) = (3)_{10} \times r_{\mathrm{pub}} = (11)_2 \times r_{\mathrm{pub}} = (2^1 + 2^0) \times r_{\mathrm{pub}} = 2r_{\mathrm{pub}} + r_{\mathrm{pub}}$. We need to carry out double and add operations for this as follows:

TABLE 8.7: Values of $2\theta_{d,F}$ mod 7

$\theta_{d,F}$	1	2	3	4
$2\theta_{d,F}$	2	4	6	8
$2\theta_{d,F}$ mod 7	2	4	6	1

TABLE 8.8: Values of $5\theta_{d,I}$ mod 7

$\theta_{d,I}$	1	2
$5\theta_{d,I}$	5	10
$5\theta_{d,I}$ mod 7	5	3

- Double of $r_{\text{pub}} \equiv (x_F, y_F)$: New $\theta_{d,F} = \left(\frac{3x_E^2+a}{2y_E}\right)$ mod $p_r = \left(\frac{3\times1^2+1}{2\times4}\right)$ mod $7 = \left(\frac{1}{2}\right)$ mod 7. That is $2\theta_{d,F} = 1$ mod $7 = 1$. For $\theta_{d,F} = 4$, the condition is satisfied as shown in Table 8.7. Therefore, $x_F = (\theta_{d,F}^2 - 2x_E)$ mod $p_r = (4^2 - 2 \times 1)$ mod $7 = 0$. Now, $y_F = (-y_E + \theta_{d,F}(x_E - x_F))$ mod $p_r = (-4 + 4(1 - 0))$ mod $7 = 0$. Hence, $2r_{\text{pub}} = (0, 0) = (x_F, y_F)$.

- Addition: $(x_E, y_E) \equiv (1, 4) + (x_F, y_F) \equiv (0, 0) = (x_H, y_H)$. $\theta_{a,H} = \left(\frac{y_E - y_F}{x_E - x_F}\right)$ mod $p_r = \left(\frac{4-0}{1-0}\right)$ mod $7 = 4$ mod $7 = 4$. $x_H = (\theta_{a,H}^2 - x_E - x_F)$ mod $p_r = (4^2 - 1 - 0)$ mod $7 = 1$ and $y_F = -y_E + \theta_{a,H}(x_E - x_H)$ mod $p_r = -4 + 4(1 - 1)$ mod $7 = -4$ mod $7 = -4 + 7$ mod $7 = 3$. Hence, $(x_H, y_H) \equiv (1, 3)$.

The secret key after key exchange for receiver is computed as follows: $r_{\text{key}} = r_{\text{priv}}s_{\text{pub}} = 2 \times (5,5) = 2 \times (x_D, y_D) \equiv (x_I, y_I)$. We need to to double operation herein.

- Double of $s_{\text{pub}} \equiv (x_I, y_I)$: New $\theta_{d,I} = \left(\frac{3x_D^2+a}{2y_D}\right)$ mod $p_r = \left(\frac{3\times5^2+1}{2\times5}\right)$ mod 7 $= \left(\frac{38}{5}\right)$ mod 7. That is $5\theta_{d,I} = 38$ mod $7 = 3$. For $\theta_{d,I} = 2$, the condition is satisfied as shown in Table 8.8. Therefore, $x_I = (\theta_{d,I}^2 - 2x_D)$ mod $p_r = (2^2 - 2 \times 5)$ mod $7 = -6$ mod $7 = -6 + 7$ mod $7 = 1$. Now, $y_I = (-y_D + \theta_{d,I}(x_D - x_I))$ mod $p_r = (-5 + 2(5 - 1))$ mod $7 = 3$. Hence, $2s_{\text{pub}} = (1, 3) = (x_I, y_I)$.

Remarks: we can also observe numerically that s_{key} and r_{key} are indeed the same as expected.

Let us do now encryption. $C_M = \{s_{\text{priv}}g, \text{Message} + s_{\text{key}} \text{ or } r_{\text{key}}\}$ as $s_{\text{key}} = r_{\text{key}}$. Therefore, $C_M = \{s_{\text{priv}}g, \text{Message} + s_{\text{priv}}r_{\text{pub}}\} = \{3 \times (3,3), (3,4) + 3 \times (1,4)\}$. Since we already have calculated $3 \times (1,4) = (1,3)$ and $3 \times (3,3) = (5,5)$. So, $C_M = \{(5,5), (3,4) + (1,3)\}$. Here, the addition of $(x_J, y_J) = (3,4)$ and $(x_K, y_K) = (1,3) \equiv (x_L, y_L)$ is needed.

- $\theta_{a,L} = \left(\frac{y_J - y_K}{x_J - x_K}\right)$ mod $p_r = \left(\frac{4-3}{3-1}\right)$ mod $7 = \left(\frac{1}{2}\right)$ mod 7. This gives $2\theta_{a,L} = 1$ mod $7 = 1$. Therefore, $\theta_{a,L} = 4$ as shown in Table 8.9. Therefore,

TABLE 8.9: Values of $2\theta_{a,L} \bmod 7$

$\theta_{a,L}$	1	2	3	4
$2\theta_{a,L}$	2	4	6	8
$2\theta_{a,L} \bmod 7$	2	4	6	1

TABLE 8.10: Values of $2\theta_{a,T} \bmod 7$

$\theta_{a,T}$	1	2	3
$2\theta_{a,T}$	2	4	6
$2\theta_{a,T} \bmod 7$	2	4	6

$x_L = (\theta_{a,L}^2 - x_J - x_K) \bmod p_r = (4^2 - 3 - 1) \bmod 7 = 5$ and $y_L = -y_J + \theta_{a,L}(x_J - x_L) \bmod p_r = -4 + 4(3 - 5) \bmod 7 = -12 \bmod 7 = -12 + 7 \times 2 \bmod 7 = 2$. Hence, $(x_L, y_L) \equiv (5, 2)$

Hence, the sender sends the ciphertext $C_M = \{(5,5), (5,2)\}$ to receiver. In order to decrypt the message, we follow the below steps:

We know that Message = (Message + $s_{\text{priv}} r_{\text{pub}}$) − $r_{\text{priv}} s_{\text{priv}} g = (5, 2) - 2 \times (5,5) = (5,2) - (1,3)$ where we use already computed $2 \times (5,5) = (1,3)$. Now, we do subtraction of $(5,2)$ and $(1,3)$. We can write using the expression of negation as: $(5, 2) + (1, -3) = (5, 2) + (1, -3 \bmod 7) = = (5, 2) + (1, -3 + 7 \bmod 7) = (5, 2) + (1, 4)$. We now need to add it. Denote $(x_O, y_O) = (5,2)$ and $(x_S, y_S) = (1,4)$. The added coordinates are denoted by $\equiv (x_T, y_T)$.

- $\theta_{a,T} = \left(\frac{y_O - y_S}{x_O - x_S}\right) \bmod p_r = \left(\frac{2-4}{5-1}\right) \bmod 7 = \left(\frac{-1}{2}\right) \bmod 7$. That is, $2\theta_{a,T} = -1 + 7 \bmod 7 = 6$. Therefore, $\theta_{a,T} = 3$ as shown in Table 8.10. Now, $x_T = (\theta_{a,T}^2 - x_O - x_S) \bmod p_r = (3^2 - 5 - 1) \bmod 7 = 3$ and $y_T = -y_O + \theta_{a,T}(x_O - x_T) \bmod p_r = -2 + 3(5 - 3) \bmod 7 = 4$.

Hence, Message $\equiv (3, 4)$. We get the decrypted message which is the original encoded message.

8.4 Blockchain

Blockchain was introduced in 2008 by Satoshi Nakamoto or a group of people with alias who developed bitcoin. He/they authored a bitcoin white paper titled 'Bitcoin: A Peer-to-Peer Electronic Cash System'. Let us understand the motivation behind blockchain technology. As we know that the bank service is not attractive. Consider an example of sending the money from one country to other. There is a tedious process for opening a bank account, high transaction fee, online scam makes vulnerable, unavailability of bank service

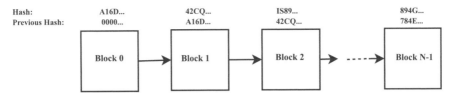

FIGURE 8.5: Illustration of a Blockchain

24×7, transfer limit in a day, and tampering of the data of a bank cannot be rolled back. We need to unwillingly trust a central authority, that is, a bank. This problem can be solved using blockchain technology.

In a centralized architecture, there is a single copy of the information. Also, there is a high maintenance cost. In contrast, the decentralized network distributes the information to all nodes. Blockchain technology decentralizes the entire network. Therefore, data can be recovered in the blockchain. Note that, a node refers to a smart device or computer connected to the network. Data cannot be tampered with in blockchain technology as it is cryptographically secured. Let us discuss some terminologies to understand blockchain technology.

8.4.1 Bitcoin

The bitcoin is a digital currency which is used for electronic payment from a sender to a receiver. Blockchain is the underlying technology to perform that. There are about 1600 digital currencies. A bitcoin can be considered as an application that uses blockchain technology. Blockchain technology can be used in a multitude of use cases.

Blockchain is a distributed digital ledger of immutable records. The meaning of immutable is that the data cannot be altered once it is recorded. Blockchain is composed of cryptographically linked blocks like a linked list of a data structure and hash as a pointer. That is, there is a chain of blocks in blockchain in chronological order. This is illustrated in Figure 8.5.

8.4.2 Hash

Hash is a function that converts input data of any size to a fixed size of alphanumeric characters. Hash represents each block uniquely. The first block has the previous hash "0000...." as there is no preceding block to it. The "previous hash" of the current block is the "Hash" of the previous block.

Hash Function and Its Properties: The blockchain performs cryptography using hash function. Given an input data, the corresponding hash value is generated. For example, if the input data is "We learn blockchain" the

corresponding hash value[1] is
2a37723e5882bbced70103fc3e17b6b3d97bb5f36d55e52f25451e1aaeff1b2b.

There are 64 digits in hexadecimal representation or 32 bytes in binary representation. Each digit is mapped to 4 bits in binary representation. Therefore, the total size is 64 × 4 equal to 256 bits. The size of input can be anything and the size of the output is a fixed size of 256 bits for the SHA-256 hashing algorithm. The SHA stands for Secure Hashing Algorithm. The properties of the hash function are as follows:

- It is a one-way function, that is, given the input, the hash value can be computed easily. However, given the hash value, it is very difficult to produce the input back. This is like a trapdoor function in ECC.

- It is deterministic, that is, for the same input, the output is also the same.

- A small change in the input, there would be a big change in the output.

8.4.3   Blockchain and Its Versions

The blockchain is shared among all the users of the networks. Each user has the same copy of it and can see the history of transactions. The details are since the first block was added to the blockchain network. The first block is also called *genesis block*. There are three versions of Blockchain. Blockchain 1.0 is used in digital currency like bitcoin or other cryptocurrencies in a decentralized system. Blockchain 2.0 is used in smart contracts and the transfer of stock and bonds. Blockchain 3.0 is used in government organizations, hospitals, and many more.

Blocks in Blockchain: The header of the block shown in Figure 8.6 has the following fields:

- **Version number**: Sequence number of the block.

- **Previous hash**: Hash of the previous block to which the current block is linked.

- **Merkle root hash**: Hashes of all transactions are structured in binary Merkle tree. The root of the tree is called Merkle root hash.

- **Timestamp**: When the block is verified and mined.

- **Nonce**: A random number used to create the hash.

- **Target**: The generated hash should be less than the target set by the network. For example, there should be 3 leading zeros.

---

[1] We refer to https://www.anders.com/blockchain for generating the hash value.

Block

Header
Version Number
Previous Hash
Merkle Root Hash
Timestamp
Nonce
Target

Transaction List

FIGURE 8.6: Header of a block

8.4.4 Miner

There are three input, namely, previous hash, Merkle root hash and the nonce to SH-256 cryptographic hashing algorithm as shown in Figure 8.7. The miner varies the nonce, while the previous hash and Merkle root remain the same, to generate a hash value lower than the target. If the hash value meets the target set by the networks, then we stop. Otherwise, the process is repeated and this is called *proof of work* consensus algorithm. All the nodes of the network agrees on the same version of the fact in the consensus algorithm.

The miner verifies and validates the transactions and adds the block. The first miner who gets the hash that meets the target is rewarded. Since the miner invests resources and computing power, he or she is rewarded for the same in terms of bitcoin or other forms of remuneration. The miner gets 12.5 bitcoins and the sum of the transaction fee of that block. The amount is halved every 2,10,00 blocks, which is approximately 4 years. Note that 1 bitcoin is equivalent to USD 51333 or 37.76 lakhs in rupees in May 2021. The miner also verifies if the sender has a sufficient amount to be transferred. The target hash is decided months in advance for every block. It is difficult to generate a nonce that satisfies the target but it is easy to verify by other miners.

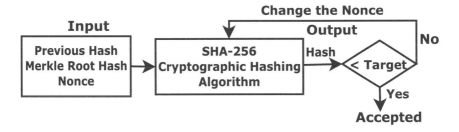

FIGURE 8.7: SHA 256 cryptographic hashing algorithm

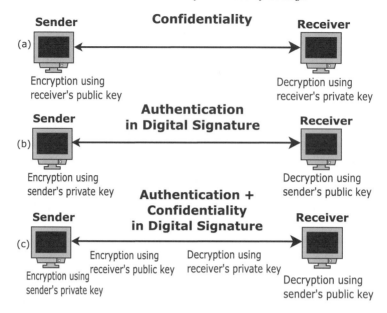

FIGURE 8.8: Confidentiality and authentication in digital signature

8.4.5   Tamper-Proof Blockchain

Let us consider that the attacker tampers the data of block number 3 of Figure 8.5. Subsequently, the hash value of this block changes. However, the previous hash value of block 4 remains intact as there is no tampering in block number 4. Consequently, the changed hash value of block number 3 due to tampering and the previous hash value of block number 4 do not match. This makes the following blocks invalid. Hence, tampering can be detected in a blockchain network. Notably, each user in the blockchain network has the same copy of the ledger. Ledger refers to the history of all transactions.

The attacker invests a lot of computing power and resources to recalculate the hash of block 3. As mentioned, the "previous hash" of block 4 does match with the recalculated hash of tampered block 3. Subsequently, the attacker needs to recalculate the hash for block 5 and so on. This requires a lot of computing power and resources, while the network is still progressing. This is nearly an impossible task in blockchain technology. Hence, this makes blockchain technology tamper-proof.

8.4.6   Role of Digital Signature in Blockchain

Confidentiality is defined as the state of keeping secret or private. This is carried out using public key for encryption and private keys for decryption as shown in Figure 8.8(a). On the other hand, authentication is defined as the process of showing something legitimate. This is achieved using digital

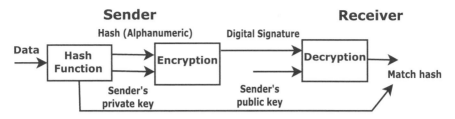

FIGURE 8.9: Digital signature

signature as shown in Figure 8.8(b). The digital signature is equivalent to handwritten signature but it is more secured. However, in authentication, we need public key, not private key, to decrypt. We make sure that received message is from the authentic sender. As shown in Figure 8.8(c), we can achieve both confidentiality and authentication. We do double encryption and decryption at both sender and receiver ends.

We can also use the SHA-256 hash function in the blockchain. First the original message is passed through an SHA-256 hash function, which gives alphanumeric characters. Subsequently, both hash message and private key of the sender is used for encryption to get a digital signature as shown in Figure 8.9. At the receiver, both the digital signature and sender's public key are used to get the hash message. If this hash message and the hash message after directly applying the hash function to the data are the same, then the message is not altered during transmission and coming from the legitimate sender.

8.4.7 Transaction in Blockchain

The transaction details are deducted amount for the sender and credited amount for the receiver. There is no actual transfer of digital currency. Only the transaction is recorded in the ledger of blockchain. The transaction detail is passed through the SHA-256 cryptographic hashing function. We know that the private key is secret with the user, while the public key is shared with all the Bitcoin users. The transaction detail is signed using the user's private key. The sender broadcasts the encrypted transactions with amount of bitcoin network to be transferred. The miner receives the transaction, verifies, and validates it. The miner then includes it in a block and propagates it to other Bitcoin users.

8.4.8 Distributed Ledger

Distributed ledger is a feature of blockchain. All users have the same copy of a ledger. A blank ledger with no data input also has some hash. Each row is a blockchain, where the "previous hash" of the current block is the "hash" of the previous block. The combination of rows and columns makes it a distributed ledger as shown in Figure 8.10. Note that each row is the same in terms of all

Peer A

Block number: 1	Block number: 2	Block number: 3	Block number: 4
Nonce: 23728	Nonce: 66882	Nonce: 19763	Nonce: 49579
Data:	Data:	Data:	Data:
Hash: 34FH...	Hash: 7GH8...	Hash: 9RJD...	Hash: 08HS...
Previous Hash:	Previous Hash: 34FH...	Previous Hash: 7GH8...	Previous Hash: 9RJD...

Peer B

Block number: 1	Block number: 2	Block number: 3	Block number: 4
Nonce: 23728	Nonce: 66882	Nonce: 19763	Nonce: 49579
Data:	Data:	Data:	Data:
Hash: 34FH...	Hash: 7GH8...	Hash: 9RJD...	Hash: 08HS...
Previous Hash:	Previous Hash: 34FH...	Previous Hash: 7GH8...	Previous Hash: 9RJD...

Peer C

Block number: 1	Block number: 2	Block number: 3	Block number: 4
Nonce: 23728	Nonce: 66882	Nonce: 19763	Nonce: 49579
Data:	Data:	Data:	Data:
Hash: 34FH...	Hash: 7GH8...	Hash: 9RJD...	Hash: 08HS...
Previous Hash:	Previous Hash: 34FH...	Previous Hash: 7GH8...	Previous Hash: 9RJD...

FIGURE 8.10: Distributed ledger

parameters. If we write something in any block of some peer, all subsequent blocks turn pink[2]. This leads to a change in "hash" and "previous hash" like a linked list. Now, clicking on mine of that block changes the nonce and regenerates the hash such that it has 4 leading zeros to meet the target. This makes that block green and the process is repeated for subsequent blocks of that row. Notably, modification of a block makes all subsequent blocks invalid and these are re-mined.

For example, when we write in the data field of block 3 (say) of Peer A, this generates a hash value that is different from block 3 of peer B or C. Note that the hash values of block 3 of peer B and C are the same as we have not modified their data fields. Hence, the data modification of a block can be easily detected. This was not possible if we have a single copy of the ledger. All the users of the network have a history of transactions since the genesis block which is the first block of the network. Even if a node (computer) gets corrupted, we do not lose the data because the same copy is with other nodes.

8.4.9   Byzantine Generals Problem

Any modification to the block must be approved by a majority of the users of the networks. This is because the modification made to the block is permanent and immutable once recorded. This makes the networks decentralized where there is no central authority like a bank. Let us assume that there are four generals, out of them, three are loyal and one is a traitor as shown in Figure 8.11. The loyal general gives the command to attack, while the traitor to not attack. The generals are not at one place, they communicate among themselves. The goal is victory even if a minority of the generals are traitors.

---

[2]Refer to https://andersbrownworth.com/blockchain/distributed for demo

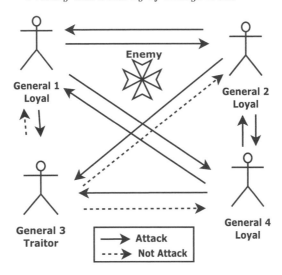

FIGURE 8.11: Byzantine general problem

In this scenario, the loyal general receives the 2 commands for attack and 1 command to not attack. The majority of commands are to attack, therefore, they attack the enemy. This is called Byzantine fault tolerance. On similar lines, in blockchain networks, the generals are the nodes and the messages are the transactions. Attack command is the legitimate transaction, while to not attack command is the invalid transaction. We arrive at the consensus in the presence of some malicious nodes.

8.4.10 Transaction Pool and Candidate Block

Transaction pool stores all the unverified transactions before getting included in a new block. Candidate block is a temporary current block that does not have valid proof of work. It is made up of transactions selected from the transaction pool. The miner picks block number 5 (say) and starts validating. However, in meantime, some other miners might get the satisfactory hash that meets the target. The block number 5 does not have a valid proof of work which is mined by miner 2 before miner 1 completes and gets the reward. Now, miner 1 starts competing for block number 6 by picking the unverified transaction from the transaction pool.

Tie in Generating Hashes or Adding Blocks by Miners: A tie is a rare event, however, we choose the one who finds the hash that meets the target first. If two miners get the hashes that meet the target at the same time, both add his or her block. However, two blockchains must not run and only one blockchain needs to be allowed. We choose the blockchain in which the other miner has added a block first and gets verified by other users in the network. Say, miner 3 adds the block in the second blockchain, then it

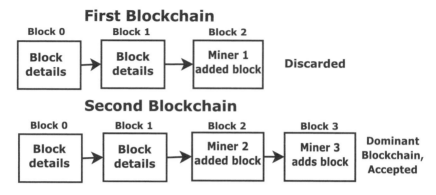

FIGURE 8.12: Tie in generating hashes

is accepted as the dominant blockchain. The first blockchain is discarded as shown in Figure 8.12.

8.4.11   Fork

The blockchain diverges into a different chain with different rules or protocols. The users of networks are not in agreement. Some improvements to be made are minor, while some are major. There are two types of forks.

- **Soft fork**: The new version works well with the old version, that is, there is backward compatibility. Hence, there is flexibility.

- **Hard fork**: This is rigid as there are different rules for different chains and the users have to choose one. Both chains are valid and cannot be discarded. Some users support the old chain, while others the new chain.

Example: We have different versions of the same coin, for instance, bitcoin (BTC) and bitcoin cash (B cash or BCH). Initially, we had a block size of 1 MB with a lesser number of transactions. With the popularity of Bitcoin, the number of transactions has been increased. Therefore, we need a larger block size of 8 MB for bitcoin cash since August 2017.

8.4.12   Bitcoin versus Ethereum

There are more than 1600 crypto-currencies. For example, Bitcoin, Bitcoin cash, Ethereum, Litecoin, and many more. Ether cash of Ethereum network is used for peer-to-peer transactions like bitcoin. In addition, it is used for the creation and execution of the smart contracts on a decentralized network. Transaction in the bitcoin network is slow and takes about 10 minutes. In the Ethereum network, it is fast and takes about 15 seconds. Bitcoin uses SHA-256 cryptographic hashing algorithm, while Ethereum uses ethash algorithm.

The *Proof of Concept* is used in the Ethereum network. One gets the chance of mining based on the number of coins he or she owns. The more the stake, the more the chance and mining power. The one with more stake likely performs genuine validation, otherwise, he or she loses stake if it is invalidated by the rest of the users. The miner gets a reward of 3 ETH and the sum of the transaction fee for the validation of the block. The reward does not get halved, unlike the bitcoin network.

8.4.13 Some Remarks on Blockchain Technology

- It is not clear whether Satoshi Nakamoto is the name of the person or group alias name. Nobody knows if Satoshi Nakamoto is alive or dead. The developers were used to communicate electronically through email or the BitcoinTalk forum created by them. Satoshi Nakamoto owns 1 million bitcoin. He disappeared from the Internet after handing over the source code of the project in 2010.

- The bitcoin refers to the unit of cryptocurrency in the transaction, while Bitcoin refers to the protocol which is a ledger to stores information related to transactions.

- 1 bitcoin is equivalent to USD 51333 or 37.76 lakhs in Indian rupees, 1 bitcoin cash is equivalent to USD 1337 or 0.98 lakhs in Indian rupees and 1 ETH is equivalent to USD 3995 or 2.93 lakh Indian rupees in May 2021.

- The blockchain network is fault-tolerant and complete (100%) availability. Blockchain is a decentralized and transparent network. There is trust between neighboring nodes that may be through gossiping. Elliptic curve is used to generate cryptographic keys.

8.4.14 Applications of Blockchain

- *Money transaction*: We know the drawback of a bank and steps for transactions between sender and receiver.

- *Know your customer (KYC)*: We do not need to submit the KYC form to each bank separately. Once KYC is recorded in a blockchain network, we can allow accessing the KYC form to each bank.

- *Voting system*: Single vote casting by an electorate; electorate identity information and votes cannot be tampered with and stored permanently.

- *Healthcare*: The medical data can be communicated more securely using blockchain technology. The data cannot be tampered with and lost in the communication channel. Importantly, there would be a single version of data. It removes duplication of medical data and saves a lot of storage capacity and of course the money.

- *Insurance claim*: The medical history of a patient can be stored in immutable records. This prevents the false claim made by the patient.

- *Smart contract*: Based on terms and conditions set using code in the Ethereum network, the smart contract automatically negotiates the parking fee, ordering some repair parts of a machine and payment through the agreement of a smart contract, negotiation of different energy (solar, wind, etc.) of a home in a smart grid system and many more. Smart contract monitors flight status and automatic payment of compensation in case flight get delayed by some hours. The sensors in a vehicle provide real-time conditions of the vehicle and automatic payment of compensation if the vehicle meets an accident.

- *Retail Management*: The sensors collect the conditions of the product. The product can be automatically tracked, and conditions at generation, shipment, and arrival can be verified through history. The contract can be executed between two vendors.

- *Government Organizations*: All the data can be secured, tamper-proof and transparent among stakeholders eliminating paper-based records.

8.4.15   Disadvantages of Blockchain

There is a perception that blockchain technology is difficult to implement. Only skilled blockchain architects and blockchain developers can do this. Only 1% of organizations currently use this technology. It is also believed that scalability is an issue. It will take longer to verify and validate a block when the network size increases. The block size is also increased from 1 MB to 8 MB. Further, we need rules and regulations from governments or organizations for regulation purposes.

8.5   Summary

In this chapter, we studied data privacy, elliptic curve cryptography, and blockchain technology. The data anonymization preserves the privacy of the user. The anonymized data must not disclose sensitive attributes like the name of disease and income of the user. Also, at the same time, we should have enough information. Next, if the RSA algorithm uses 3072 bits public key, then the ECC algorithm uses only 256 bits public key for a comparable level of security. ECC algorithm uses a smaller key size and hence suitable for IoT networks. Finally, the data cannot be tampered with in blockchain technology as it is cryptographically secured.

8.6 Exercises

1. Apply k-anonymity and l-diversity anonymization techniques for dataset of Table 8.11.

TABLE 8.11: Dataset for k-anonymity and l-diversity anonymization

	Non Sensitive	Non Sensitive	Non Sensitive	Sensitive
Record No.	**Name**	**Age**	**Area Code**	**Income (Lakh)**
1	David	27	101	10
2	Diya	32	120	25
3	Krish	41	192	18
4	Priyansh	22	148	14

2. (a) What could be the original pin code if we generalize pin code in k-anonymity as 844***?

   (b) What could be the original gender if we generalize gender in k-anonymity as *?

3. How does the key exchange happen in ECC when the receiver does not know the sender?

4. Generate an elliptic curve $(y^2 = x^3 + ax + b)$ over a finite field for $a = 1$, $b = -1$ and $p_r = 5$.

5. Crack the number of jumps using brute-force method if we start from the point (2, 3) and end at the point (1, 4) on the elliptic curve of the last Problem 4 one by one. It is possible herein because n_r is a small number.

6. Carry out the encryption for the elliptic curve discussed in the Problem 4 for $g = (1, 4)$, Message $= (3, 2)$. The private keys for sender and receiver are 5 and 2, respectively.

7. Carry out the decryption for the elliptic curve discussed in the Problem 4 for $g = (1, 4)$, Message $= (3, 2)$. The private keys for sender and receiver are 5 and 2, respectively.

8. **Do It Yourself**: Study and modify the example of transactions of Token available at https://andersbrownworth.com/blockchain/tokens

Chapter 9

Applications of IoT

9.1 Introduction

In a smart environment, heterogeneous things send data to the gateway, fog node, or cloud using wireless protocols. Encryption of data is carried out in a secured smart environment. Further, things data analytic is used for automated decisions and making our life easier. The chapter discusses two use cases of smart environments, namely, smart healthcare, and smart city. This helps us in the visualization of the learned concepts of previous chapters. In particular, human activity recognition using wearable sensors and channel state information in a smart healthcare system is presented. The channel state information provides a device-free solution and hence, better than wearable sensors and image/video-based. The image and video-based approach breach the privacy of the user and require a large transmit bandwidth. The chapter also presents smart parking, smart farming, and smart air pollution monitoring for smart city applications. The smart system facilitates improved services to the users without any human intervention.

9.2 Smart Healthcare

Three applications are presented herein for a smart healthcare system: human activity recognition using wearable sensors, Channel State Information (CSI) based human activity recognition, and human health monitoring.

9.2.1 Human Activity Recognition Using Wearable Sensors

In this section, we present a human activity recognition (HAR) application using wearable sensors. The applications of HAR include remote patient monitoring, elderly people monitoring, and transportation amongst others. The wearable biomedical sensors are the following:

- Electromyography (EMG): To assess the health of muscles.

DOI: 10.1201/9781003225584-9

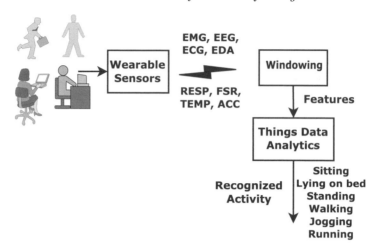

FIGURE 9.1: Human activity recognition using wearable sensors

- Electroencephalograph (EEG): To detect abnormalities in the brain waves.

- Electrocardiogram (ECG): To record electrical activity of the heart.

- Accelerometer (ACC): To measure acceleration of the body.

- Electrodermal Activity (EDA): To measure changes in the electrical properties of the skin.

- Respiration (RESP): To measures breathing rate.

- Force (FSR): To detect numbness of the body.

- Temperature (TEMP): To measure body temperature.

The other biomedical sensors are blood pressure sensor, Galvanic skin response sensor, airflow sensor, sound generator, body position sensor, snore sensor, alert patient button, spirometer, glucometer, and SPO2 pulse oximeter. The data from the things are sent using wireless technology such as Bluetooth, Wi-Fi, or LoRaWAN to the gateway, fog node or cloud for computational purpose securely. The activities that can be detected are classified into several categories. Those can be (a) sitting, (b) lying on a bed, (c) standing, (d) walking, (e) jogging, and (f) running to name a few. Wearable sensors based HAR is shown in Figure 9.1. The wearable sensors data change uniquely according to the activity. For example, the heart rate and body temperature increase from rest to intense activity conditions. The acceleration sensor gives the body accelerations in x, y, and z directions. There are several smart healthcare kits such as Biosignalplux, and eHealth Medical Development Platform for Arduino—MySignals HW Complete Kit to measures biomedical signals.

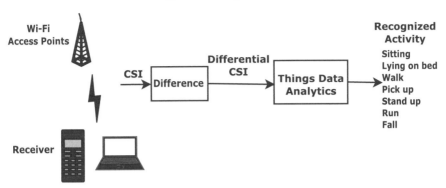

FIGURE 9.2: Human activity recognition using differential CSI

One can choose a biomedical kit depending on the requirements of specific biomedical signals, sampling rate, computation and storage facilities, ease of use, and cost amongst others.

We utilize data analytic technique for classification of different activities using wearable sensor data. If we use machine learning algorithm, we can extract features of wearable biomedical data for different activities. For instance, we compute mean, variance, standard deviation, skewness, kurtosis, minimum and maximum value, and many more as features. Notably, the deep learning algorithm automatically extracts features. In order to have multiple instances of a specific biomedical signal, the concept of windowing is used. The original time-series data is windowed to get different overlapping segments of a single time-series data. The feature is computed for each windowed signal. Subsequently, the features are fed to a classifier like kNN, naive Bayes, or support vector machine (SVM) algorithm. Finally, the activities are recognized based on the wearable sensor data. Notably, we can use fewer sensors also, however, multiple sensors provide complementary information and generally increases the activity recognition accuracy at the cost of computational complexity.

9.2.2 Human Activity Recognition Using Channel State Information

HAR algorithms may be classified into three categories: wearable sensor based, image/video-based and wireless link based. In the last section, we discussed wearable sensor-based activity recognition. However, wearable sensors may cause discomfort to humans. Image/video-based HAR consumes a lot of bandwidth during transmission and breaches the privacy of users. Therefore, we discuss wireless link-based HAR in this section.

We use CSI between transmitter and receiver to recognize the activity of a person as shown in Figure 9.2. Wi-Fi access points present in the environment act as a transmitter and smart device as a receiver. The medium between a transmitter and a receiver is called a channel. The CSI is a complex number and hence has both magnitude and phase. These magnitude and phase give a unique signature for different activities. A public dataset of CSI for activity recognition is of Stanford data dump of Ermon Group. Linux 802.11n CSI Tool is used to get CSI at 1000 Hz. The tool is built using Intel Wi-Fi Wireless Link 5300 802.11n MIMO. There are 90 subcarriers and each subcarrier has amplitude and phase. The first column of the CSI dataset is time-stamp. The second to ninety-first columns are amplitude data. Finally, ninety-second to one hundred eighty-first columns is phase data for 30 subcarriers times 3 antennas of a MIMO system.

Generally, the CSI contains the carrier frequency offset and sampling frequency offset as per literature. If we take the difference of two CSI for the same activity, the offset can be easily canceled. This soft computing approach enhances the activity recognition performance. The differential CSI is further fed to things data analytic for classification of different activities. The different classified activities are sitting, lying on the bed, walk, pick up, stand up, run and fall. One application of the sensed activities can be in a pacemaker for maintaining the required heart rate using a controller.

9.2.3 Human Health Monitoring

We detect anomalies in ECG and EEG data of a smart healthcare system. In particular, arrhythmia and seizure are detected using ECG and EEG signals, respectively. There are three main components of an ECG signal: P wave, QRS complex, and T wave. The P wave, QRS complex, and R peak represent atrial depolarization, ventricular depolarization, and ventricular repolarization, respectively. There are 48 patients data in MIT-BIH arrhythmia database. The data has been collected using two-lead sampled at 360 Hz.

As we know QRS complex gives information about cardiac arrhythmias. The R peak is detected using the Pan-Tompkins algorithm. Subsequently, the classification of normal, ventricular, and super-ventricular beats are carried out. The challenge is that normal beat and superventricular beats are similar. Therefore, 2-stage data analytic is used as shown in Figure 9.3. In the first stage, ventricular beat is separated from the normal plus super-ventricular beats. In the next stage, the normal and super-ventricular beats are separated.

There is a class imbalance problem because of the abundance of normal beats and scarcity of abnormal beats. In order to balance the number of samples of both classes, upsampling of abnormal class data is done to increase the number of samples of this class. Similarly, the CHB-MIT dataset has scalp EEG recordings of 916 hours for 24 seizure patients. The dataset is used for the detection of seizures. Other biomedical signals from a smart healthcare system can also be integrated into the framework for anomaly detection using multi-sensor healthcare data.

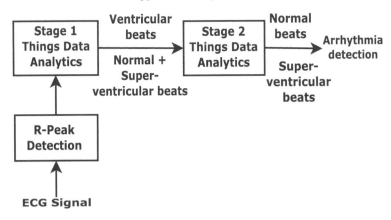

FIGURE 9.3: Arrhythmia detection using ECG signal

9.3 Smart City

We present herein three applications of a smart city project: smart parking, smart farming, and smart air pollution monitoring systems.

9.3.1 Smart Parking

In the metropolitan areas with big shopping malls and offices, we have a large number of vehicles with small and costly parking spaces. This leads to wastage of time and fuel, and traffic congestion in manual search of a parking space. A smart parking system is the solution in this regard for an urban area. In a smart parking system, the driver gets live information of vacant parking slots on his/her smartphone application.

The occupied or free slot in a parking area is detected using pressure or infrared sensors. The cost of an infrared sensor is low and transmits information using IoT protocols. When a car arrives at the entry, it is auto navigated to the nearest free parking slot as shown in Figure 9.4. The location tracking of the vehicle is carried out using RSS based localization algorithm. Note that, in underground or multi-story complex buildings, GPS does not work well. Therefore, we need to resort to the low cost and ubiquitous RSS measurements for the localization task. The location information helps in navigating the driver in a large underground parking area. On exit, the number of free slots is incremented by one. If the blockchain technology is adopted, the system negotiates the parking fee and payment is done securely without any human intervention.

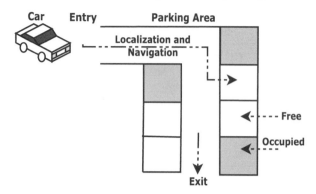

FIGURE 9.4: Smart parking system

9.3.2 Smart Farming

We use Meshlium 4G 868/900 AP based smart agriculture IoT vertical kit for data collection, data processing, and drawing inferences. This helps in enhancing crop productivity, measuring climate change, and animal health monitoring in real-time. Smart Agriculture PRO 868/900 PRO 5 DBi is a plug and sense kit and uses 6600 ma-h rechargeable battery and an external solar panel. The smart agriculture kit measures the following:

- Temperature

- Humidity

- Pressure

- Soil temperature

- Soil moisture up to 1.5 m and 4.5 m

- Leaf wetness

- Wind speed using anenometer, wind vane, and pluviometer

- Solar radiation

Similar to other smart systems, sensors measure soil and water (moisture) health, temperature, humidity, and light. We can also make use of a drone for data gathering from a large agriculture field. The collected data is further sent to the gateway, fog node or cloud using IoT protocols for processing as shown in Figure 9.5. Things data analytic is used for decision-making purposes. The location of animals grazing in the field is tracked using a localization algorithm. The overall cost reduces and the productivity increases in smart farming.

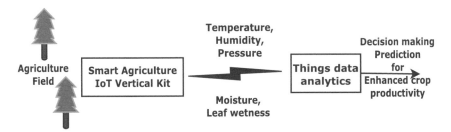

FIGURE 9.5: Smart farming system

9.3.3 Smart Air Pollution Monitoring System

Air pollution is caused by urbanization, transportation, industrial emission, dust, wildfire, and burning of fossil fuels. The solid and liquid particles of gases are suspended in air pollution. We use a smart pollution monitoring system for pollution control measures. We use air quality index as shown in Figure 9.6 like

- Ozone (O_3)

- Particulate Matter (PM) 2.5 and PM10

- Nitric dioxide (NO_2)

- Sulphur dioxide (SO_2) and

- Carbon monoxide (CO)

We use Meshlium 4G 802.15.4 AP-based smart cities IoT vertical kit which is simply a plug and sense kit. The power option is provided by 6600 ma-h rechargeable battery and external solar panel. The air quality indices are estimated on hourly, day wise and week wise basis. The data are sent to

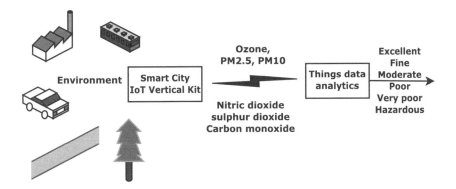

FIGURE 9.6: Smart air pollution monitoring system

the gateway, fog node or cloud node using IoT protocols. Subsequently, the following values are computed and mapped are

1. Excellent, range: 0 to 50

2. Fine, range: 51 to 100

3. Moderate, range: 101 to 150

4. Poor, range: 151 to 200

5. Very poor, range: 201 to 300 and

6. Hazardous, range: 301 to 500.

Hence, we designate our environment with one of these classes and know whether it is safe to live or not.

9.4 Summary

In this chapter, we presented two broad use cases of IoT networks, namely, smart healthcare and smart city. In particular, HAR using wearable sensors and CSI in a smart healthcare system are described. Further, human health monitoring using ECG and EEG signals are illustrated. Finally, smart parking, smart farming, smart air pollution monitoring systems are discussed in the smart city use case. These IoT applications are used for improved monitoring, improved control and operation processes, and automation purposes.

9.5 Exercises

1. Can we have wired things connected to IoT gateway?

2. Can we use 4G-LTE for data transfer from things to the gateway, fog node, or cloud?

3. Why do we not prefer undersampling to solve the class imbalance problem?

4. How do you take RSS measurements for localization in smart parking?

5. Which navigation algorithm do you leverage in smart parking?

6. What are the effects of air pollution on human health? Which community of the people are more vulnerable?

7. How do you determine the most polluted areas given air quality data on a city map?

8. What actions can be taken in case of the polluted areas?

9. In which application among healthcare and air pollution monitoring, a low computational time is desirable?

10. **Do It Yourself**: Design the IoT projects for some smart environments.

Bibliography

[1] CHB-MIT scalp EEG database. https://physionet.org/content/chbmit/1.0.0/. (accessed June 12, 2021).

[2] Dijkstra's algorithm. https://www.youtube.com/user/barngrader/featured. (accessed June 12, 2021).

[3] Libelium-IoT solution. https://www.libelium.com/. (accessed June 12, 2021).

[4] LISP host mobility - LISP host mobility solution. https://www.cisco.com/c/en/us/td/docs/solutions/Enterprise/Data_Center/DCI/5-0/LISPmobility/DCI_LISP_Host_Mobility.html. (accessed June 12, 2021).

[5] Locator ID separation protocol (LISP) overview. https://www.cisco.com/c/en/us/td/docs/ios-xml/ios/iproute_lisp/configuration/xe-16-8/irl-xe-16-8-book/irl-overview.pdf. (accessed June 12, 2021).

[6] MIT-BIH arrhythmia database. https://www.physionet.org/content/mitdb/1.0.0/. (accessed June 12, 2021).

[7] Overview of MAC mobility. https://www.juniper.net/documentation/us/en/software/junos/evpn-vxlan/topics/concept/mac-mobility.html. (accessed June 12, 2021).

[8] Realpars. https://www.youtube.com/c/realpars/featured. (accessed June 12, 2021).

[9] Simplilearn. https://www.youtube.com/c/SimplilearnOfficial/featured. (accessed June 12, 2021).

[10] Sunny classroom. https://www.youtube.com/user/sunnylearning. (accessed June 12, 2021).

[11] Technical guftgu. https://www.youtube.com/c/TechnicalGuftgu/featured. (accessed June 12, 2021).

[12] LoRa Alliance. LoRaWAN 1.0. 3 specification. *lora-alliance. org*, 1:2018–07, 2018.

[13] Mohammed H Alsharif, Sunghwan Kim, and Nuri Kuruoğlu. Energy harvesting techniques for wireless sensor networks/radio-frequency identification: A review. *Symmetry*, 11(7):865, 2019.

[14] Navid Amini, Alireza Vahdatpour, Wenyao Xu, Mario Gerla, and Majid Sarrafzadeh. Cluster size optimization in sensor networks with decentralized cluster-based protocols. *Computer communications*, 35(2):207–220, 2012.

[15] Saiful Azad and Al-Sakib Khan Pathan. *Practical cryptography: algorithms and implementations using C++*. CRC Press, 2014.

[16] Victor Banos, Muhammad Shahwaiz Afaqui, Elena Lopez, and Eduard Garcia. Throughput and range characterization of IEEE 802.11 ah. *IEEE Latin America Transactions*, 15(9):1621–1628, 2017.

[17] Victor Baños-Gonzalez, M Shahwaiz Afaqui, Elena Lopez-Aguilera, and Eduard Garcia-Villegas. Throughput and range characterization of IEEE 802.11 ah. *arXiv preprint arXiv:1604.08625*, 2016.

[18] Ben Bellekens, Le Tian, Pepijn Boer, Maarten Weyn, and Jeroen Famaey. Outdoor IEEE 802.11 ah range characterization using validated propagation models. In *GLOBECOM 2017-2017 IEEE Global Communications Conference*, pages 1–6. IEEE, 2017.

[19] Igor Bisio, Fabio Lavagetto, Andrea Sciarrone, Terrence Penner, and Mina Guirguis. Context-awareness over transient cloud in D2D networks: energy performance analysis and evaluation. *Transactions on Emerging Telecommunications Technologies*, 28(2):e3002, 2017.

[20] Nirupama Bulusu, John Heidemann, and Deborah Estrin. GPS-less low-cost outdoor localization for very small devices. *IEEE personal communications*, 7(5):28–34, 2000.

[21] James J Caffery and Gordon L Stuber. Overview of radiolocation in CDMA cellular systems. *IEEE Communications Magazine*, 36(4):38–45, 1998.

[22] Subhash Challa and Don Koks. Bayesian and Dempster-Shafer fusion. *Sadhana*, 29(2):145–174, 2004.

[23] Hongyang Chen, Kaoru Sezaki, Ping Deng, and Hing Cheung So. An improved DV-hop localization algorithm for wireless sensor networks. In *2008 3rd IEEE Conference on Industrial Electronics and Applications*, pages 1557–1561, 2008.

[24] Zhenghua Chen, Le Zhang, Chaoyang Jiang, Zhiguang Cao, and Wei Cui. WiFi CSI based passive human activity recognition using attention based BLSTM. *IEEE Transactions on Mobile Computing*, 18(11):2714–2724, 2018.

[25] David Culler, Samita Chakrabarti, and IP Infusion. 6LoWPAN: Incorporating IEEE 802.15.4 into the IP architecture. *White paper*, 2009.

[26] Jasenka Dizdarević, Francisco Carpio, Admela Jukan, and Xavi Masip-Bruin. A survey of communication protocols for internet of things and related challenges of fog and cloud computing integration. *ACM Computing Surveys (CSUR)*, 51(6):1–29, 2019.

[27] Dinh-Thuan Do. Time power switching based relaying protocol in energy harvesting mobile node: optimal throughput analysis. *Mobile Information Systems*, 2015, 2015.

[28] Dinh-Thuan Do. Optimal throughput under time power switching based relaying protocol in energy harvesting cooperative networks. *Wireless Personal Communications*, 87(2):551–564, 2016.

[29] Lina Elmorshedy, Cyril Leung, and S Ali Mousavifar. RF energy harvesting in DF relay networks in the presence of an interfering signal. In *2016 IEEE international conference on communications (ICC)*, pages 1–6. IEEE, 2016.

[30] William H Equitz. A new vector quantization clustering algorithm. *IEEE transactions on acoustics, speech, and signal processing*, 37(10):1568–1575, 1989.

[31] Mehmet Ali Ertürk, Muhammed Ali Aydın, Muhammet Talha Büyükakkaşlar, and Hayrettin Evirgen. A survey on LoRaWAN architecture, protocol and technologies. *Future Internet*, 11(10):216, 2019.

[32] Dino Farinacci, Vince Fuller, Dave Meyer, and Darrel Lewis. The locator/id separation protocol (LISP). *Internet Engineering Task Force (IETF), Request for Comments: 6830*, 2013.

[33] Behrouz A Forouzan. *Data communications and Networking, Networking series*. Tata Mcgraw-Hill publishers, New York, USA, 2008.

[34] Jacob Fraden. *Handbook of modern sensors: physics, designs, and applications*. American Association of Physics Teachers, 1998.

[35] Zoran Gajic. Discrete-time state space analysis. `http://eceweb1.rutgers.edu/~gajic/solmanual/slides/chapter8_DIS.pdf`. (accessed June 12, 2021).

[36] Eduard Garcia, Josep L Ferrer, Elena Lopez-Aguilera, Rafael Vidal, and Josep Paradells. Client-driven load balancing through association control in IEEE 802.11 WLANs. *European Transactions on Telecommunications*, 20(5):494–507, 2009.

[37] Ruchi Garg and Sanjay Sharma. Modified and improved IPv6 header compression (MIHC) scheme for 6LoWPAN. *Wireless Personal Communications*, 103(3):2019–2033, 2018.

[38] Abebe Geletu. Quadratic programming problems-a review on algorithms and applications (active-set and interior point methods). https://www.tu-ilmenau.de/fileadmin/media/simulation/Lehre/Vorlesungsskripte/Lecture_materials_Abebe/QPs_with_IPM_and_ASM.pdf. (accessed June 12, 2021).

[39] Jacek Gondzio. Interior point methods for convex quadratic programming. https://www.maths.ed.ac.uk/hall/NATCOR_2016/IPMsQP.pdf. (accessed June 12, 2021).

[40] Ian Goodfellow, Yoshua Bengio, Aaron Courville, and Yoshua Bengio. *Deep learning*, volume 1. MIT press Cambridge, 2016.

[41] Yanju Gu and Sonia Aissa. RF-based energy harvesting in decode-and-forward relaying systems: Ergodic and outage capacities. *IEEE Transactions on Wireless Communications*, 14(11):6425–6434, 2015.

[42] David L Hall and Alan Steinberg. Dirty secrets in multisensor data fusion. Technical report, PENNSYLVANIA STATE UNIV UNIVERSITY PARK APPLIED RESEARCH LAB, 2001.

[43] Greg Hankins. Ethernet VPN (EVPN) overlay networks for ethernet services. https://archive.nanog.org/sites/default/files/monday_general_hankins_vpn_2.pdf. (accessed June 12, 2021).

[44] Trevor Hastie, Robert Tibshirani, and Martin Wainwright. *Statistical learning with sparsity: the LASSO and generalizations*. Chapman and Hall/CRC, 2019.

[45] Tian He, Chengdu Huang, Brian M Blum, John A Stankovic, and Tarek Abdelzaher. Range-free localization schemes for large scale sensor networks. In *Proceedings of the 9th annual international conference on Mobile computing and networking*, pages 81–95, 2003.

[46] Wendi B Heinzelman, Anantha P Chandrakasan, and Hari Balakrishnan. An application-specific protocol architecture for wireless microsensor networks. *IEEE Transactions on wireless communications*, 1(4):660–670, 2002.

[47] Jangeun Jun, Pushkin Peddabachagari, and Mihail Sichitiu. Theoretical maximum throughput of IEEE 802.11 and its applications. In *Second IEEE International Symposium on Network Computing and Applications, 2003. NCA 2003.*, pages 249–256. IEEE, 2003.

[48] Steven M Kay. *Fundamentals of statistical signal processing*. Prentice Hall PTR, 1993.

[49] Michael Kern. Anonymity: A formalization of privacy-l-diversity. In *Proceeding zum Seminar Future Internet (FI), Innovative Internet Technologien und Mobilkommunikation (IITM) und Autonomous Communication Networks (ACN)*, volume 49. Citeseer, 2013.

[50] Pritam Khan, Yasin Khan, and Sudhir Kumar. Tracking and stabilization of heart-rate using pacemaker with FOF-PID controller in secured medical cyber-physical system. In *2020 International Conference on COMmunication Systems & NETworkS (COMSNETS)*, pages 658–661. IEEE, 2020.

[51] Pritam Khan, Yasin Khan, and Sudhir Kumar. Activity-based tracking and stabilization of human heart rate using fuzzy FO-PID controller. *IEEE Journal of Emerging and Selected Topics in Industrial Electronics*, pages 1–10, 2021.

[52] Pritam Khan, Bathula Shiva Karthik Reddy, Ankur Pandey, Sudhir Kumar, and Moustafa Youssef. Differential channel-state-information-based human activity recognition in IoT networks. *IEEE Internet of Things Journal*, 7(11):11290–11302, 2020.

[53] Lawrence A Klein. *Sensor and data fusion: a tool for information assessment and decision making*, volume 138. SPIE press, 2004.

[54] Mikko Kohvakka, Mauri Kuorilehto, Marko Hännikäinen, and Timo D Hämäläinen. Performance analysis of IEEE 802.15.4 and ZigBee for large-scale wireless sensor network applications. In *Proceedings of the 3rd ACM international workshop on Performance evaluation of wireless ad hoc, sensor and ubiquitous networks*, pages 48–57, 2006.

[55] Paweł Kułakowski, Javier Vales-Alonso, Esteban Egea-López, Wiesław Ludwin, and Joan García-Haro. Angle-of-arrival localization based on antenna arrays for wireless sensor networks. *Computers & Electrical Engineering*, 36(6):1181–1186, 2010.

[56] Sudhir Kumar. Compartmental modeling of opportunistic signals for energy efficient optimal clustering in WSN. *IEEE Communications Letters*, 22(1):173–176, 2017.

[57] Sudhir Kumar. Joint malicious source detection and target localization using compartmental model in cluster-based networks. In *2018 IEEE International Conference on Advanced Networks and Telecommunications Systems (ANTS)*, pages 1–5. IEEE, 2018.

[58] Sudhir Kumar. Performance analysis of RSS-based localization in wireless sensor networks. *Wireless Personal Communications*, 108(2):769–783, 2019.

[59] Sudhir Kumar and Sajal K Das. Target detection and localization methods using compartmental model for internet of things. *IEEE Transactions on Mobile Computing*, 19(9):2234–2249, 2019.

[60] Sudhir Kumar and Rajesh M Hegde. Indoor node localization using geometric dilution of precision in ad-hoc sensor networks. In *2014 48th Asilomar Conference on Signals, Systems and Computers*, pages 1525–1529. IEEE, 2014.

[61] Sudhir Kumar and Rajesh M Hegde. An efficient compartmental model for real-time node tracking over cognitive wireless sensor networks. *IEEE Transactions on Signal Processing*, 63(7):1712–1725, 2015.

[62] Sudhir Kumar and Rajesh M Hegde. Multi-sensor data fusion methods for indoor localization under collinear ambiguity. *Pervasive and mobile computing*, 30:18–31, 2016.

[63] Sudhir Kumar and Rajesh M Hegde. A review of localization and tracking algorithms in wireless sensor networks. *arXiv preprint arXiv:1701.02080*, 2017.

[64] Sudhir Kumar, Rajesh M. Hegde, and Niki Trigoni. Gaussian process regression for fingerprinting based localization. *Ad Hoc Networks*, 51:1–10, 2016.

[65] Sudhir Kumar, Vatsal Sharan, and Rajesh M Hegde. Energy efficient optimal node-source localization using mobile beacon in ad-hoc sensor networks. In *2013 IEEE global communications conference (GLOBE-COM)*, pages 487–492. IEEE, 2013.

[66] Sudhir Kumar, Shriman Narayan Tiwari, and Rajesh M Hegde. Sensor node tracking using semi-supervised hidden Markov models. *Ad Hoc Networks*, 33:55–70, 2015.

[67] James F Kurose. *Computer networking: A top-down approach featuring the internet, 3/E*. Pearson Education India, 2005.

[68] Aseem Kushwah, Sudhir Kumar, and Rajesh M Hegde. Multi-sensor data fusion methods for indoor activity recognition using temporal evidence theory. *Pervasive and Mobile Computing*, 21:19–29, 2015.

[69] Bhagwandas Pannalal Lathi. *Modern digital and analog communication systems*. Oxford university press, New York, USA, 1998.

[70] Ngoc Phuc Le, Nguyen-Son Vo, Minh-Tiep Hoang, and Duc-Dung Tran. Unified analysis of energy harvesting-based MIMO relay wireless systems over Nakagami-m fading channels. *Transactions on Emerging Telecommunications Technologies*, 28(10):e3160, 2017.

[71] Alberto Leon-Garcia and Indra Widjaja. *Communication networks: fundamental concepts and key architectures*, volume 2. McGraw-Hill New York, 2000.

[72] Ninghui Li, Tiancheng Li, and Suresh Venkatasubramanian. t-closeness: Privacy beyond k-anonymity and l-diversity. In *2007 IEEE 23rd International Conference on Data Engineering*, pages 106–115. IEEE, 2007.

[73] M. Liggins, D. Hall, and J. Llinas. *Handbook of Multisensor Data Fusion: Theory and Practice, Second Edition*. CRC Press, 2017.

[74] Yoseph Linde, Andres Buzo, and Robert Gray. An algorithm for vector quantizer design. *IEEE Transactions on communications*, 28(1):84–95, 1980.

[75] Ashwin Machanavajjhala, Daniel Kifer, Johannes Gehrke, and Muthuramakrishnan Venkitasubramaniam. L-diversity: Privacy beyond k-anonymity. *ACM Trans. Knowl. Discov. Data*, 1(1):3–es, 2007.

[76] Guoqiang Mao, Barış Fidan, and Brian DO Anderson. Wireless sensor network localization techniques. *Computer networks*, 51(10):2529–2553, 2007.

[77] Mónica Martí, Carlos Garcia-Rubio, and Celeste Campo. Performance evaluation of CoAP and MQTT_SN in an IoT environment. *Proceedings*, 31(1):49, 2019.

[78] S. Misra, A. Mukherjee, and A. Roy. *Introduction to IoT*. Cambridge University Press, 2020.

[79] Akif Mufti. https://www.youtube.com/user/warcroft23/featured. (accessed June 12, 2021).

[80] Nandini Mukherjee, Sarmistha Neogy, and Sarbani Roy. *Building wireless sensor networks: theoretical and practical perspectives*. CRC Press, 2017.

[81] VPS Naidu, G Girija, JR Raol, and Raj R Appavu. Data association and fusion algorithms for tracking in presence of measurement loss. *Journal of the Institution of Engineers (I)*, 86:17–28, 2005.

[82] Parham H Namin and Mohammad A Tinati. Localization of irregular wireless sensor networks based on multidimensional scaling. In *2009 International Conference on Advanced Technologies for Communications*, pages 79–83. IEEE, 2009.

[83] Dragoş Niculescu and Badri Nath. DV based positioning in ad hoc networks. *Telecommunication Systems*, 22(1):267–280, 2003.

[84] Jonas Olsson. 6LoWPAN demystified. *Texas Instruments*, 13, 2014.

[85] Ankur Pandey, Ryan Sequeria, Preetam Kumar, and Sudhir Kumar. A multistage deep residual network for biomedical cyber-physical systems. *IEEE Systems Journal*, 14(2):1953–1962, 2019.

[86] Ankur Pandey, Piyush Tiwary, Sudhir Kumar, and Sajal K Das. Adaptive mini-batch gradient ascent based localization for indoor IoT networks under Rayleigh fading conditions. *IEEE Internet of Things Journal*, 2020.

[87] Ankur Pandey, Raghu Vamsi, and Sudhir Kumar. Handling device heterogeneity and orientation using multistage regression for GMM based localization in IoT networks. *IEEE Access*, 7:144354–144365, 2019.

[88] Ankur Pandey, Piyush Tiwary, Sudhir Kumar, and Sajal K Das. Residual neural networks for heterogeneous smart device localization in IoT networks. In *2020 29th International Conference on Computer Communications and Networks (ICCCN)*, pages 1–9. IEEE, 2020.

[89] Shailaja Patil, Mukesh Zaveri, et al. MDS and trilateration based localization in wireless sensor network. *Wireless Sensor Network*, 3(06):198, 2011.

[90] Neal Patwari, Alfred O Hero, Matt Perkins, Neiyer S Correal, and Robert J O'dea. Relative location estimation in wireless sensor networks. *IEEE Transactions on signal processing*, 51(8):2137–2148, 2003.

[91] Fang Pen. Elliptic curve cryptography explained. https://fangpenlin.com/posts/2019/10/07/elliptic-curve-cryptography-explained/. (accessed June 12, 2021).

[92] Tommaso Polonelli, Davide Brunelli, Achille Marzocchi, and Luca Benini. Slotted ALOHA on LoRaWAN-design, analysis, and deployment. *Sensors*, 19(4):838, 2019.

[93] H Vincent Poor. *An introduction to signal detection and estimation.* Springer Science & Business Media, 2013.

[94] J.G. Proakis and M. Salehi. *Digital Communications.* McGraw-Hill, New York, USA, 2008.

[95] Orod Raeesi, Juho Pirskanen, Ali Hazmi, Toni Levanen, and Mikko Valkama. Performance evaluation of IEEE 802.11 ah and its restricted access window mechanism. In *2014 IEEE international conference on communications workshops (ICC)*, pages 460–466. IEEE, 2014.

[96] Orod Raeesi, Juho Pirskanen, Ali Hazmi, Jukka Talvitie, and Mikko Valkama. Performance enhancement and evaluation of IEEE 802.11 ah multi-access point network using restricted access window mechanism.

In *2014 IEEE International Conference on Distributed Computing in Sensor Systems*, pages 287–293. IEEE, 2014.

[97] P Rao. *DIGITAL COMMUNICATION*. Tata McGraw-Hill Education, New Delhi, India, 2011.

[98] Jitendra R Raol. *Multi-sensor data fusion with MATLAB®*. CRC press, 2009.

[99] Jitendra R Raol. *Data fusion mathematics: theory and practice*. CRC Press, 2015.

[100] Ammar Rayes and Samer Salam. *Internet of things from hype to reality*. Springer, 2017.

[101] Derek Rowell. Time-domain solution of LTI state equations. `http://web.mit.edu/2.14/www/Handouts/StateSpaceResponse.pdf`. (accessed June 12, 2021).

[102] Ali Sajassi, R Aggarwal, N Bitar, A Isaac, J Uttaro, J Drake, and W Henderickx. BGP MPLS-based Ethernet VPN, 2015.

[103] Saritha Saritha and V Sarasvathi. A study on application layer protocols used in IoT. In *2017 International Conference on Circuits, Controls, and Communications (CCUBE)*, pages 155–159. IEEE, 2017.

[104] Chris Savarese, Jan M Rabaey, and Jan Beutel. Location in distributed ad-hoc wireless sensor networks. In *2001 IEEE international conference on acoustics, speech, and signal processing. proceedings (Cat. No. 01CH37221)*, volume 4, pages 2037–2040. IEEE, 2001.

[105] Khalid Sayood. *Introduction to data compression*. Newnes, 2012.

[106] Andrea Sciarrone, Claudio Fiandrino, Igor Bisio, Fabio Lavagetto, Dzmitry Kliazovich, and Pascal Bouvry. Smart probabilistic fingerprinting for indoor localization over fog computing platforms. In *2016 5th IEEE International Conference on Cloud Networking (Cloudnet)*, pages 39–44. IEEE, 2016.

[107] Muhammad Shafiq, Maqbool Ahmad, Azeem Irshad, Moneeb Gohar, Muhammad Usman, Muhammad Khalil Afzal, Jin-Ghoo Choi, and Heejung Yu. Multiple access control for cognitive radio-based IEEE 802.11 ah networks. *Sensors*, 18(7):2043, 2018.

[108] Syed Tariq Shah, Kae Won Choi, Syed Faraz Hasan, and Min Young Chung. Throughput analysis of two-way relay networks with wireless energy harvesting capabilities. *Ad Hoc Networks*, 53:123–131, 2016.

[109] Zach Shelby and Carsten Bormann. *6LoWPAN: The wireless embedded Internet*, volume 43. John Wiley & Sons, 2011.

[110] Zach Shelby, Klaus Hartke, and Carsten Bormann. The constrained application protocol (CoAP). *Internet Engineering Task Force (IETF), Request for Comments: 7252*, 2014.

[111] Xiaohong Sheng and Yu-Hen Hu. Maximum likelihood multiple-source localization using acoustic energy measurements with wireless sensor networks. *IEEE Transactions on Signal Processing*, 53(1):44–53, 2004.

[112] Ke Shi, Lin Zhang, Zhiying Qi, Kang Tong, and Hongsheng Chen. Transmission scheduling of periodic real-time traffic in IEEE 802.15.4e TSCH-based industrial mesh networks. *Wireless Communications and Mobile Computing*, 2019, 2019.

[113] Rajeev Shorey, A Ananda, Mun Choon Chan, and Wei Tsang Ooi. *Mobile, wireless, and sensor networks: technology, applications, and future directions*. John Wiley & Sons, 2006.

[114] Ian Sinclair. *Sensors and transducers*. Elsevier, 2000.

[115] José VV Sobral, Joel JPC Rodrigues, Ricardo AL Rabêlo, Jalal Al-Muhtadi, and Valery Korotaev. Routing protocols for low power and lossy networks in internet of things applications. *Sensors*, 19(9):2144, 2019.

[116] Houbing Song, Danda B Rawat, Sabina Jeschke, and Christian Brecher. *Cyber-physical systems: foundations, principles and applications*. Morgan Kaufmann, 2016.

[117] Nandan Sriranga, Kyatsandra G Nagananda, Rick S Blum, A Saucan, and Pramod K Varshney. Energy-efficient decision fusion for distributed detection in wireless sensor networks. In *2018 21st International conference on information fusion (FUSION)*, pages 1541–1547. IEEE, 2018.

[118] William Stallings. *Cryptography and network security, 4/E*. Pearson Education India, 2006.

[119] William Stallings. *Data and computer communications*. Pearson Education India, 2007.

[120] Kamil Staniec and Michał Kowal. LoRa performance under variable interference and heavy-multipath conditions. *Wireless communications and mobile computing*, 2018, 2018.

[121] Weiping Sun, Munhwan Choi, and Sunghyun Choi. IEEE 802.11 ah: A long range 802.11 WLAN at sub 1 GHz. *Journal of ICT standardization*, 1(1):83–108, 2013.

[122] Ahmad F Taha. Optimization and control of cyber-physical systems. https://engineering.utsa.edu/ataha/teaching/ee-5243-optimization-and-control-of-cyber-physical-systems/. (accessed June 12, 2021).

[123] Andrew S. Tanenbaum. *Computer Networks*. Pearson Education, Upper Saddle River, New Jersey, 2003.

[124] Herbut Taub, Donald L. Schilling, and Goutam Saha. *Principles Of Communication Systems*. McGraw-Hill Education (India) Pvt Limited, 2008.

[125] Georgios Tsivgoulis. Source localization in wireless sensor networks with randomly distributed elements under multipath propagation conditions. Technical report, NAVAL POSTGRADUATE SCHOOL MONTEREY CA, 2009.

[126] Jean-Philippe Vasseur and Adam Dunkels. *Interconnecting smart objects with IP: The next internet*. Morgan Kaufmann, 2010.

[127] Hemant Verma, Debdeep Paul, Shiva Reddy Bathula, Shreya Sinha, and Sudhir Kumar. Human activity recognition with wearable biomedical sensors in cyber physical systems. In *2018 15th IEEE India Council International Conference (INDICON)*, pages 1–6. IEEE, 2018.

[128] Liuping Wang. *Model predictive control system design and implementation using MATLAB®*. Springer Science & Business Media, 2009.

[129] Thomas Watteyne, Maria-Rita Palattella, and Luigi Alfredo Grieco. Using IEEE 802.15.4e time-slotted channel hopping (TSCH) in the internet of things (IoT): Problem statement. *Internet Engineering Task Force*, 2015.

[130] Tim Winter, Pascal Thubert, Anders Brandt, Jonathan W Hui, Richard Kelsey, Philip Levis, Kris Pister, Rene Struik, Jean-Philippe Vasseur, Roger K Alexander, et al. RPL: IPv6 routing protocol for low-power and lossy networks. *RFC*, 6550:1–157, 2012.

[131] Siamak Yousefi, Hirokazu Narui, Sankalp Dayal, Stefano Ermon, and Shahrokh Valaee. A survey on behavior recognition using WiFi channel state information. *IEEE Communications Magazine*, 55(10):98–104, 2017.

[132] Stanislaw H. Zak. An introduction to model-based predictive. `https://engineering.purdue.edu/~zak/ECE680/MPC_handout.pdf`. (accessed June 12, 2021).

[133] Reza Zekavat and R Michael Buehrer. *Handbook of position location: Theory, practice and advances*, volume 27. John Wiley & Sons, 2011.

[134] Qiliang Zhu, Baojiang Si, Feifan Yang, and You Ma. Task offloading decision in fog computing system. *China Communications*, 14(11):59–68, 2017.

[135] Dimitrios Zorbas, Georgios Z Papadopoulos, and Christos Douligeris. Local or global radio channel blacklisting for IEEE 802.15.4-TSCH networks? In *2018 IEEE International Conference on Communications (ICC)*, pages 1–6. IEEE, 2018.

Index

6LowPAN, 70–72, 74

absolute slot number, 53
acceleration, 234
accelerometer, 5, 132, 199, 234
access point, 40
accuracy, 5, 187, 188
acknowledgment, 42, 71, 79
activation function, 179
actuator, 6, 192
adaptation layer, 72–74
adaptive data rate, 65
address resolution protocol, 15, 197
addressing field, 71
age, 21
AID hierarchy, 40
air quality index, 239
air quality sensor, 4
airflow sensor, 234
Akaike information criterion, 173
ALOHA, 65
analytic, 165, 192, 235, 236, 238
anchor, 122, 128, 131, 133, 134
angle-of-arrival, 123, 127
antenna array, 128
application layer, 1, 12, 71
application layer protocol, 12, 77
approximate point in triangle test, 132, 134
area, 25
area border router, 25
arrhythmia, 236
artificial intelligence, 165
artificial neural network, 178
association identifier, 40

assumption based coordinates, 132, 135
asymmetric key, 210
asymmetric key cryptography, 210
atrial depolarization, 236
attribute, 208
authentication, 224, 225
autonomous system, 19, 23, 27
autonomous system number, 27
axon, 178

backbone router, 25
backoff, 65, 68
backoff stage, 44
backoff time, 42
backpropagation, 182, 183
balance property, 47
bandwidth, 35, 59, 61, 65, 191, 199, 203, 235
bandwidth-delay product, 28
base station, 94
batch gradient descent, 185
batchsize, 185
Bayes theorem, 99, 101, 112, 170
Bayesian information criterion, 173
Bayesian method, 104
beacon, 122
belief, 104
Bellman-Ford algorithm, 19, 75
bias and variance tradeoff, 176
binary phase-shift keying, 56
binary step function, 180
Binomial distribution, 112, 113
biological neural network, 178
bipolar sigmoid, 180

bit rate, 60, 61
bitcoin, 220, 221, 223, 225, 228, 229
bitcoin cash, 228
blockchain, 220, 224, 225, 227, 229, 230, 237
blockchain technology, 1
blockchain version, 222
blocking technique, 54
blood pressure sensor, 234
bluetooth, 55, 234
body position sensor, 234
body temperature, 234
border gateway protocol, 20, 26, 196
box and whisker plot, 137, 138
BPSK modulator, 49
bridge, 13
broadcast ID, 17
Byzantine generals problem, 226

capacitive sensor, 4
carbon monoxide, 239
carrier sense multiple access, 9
carrier sense multiple access-collision avoidances, 51
carrier signal, 63
cell body, 178
centralized architecture, 110, 112, 114, 115, 117
centralized detection, 112
centralized fusion, 99
centroid algorithm, 132
cftool toolbox, 176
channel, 51
channel access scheme, 51
channel bandwidth, 34
channel gain, 144
channel hopping, 52
channel offset, 53
channel state information, 233, 235, 236
child, 75
chip, 60

chip duration, 59, 60
chip rate, 60, 61
chirp, 63
chirp spread spectrum, 56, 63
chirp spread spectrum modulation, 59
circuit switching, 14
class A, 15, 16, 57
class B, 15, 16, 57
class C, 15–17, 57
class D, 15, 16
class E, 15, 16
class imbalance problem, 236
classful address, 18
classful IPv4 address, 15
classification, 166, 167, 235, 236
classless interdomain routing, 18
client, 77
closest point-based method, 132, 133
cloud computing, 191, 192, 194, 200, 234, 238, 240
cluster, 97, 173
cluster head, 88, 93, 94
cluster-tree topology, 52
clustering, 87, 166, 173
code rate, 60
coding efficiency, 62
coding rate, 62
computation, 192, 199, 200
computational power, 203
confidentiality, 224, 225
confirmable, 79, 80
connection control, 11
consensus algorithm, 223
constellation, 35, 36
constrained application protocol, 1, 71, 78
constrained MPC, 154, 156, 157
container, 194
contention window size, 43
control action, 149, 153, 157–160
controller, 149, 236
convergence, 44, 186
convex function, 160

correlation property, 47
cost, 203
count-to-infinity, 20
coverage, 65, 203
Cramer-Rao lower bound, 137
cross correlation, 127
cross-entropy, 181
cross-validation, 187
cryptography, 221
CSMA/CA, 70
CSMA/CD, 70
cumulative distribution function, 137, 139
customer edge, 196
cyclic redundancy check, 9, 62, 71

DAO acknowledgment, 76
data aggregation, 93
data anonymization, 1, 207
data fusion, 98, 104, 173
data interframe spacing, 42
data link layer, 8, 14, 70
data packet, 71
data rate, 8, 60, 61
data rate optimization, 62
datagram offset, 74
datagram size, 73
datagram tag, 73
datagram transport layer security, 79
decentralized, 93
decentralized architecture, 221, 222, 226, 228, 229
decision fusion, 110
decryption, 216–218, 220, 224, 225
deep learning, 165, 235
deep neural network, 178
default IP gateway, 197
delay, 27
demodulator, 35, 49
Dempster-Shafer theory, 104
dendrite, 178
designated router, 25
desired source, 144, 147, 148
despreader, 50

destination address, 72, 74
destination oriented directed acyclic graph, 75
detection, 36, 236
deviance information criterion, 173
digital currency, 221, 225
digital signature, 224, 225
Dijkstra algorithm, 22
dimensionality reduction, 174
direct sequence spread spectrum, 48, 56
directed acyclic graph, 75
direction-of-arrival, 123
discrete logarithm problem, 214
distance vector, 19, 20
distance vector routing, 21, 23
distance vector-HOP, 132, 133
distance-based, 122, 123
distance-free, 122, 131
distributed architecture, 110, 114–117
distributed detection, 114
distributed fusion, 99
distributed ledger, 221, 224–226
DODAG, 75
DODAG advertisement object, 76
DODAG information object, 76
DODAG information solicitation, 76
domain naming system, 71
dot operation, 212
doubling operation, 212–216, 218, 219
duty cycle, 69
dwell time, 69

ECC algorithm, 210
edge, 191, 195, 197
edge computing, 200
egress tunnel routers, 198
eigenvalue, 130, 160, 175
eigenvector, 130, 175, 176
elbow method, 173
electric actuator, 6

electrocardiogram, 234, 236
electrodermal activity, 234
electroencephalograph, 234, 236
electromyography, 233
elliptic curve, 211, 216–218, 229
elliptic curve cryptography, 1, 210
elliptic curve discrete logarithm,
     216
emulator, 193
encapsulation, 12
encapsulation header, 71
encryption, 216, 218, 219, 224, 225
endpoint identifiers, 198
energy, 93, 95–98, 143, 200, 203,
     204
energy efficient clustering, 93
energy harvesting, 1, 143, 148, 149
error control, 9, 11
ethereum, 228
Ethernet virtual private network,
     195, 196
even sequence, 35
event detection, 110
extensible messaging and presence
     protocol, 71, 83
exterior routing protocol, 19

f1-score, 187, 188
false negative, 188
false positive, 188
feature, 165, 167, 173, 235
file transfer protocol, 11, 71
fingerprinting based localization,
     199, 200
Fisher information matrix, 137
flood, 21
flow control, 9, 11
flow label, 72
flow sensor, 4
fog computing, 1, 191, 192, 194,
     196, 200, 238
fog node, 192, 202–205, 234, 240
fog orchestration, 199
force, 234
fork, 228

fragment header, 72, 73
frame, 8
frame check sequence, 42, 71
frame control, 42, 71
frame transmission time, 67
frequency, 53
frequency hopping spread
     spectrum, 48
Friss transmission, 137, 203
full function device, 51, 74
fused belief, 105

galvanic skin response sensor, 234
gateway, 1, 14, 56, 77, 234, 238,
     240
Gaussian distribution, 111,
     126–128, 137, 144, 146
Gaussian frequency-shift keying,
     56
generalization, 208
generator, 211, 215, 216
generator point, 218
genesis block, 222, 226
global blocking, 55
global decision, 110, 112, 114, 115
global positioning system, 1, 237
global threshold, 116
glucometer, 234
gradient, 184
gradient descent, 184, 185
gyroscope, 132, 199

hard fork, 228
hash, 221, 224–227
header, 43, 222
header compression, 74
heart rate, 234, 236
heaviside function, 180
Hessian, 185
high bias, 176
high variance, 176, 186
holdout set, 187
hop limit, 74
hop time, 69
host ID, 15, 17

HTTP, 77, 78
hub, 13
human activity recognition,
    233–236
human health monitoring, 233,
    236
humidity, 238
humidity sensor, 4
hybrid architecture, 110
hybrid fusion, 99
hydraulic actuator, 6
hyperparameter, 186, 187
hypertext transfer protocol, 12, 71
hypervisor, 193
hysteresis, 6

identity address, 198
identity element, 214
identity function, 179
IEEE 802.11, 33
IEEE 802.11ah, 33
IEEE 802.15.4, 45, 51, 70, 73
imaging sensor, 5
improved header compression, 72
inductive sensor, 4
inertial based, 132, 199
information detection, 147
information element, 40
information transmission, 144
infrared sensor, 4, 237
ingress tunnel routers, 198
insurance, 230
intelligent decision, 165
interference, 52, 192
interfering source, 144, 146–148
interior gateway routing protocol,
    23
interior routing protocol, 19, 24
Internet, 7, 192
Internet control message protocol,
    15
Internet group message protocol,
    15
Internet of Things, 1
Internetworking protocol, 14

intialization, 90
IP address, 14, 195
IP version 4, 15
IP version 6, 15
IPv6 address, 18, 70, 72
IPv6 routing protocol, 74

Jacobian, 161, 162

k-anonymity, 208–210
k-nearest neighbor, 168
k-nearest neighbors, 235
Karush-Kuhn-Tucker conditions,
    161
key generation, 216
know your customer, 229
Kullback-Leibler divergence, 182

l-diversity, 208–210
label, 166, 167, 173
Lagrange function, 161
landmark, 122
Laplace transform, 151
latency, 82, 192, 200
LEACH, 93
learning, 165
learning rate, 185, 186
least square, 128, 129
leave-one-out cross-validation, 187
level sensor, 4
likelihood, 100
line-of-sight, 133, 144
linear activation, 179
linear regression, 172
link budget, 59
link layer, 70
link margin, 59
link state packet, 25
link state routing, 20, 75
litecoin, 228
local area network, 8
local blocking, 54
local decision, 99, 110, 111, 114
local threshold, 116
localization, 1, 122, 192, 199, 237,
    238

localization error, 137
location address, 198
locator/identifier separation
    protocol, 198
logarithmic barrier function, 161
logical address, 10, 15
logistic regression, 171, 172
long range wide area networks, 55
LoRaWAN device class, 57
loss function, 181, 183, 185, 186
low power and lossy networks, 74
low-energy adaptive clustering
    hierarchy, 93
low-power wide-area network, 55

MAC address, 9, 15, 195–197
MAC layer, 33, 46, 70, 72
machine learning, 165, 167, 235
magnetometer, 199
majority voting, 168, 169
mass, 104
maximum a posteriori estimate,
    99
maximum likelihood estimate, 99,
    100
maximum-length PN sequence, 47
mean absolute error, 181
mean squared error, 181
media access control address, 8
Merkle root hash, 222, 223
mesh addressing header, 74
mesh header, 72
mesh topology, 51
mesh under routing, 74
message header, 80
message ID, 82
message queue telemetry support,
    71
message queue telemetry
    transport, 1, 78, 82
micro controller, 2
middleware, 1
miner, 223, 225, 227
minibatch gradient descent,
    184–186

minibatch size, 186
mobility, 192, 197
model predictive control, 149
modulated chirp, 63
modulation, 34, 48, 94
modulation and coding scheme, 34
modulator, 35, 49
moisture, 238
monic polynomial, 213
Moore's law, 192
moving horizon control, 149
multicast, 72, 78
multidimensional scaling, 123, 129
multilateration, 123, 124, 128
multipath fading, 52, 192

n-fold cross-validation, 187
naive Bayes, 235
Naive Bayes classification, 169
negation, 214, 218, 220
network ID, 15, 17
network layer, 1, 8, 10, 70
next header, 72
Nielsen's law, 192
nitric dioxide, 239
non-confirmable, 79, 80
non-line-of-sight, 144
non-storing node, 76
nonce, 222, 223, 226

odd sequence, 35
offload, 192, 200–202, 204, 205
offset QPSK, 36, 48
one way function, 211, 222
open shortest path first, 19, 24
operating system, 193, 194
optimal capacity, 176
orthogonal frequency division
    multiplexing, 34, 56
OSI model, 7
outlier, 138
over-fitting, 176
ozone, 239

P wave, 236
packet, 14

packet errror retransmission, 44
packet length, 61
packet loss, 28
packet switching, 14
PAN coordinator, 51
Pan-Tompkins algorithm, 236
parent, 75
particulate matter, 239
path loss, 45, 58
path loss exponent, 129
payload, 42, 80
perceptron, 165
perceptron model, 178
phase shift keying, 35, 48
physical address, 9, 15
physical layer, 7, 34, 46, 70
piezoelectric pressure sensor, 3
piggyback, 80
plausibility, 108
pneumatic actuator, 6
point addition, 212, 214–216, 218,
    219
Poisson distribution, 67
port number, 11
positive definite matrix, 160
posterior probability, 103
power loss, 95
power saving, 40
power set, 105
power spectral density, 48
power-splitting based relay, 144,
    147
preamble, 43, 71
precision, 5, 187, 188
prediction horizon, 149
pressure, 238
pressure sensor, 3, 237
previous hash, 222–226
principal component analysis, 173,
    174
prior probability, 100, 110, 113
privacy, 207, 235
privacy and security, 1
private key, 210, 211, 215–218,
    224, 225

probability, 100, 169, 171
probability density function, 96,
    100
probability mass function, 112,
    113
probability of detection, 111,
    113–115, 117
probability of error, 111, 113, 115,
    117
probability of false alarm, 112,
    113, 115
probability of missed detection,
    113
processing gain, 50
processing time, 27
proof of concept, 229
proof of work, 223, 227
propagation time, 28, 68
protocol, 1, 237, 238, 240
provider edge, 196, 197
proximity sensor, 3
pseudo-inverse, 125
pseudo-noise sequence, 46, 48
pseudo-random, 69
public key, 210, 211, 215, 216,
    218, 224, 225
public key cryptography, 210
publish subscribe model, 77
publisher, 77
pulse amplitude modulation, 39
pure ALOHA, 65

QPSK, 35
QRS complex, 236
quadprog function, 160
quadrature amplitude
    modulation, 39
quadrature amplitude shift
    keying, 39
quadrature phase-shift keying, 35,
    56
quality of service, 41, 82
queuing time, 27

R peak, 236

radio frequency identification, 123
reassembly, 11
reassembly timer, 74
recall, 187, 188
receding horizon control, 149
received signal, 111, 144, 146, 147
received signal strength, 123, 128, 237
received signal strength indicator, 59, 167
receiver sensitivity, 59
record, 208
rectified linear unit activation function, 181
reduced function device, 51, 74
regression, 166, 167, 170, 171
reinforcement learning, 166
relay, 144–148
relay protocol, 143
repeater, 13
request response model, 77
reset, 79
resistance temperature detector, 3
resolution, 5
resource allocation frame, 41
resource pooling, 191
respiration, 234
restricted access window, 41
retail management, 230
reverse address resolution protocol, 15
RFID interrogator, 123
RFID reader, 123
RFID transponder, 123
root, 75
router, 14, 20
routing, 10, 74
routing information protocol, 19, 23
routing locators, 198
routing table, 19, 24
RPL instance, 76
RSA algorithm, 210

sample and hold circuit, 150

scalability, 191
secret key, 216, 218, 219
security, 207
security header, 71, 72
segment, 11
segmentation, 11
seizure, 236
semi-supervised learning, 166
semiconductor temperature sensor, 3
sensitive attributes, 207, 209, 210
sensitivity, 5
sensor, 1, 77, 93, 99, 104, 106, 110–112, 114, 126, 127, 133, 233–236
sequence number, 11, 14, 21, 71, 196, 197, 222
server, 77
session layer, 12
SHA-256 hashing algorithm, 222, 223, 225, 228
short header, 41
short inter-frame space, 42
shortest path, 22
sigmoid activation function, 180, 182
sigmoid function, 172
signal, 125, 235
signal detection, 110
signal model, 111, 144, 147
signal-to-interference-plus-noise ratio, 144, 148
signal-to-noise ratio, 35, 59, 146, 148, 149
simple mail transfer protocol, 71
slack variable, 161
slotted ALOHA, 68
smart agriculture, 238
smart air pollution monitoring, 239
smart city, 239
smart contract, 228, 230
smart environment, 166, 192
smart farming, 238
smart healthcare, 233, 236

smart object, 2
smart parking, 237
snore sensor, 234
soft fork, 228
solar panel, 238, 239
solar radiation, 238
soma, 178
sound generator, 234
source, 122
source address, 72, 74
speed frame exchange, 42
spirometer, 234
SPO2 pulse oximeter, 234
spread spectrum technique, 63
spreader, 50
spreading factor, 60, 61, 65
squashing function, 179
star topology, 13, 51
start of frame delimiter, 71
state, 102, 149
state-space model, 149–151, 153, 155
stateless communication, 77
stateless header compression, 72
stochastic gradient descent, 184, 186
storage, 191, 192, 199
storing node, 76
stub network, 25
subnet, 17
subnet mask, 15, 16
subscriber, 77
sulphur dioxide, 239
super-ventricular, 236
supernet, 18
supervised learning, 166–168
support, 107
suppression, 208
switch, 13
symbol, 60
symbol duration, 60, 61
symbol rate, 60, 61
symmetric key cryptography, 210
synapse, 178
synchronization, 52, 123, 125, 127

T wave, 236
t-closeness, 208
tamper-proof blockchain, 224
tanh activation function, 180
target, 102, 111, 222, 223, 226, 227
target detection, 110
task offload, 203
Taylor series, 151, 185
TCP, 71
TCP/IP model, 13
temperature, 234, 238
temperature sensor, 2
testing data, 167, 168, 187, 199
thermal actuator, 6
thermistor, 3
thermocouple, 3
things, 1, 77, 143
threshold, 111, 112, 115, 145, 180, 200
throughput, 28, 41–43, 69, 82
time of air, 61, 62, 65, 69
time slot, 52
time-difference-of-arrival, 123, 126
time-of-arrival, 123, 125
time-slotted channel hopping, 52
time-switching based relay, 144
timestamp, 222
token, 80
token length, 82
topic, 82
tracking, 122
traffic class, 72
traffic congestion, 237
traffic indication map, 40
traffic intensity, 28
training data, 166–168, 187, 199
transaction, 229
transaction details, 225
transaction pool, 227
transducer, 2
transit network, 25
transmission control protocol, 11
transmission rate, 8, 29
transmission time, 27, 28
transport layer, 11, 71

transport layer security, 79
trapdoor function, 211, 214, 222
true negative, 188
true positive, 188
tuple, 208

UDP, 71
ultrasonic sensor, 4
uncertainty interval, 109
unconstrained MPC, 155, 158
under-fitting, 176
unicast, 72
unsupervised learning, 166, 173, 174
upsampling, 236
user datagram protocol, 11

validation set, 187
ventricular, 236

ventricular depolarization, 236
ventricular re-polarization, 236
version number, 222
virtual machine, 194, 197, 198
virtualization technology, 192
visual based, 123
voting system, 229
vulnerable time, 68

weight, 125, 167, 170, 171, 178, 182, 185, 186, 201, 203
wetness, 238
wild card, 82
wind speed, 238
world wide web, 11, 12

Zigbee coordinator, 51
Zigbee device, 51
Zigbee router, 51